ST. BENEDICT
AND THE SIXTH CENTURY

SAINT BENEDICT
AND THE
SIXTH CENTURY

BY
DOM JOHN CHAPMAN

GREENWOOD PRESS, PUBLISHERS
WESTPORT, CONNECTICUT

The Library of Congress cataloged this book as follows:

Chapman, John, Father, 1865–1933.
    Saint Benedict and the sixth century. Westport, Conn.,
Greenwood Press [1971]

      vi, 239 p. 23 cm.

      Reprint of the 1929 ed.
      Includes bibliographical references.

    1. Benedictus, Saint, Abbot of Monte Cassino. 2. Benedictus,
Saint, Abbot of Monte Cassino. Regula. 3. Monasticism and religious
orders. I. Title.

BX4700.B3C5 1971   271'.1'0924 [B]   79–109719
ISBN 0–8371–4209–1   MARC

Library of Congress   72 [4]

BX
4700
. B3
C5
1971

Originally published in 1929 by Longmans, Green and Co., Ltd.,
London, New York, Toronto

Reprinted in 1971 by Greenwood Press, Inc.
51 Riverside Avenue, Westport, CT 06880

Library of Congress catalog card number 79-109719
ISBN 0-8371-4209-1

Printed in the United States of America

10 9 8 7 6 5 4 3 2

PREFACE

At the beginning of this year, when I was preparing a lecture on Justinian, I noticed that Emperor's quotations from the Rule of St. Benedict, and also the use of the word *conuersatio* in the official translation of the Novellae. This set me to write the fourth and twelfth chapters of this book, and these led me further into the sixth century. The fact that St. Benedict is never mentioned by name until St. Gregory in 593, forty years after his death, is the real motive of the studies in this volume.

I had previously dipped fairly often into sixth century matters by accident, rather than design,—in studying the Monophysites, in writing on the reunion of East and West in 519, on the fifth General Council, on Justinian, and on Fulgentius,—in my labours at the history of Vulgate MSS., which interested me in Victor of Capua and Eugippius, and especially in Cassiodorus, for whom I long ago conceived a warm affection;—I had also worked long ago at the text of the Rule and St. Benedict's posthumous fame in martyrologies and kalendars. I have now worked up various points, which have attracted me for half a year from the N.T. studies which I prefer, because I feel it a pity that Benedictine monks should write so little about St. Benedict. I hope others may be induced to complete the picture of the Patriarch of Monks in his own century ; as I have only dashed a few blobs of paint here and there, and intensive study could doubtless be expended on many other connected subjects.

I acknowledge my debt to Abbot Butler's edition of the Rule, without which I could not have done anything ; also to Moricca'a edition of the Dialogues of St. Gregory the Great. I have written almost entirely from sixth century sources. The excellent indexes of Hartmann to St. Gregory's

v

Registrum, and of Mommsen and Traube to the *Variae* of Cassiodorus, have greatly lightened my labour.

The chapter on Cassiodorus does not contain much that is new, but old data are marshalled, I hope, with new force. To monks of St. Benedict, whether Black or White, I trust the last chapter will be of interest. It is conclusive, and therefore important, as it is a new item in lexicography and a new light on the Benedictine vows.

H. JOHN CHAPMAN.

Downside Abbey,
August 11th, 1928.

CONTENTS

ERRATUM

Page 25. Note 2.

for " A Benedictine novice ought not to say . . ."

read " A Benedictine novice ought to say. . ."

ST. BENEDICT
AND THE SIXTH CENTURY

CHAPTER I

THE CONTEMPORARY CELEBRITY OF ST. BENEDICT

ST. BENEDICT first mentioned by St. Gregory—The carefulness of St. Gregory—He wrote his stories from notes of depositions made by witnesses—They are not ' legends '—Procopius compared with Gregory — Evidence for miracles — The small number of them in the sixth century—St. Benedict's celebrity in his own time was due to his miracles when still in his cave, and then as an Abbot at Subiaco—An omission of the miraculous or of the belief in the miraculous in history is a cause of serious error—St. Benedict's place in the sixth century is primarily that of a wonder-worker.

IT is a strange fact that St. Benedict is not mentioned in any contemporary document that has come down to us. We first[1] hear of him from St. Gregory the Great, whose Dialogues are the work of a man of great experience of life and of solid common sense, who has sifted his data with care. He does not depend on any written sources, but entirely on oral information. He is well aware of the uncertainty of second and third hand evidence, as well as of the infirmities of human nature which may cause even direct reports to be doubtful.

[1] The poem of Marcus on St. Benedict was regarded by Traube as anterior to St. Gregory. On its probable date, see note at end of Chapter IX.

I

He is also aware that the particular matters he is relating are startling and unexpected, for they are chiefly miraculous events of fairly recent date.

Now the Italians of his day were not so silly as to disbelieve in miracles; but they were sufficiently uneducated and behindhand to be ready to accept only the accustomed and the traditional. That St. Martin did signs and wonders in Gaul two hundred years earlier was a well-known fact; all sorts of miraculous interventions took place in the stories of the martyrs a century further back still; at their shrines graces and cures might still be obtained. But that real saints had been living in their own time, not in Eastern deserts, but at home, in Italy—bishops and abbots whom they might themselves have met—this would seem incredible. St. Gregory puts this objection in the mouth of his interlocutor, Peter the deacon (though Peter of course knew better), in order to give the answer:

Dial. I Præf. ' I was not aware that any had shone (*fulsisse*) by miracles in Italy to any remarkable extent, so that I do not know with whom you are comparing yourself. I do not doubt that there have been good men in this country, but I do not imagine that they have performed any signs and wonders; if they did, these events have been so hidden in silence that we do not know whether they took place.'

Gregory. ' If I should relate merely what my own humble self has come to know by the witness of perfect and proved men, or good and orthodox men, or by personal experience, the day would be finished, I ween, before my talk was at an end.'

Peter thereupon begs to hear these tales, as example is more potent than precept. The Pope assures him that hearing as well as seeing may be good evidence:

' I will without hesitation relate what I have come to know by the narratives of venerable men; and I will do so according

to the precedent set by Holy Writ, since it is perfectly clear to
me that Mark and Luke learned what they wrote, from hearing
not from seeing.

But in order that I may remove from my readers any occasion
of doubt, I make it plain, with regard to each fact which I relate,
from what source I have obtained it. But I want you to understand that *in some cases I retain the sense only, whereas in other
cases I retain the words together with the sense.* For if I had wished
to retain even the exact words of all my informants, these being
spoken in a rustic dialect would not have been suitable to a
written style.'

These words clearly imply that St. Gregory is writing
from his own copious notes. He does not simply relate
from memory what his informants had told him, but he
had taken down what they said in their own language.
But when they were peasants he has now put their words
into a more literary form.

This is perhaps confirmed by the resemblance of wording
when St. Gregory tells the same story over again; for
some stories in the first three books are referred to again
in the fourth, and a good many are repeated at length in
the Saint's Homilies on the Gospels. It is probable that
in going over the same tale, he has not consulted his earlier
published work, but has used his original notes over again.

Signor Umberto Moricca, in his admirable preface to
the Dialogues, has made a list of all the authorities quoted
by St. Gregory. In thirty-seven cases the Pope does not
give their names, as they would be unknown to his readers;
there are two bishops among these; fifteen cases are told
by monks; others by elders, grave and orthodox (*fideles*)
persons, ' some of my neighbours', many, a good many,
the inhabitants of Narni, the people, a poor old man,
masons, dyers, etc.

The rest of the stories,—the greater number,—are told
on the authority of well-known persons, chiefly bishops

and abbots, with some monks, priests, a subdeacon, a defensor, a sacristan, their names being given. St. Gregory had received a legal education, and had been a judge as Prefect of Rome. He knew how to interrogate witnesses and write down their depositions.

The events he relates are in a few cases strange to us, because they belong to a different age.[1] The larger portion of them, however, is more credible in the twentieth century than it was in the sixth. Most of the fourth book is concerned with ' phantasms of the dying ': such apparitions at the moment of death (and even in moments of peril) are too well attested to be regarded as supernatural in most cases. Other visions will be recognised as at least partly imaginary. Most of the cures of the sick and the telepathic, prophetic or thought-reading phenomena are so like those which are attested under oath in hundreds of ' processes ' of beatification and canonisation, that nobody who knows anything of such matters will be surprised at them.[2] There are also a few very extraordinary stories such as the raising to life of a young monk who was so crushed under a fallen wall that his body was carried to St. Benedict in a sack. We cannot control the details; and of course they may have been exaggerated. Other tales relate providential coincidences in answer to prayer,

[1] For example, Dial. II 24, the boy monk whose body was cast out of the grave; St. Benedict sends a consecrated Host to be laid upon it with great reverence.

[2] It is difficult to give instances of miracles of Saints, on account of the great number of examples, I suggest for example the lives of St. John Joseph of the Cross or of St. Gerard Majella or the Jesuit St. Francis Jerome. If the Mediæval is preferred, I suggest St. Francis de Paula or St. Dominic. The late Dr. E. A. Abbot, who disbelieved in miracles, published two volumes on the posthumous miracles of St. Thomas of Canterbury; he regarded the facts as on the whole unassailable. Similar to these are the miracles done by the relics of St. Stephen in Africa, as related by St. Augustine and his friend St. Evodius. A good work to consult would be the life of St. Joseph of Cupertino by Bernini; as it is simply written from sworn evidence. It is not easy to procure; but the life given by the Bollandists with additions from Bernini will do almost as well. Either is very charming reading, and very extraordinary and incredible!

as for example when St. Benedict finds sacks of corn at the door, left by an unknown donor.[1]

Had St. Gregory been credulous (like the people who believe that miracles do not happen, on the authority of those who know nothing about the evidence for them) he might doubtless have written ten books instead of four; for the wonders related to him as a collector, at third hand and as reports and traditions, must have been very much more numerous than the sober witness which he was willing to accept.

I regret, therefore, to see that even Moricca compares the Dialogues to the *Gesta* of the Roman martyrs (which after Dufourcq he regards as the oral traditions of the Roman cemeteries), and speaks of the stories as ' legends ', just as less critical writers have done. Even the furthest back of them, such as the stories of Paulinus and of the early years of St. Benedict, are scarcely ' legends ' in the ordinary sense of the word. Almost all the tales are depositions, which may be lies, or inaccurate or exaggerated, but are neither traditions nor legends any more than they are ' Nature-Myths ', or parables, or romances.

Nor are they History, in the general sense, but disconnected tags. In the sixth century we have one ' great

---

[1] The arguments urged against St. Gregory's accuracy by Dudden have been carefully and effectively refuted by Signor Moricca. Attention must especially be drawn to his suggestion, or rather proof, that the Dialogues have mixed up Paulinus III bishop of Nola with the famous Paulinus I (Pref. p. xxxvii). As to the martyrdom of Hermenegild, I have always held that the account given by St. Leander to St. Gregory must be the truth, and that the other less exactly contemporary accounts must be judged by it. But here even Dudden can only say that Gregory followed Leander, and was merely wrong in supposing Leander to possess correct and unbiased information. Supposing Dr. Dudden's story (*Gregory the Great*, vol. I, pp. 403-7) were more accurate than that of the bishop of Seville, it would follow that St. Gregory had for once been wrong in judging the character of his informant. As Leander had received Hermenegild into the Church, and knew him intimately, whereas Joannes Biclarensis and Gregory of Tours did not, it is not clear that their posterior evidence is of greater value. Anyhow I do not share Dr. Dudden's nineteenth century view that changes of religion are to be explained by political reasons: in the sixth century it is often more prudent conversely to explain changes of policy by religious reasons.

historian ', as Professor Bury says, and it is interesting to compare Procopius with St. Gregory. Now Procopius was present occasionally at the events he relates, just as St. Gregory gives six stories in the Dialogues from his own knowledge, besides some more in his letters. For the rest of Procopius's work we presume he had good authorities, whether of eye-witnesses or of hearsay. It is difficult to judge how far he is influenced by political opinions, or by prejudice. Sometimes he seems to speak his mind freely. In the ' Buildings ' he is a mere flatterer: in the Secret History he is ridiculous. I quote a passage[1] in order to compare his treatment of the miraculous with. that of St. Gregory:

Procopius, Hist. Arcana, 12. ' To myself and to many of us, [Justinian and Theodora] have never seemed to be human beings but evil demons and, as the poets say, ' plagues to men ', who took counsel together that they might be able to destroy all the races and the works of mankind, and for this purpose assumed a human body and became anthropodaemons, and have in this way turned the whole world upside down. . . .

Some of those who attended him at a distance at night and were present in the palace, whose soul was in a state of purity, thought they saw a strange diabolical phantasm instead of him. One of these persons used to say that he would suddenly rise from his throne and take walks (for he was never accustomed to sit down for long) and that at this moment the head of Justinian would disappear while his body seemed to make these long perambulations, and the witness would stand in doubt and hesitation, thinking his eyes must have failed him. Later, however, the head would return to the body, so that what was till then wanting was unexpectedly supplied.

Another related that he was standing by Justinian, who was eposing, when suddenly his face became like a featureless

---

[1] I assume that the *Historia Arcana* is really by Procopius, with Diehl and Pargoire and Bury, and practically all recent writers. I have not investigated the question myself by comparison of style. There are however plenty of strange stories in the ' Wars ' of Procopius, told on no particular authority, as well as in the Secret History.

lump of flesh, for it had no eyebrows or eyes where they ought
to be, or any other feature; but after a time the form of his
visage returned and was visible.

And they say that a certain monk, especially dear to God,
was persuaded by his companions in the desert to come to
Byzantium, to espouse the cause of their countrymen, who were
suffering injustice and violence beyond bearing. On his arrival
he at once obtained an audience of the emperor. As he was
about to enter within, when he touched the threshold with one
of his feet, he suddenly leapt back. The eunuch who was
introducing him and the bystanders urged him to go forward;
but without any reply, like one distraught he returned to his
lodging. Those who followed him asked him why he behaved
thus; and they say that he declared he saw before him the Prince
of the Devils upon the throne in the palace; such a one he would
not approach, nor ask him any favour.'

These very unusual happenings are related on the
vaguest authority. Who were these witnesses who had
such strange experiences or hallucinations in the dark?
It is hardly satisfying to be assured that their soul was pure.
From what desert, from what country, from what community did the monk dear to God arrive? Pope Gregory
would have taken down his evidence, told us his biography
and the street, perhaps, where his δωμάτιον was situated.
But the great historian is satisfied with *on dit*.

In this case of Procopius we feel sure that these miracles
did not happen, and we are not even sure that anyone even
thought he had seen them happen. In St. Gregory's
case we are at least sure that the facts were related to the
Pope. In the case of legends, as for example Jacobus de
Voragine, we have no certainty whatever. In the case of
ordinary evidence, we may distrust some of the witnesses,
but we cannot doubt that on the whole they were believed.
For instance, we may disbelieve in the miraculous cures
at Lourdes; but it would be rash to deny that the railway
companies have to run an extra number of trains to Lourdes

because so many do believe in them. It would similarly (due proportion being preserved) be rash to doubt that St. Benedict, even if he did no miracles, was believed by his contemporaries to do them in considerable numbers.

We may be surprised, perhaps, at the small number of miracles (including visions and apparitions) that St. Gregory was able to collect for the whole of Italy, for they cover about a century, though most of them were within fifty years of the date of his book. Suppose the learned Pope Pius XI were to collect the miraculous events in Italy during the last hundred years, and to relate them in a series of Dialogues with Cardinal Gasparri, we should certainly expect ten times as many books, or twenty times. The period would include not merely famous and popular names like Anna Maria Taigi, St. Benedict Joseph Labre, St. Gabriel dell' Annunziatta, Gemma Galgani, Girolamo Cottolengo, Don Bosco, Cardinal Ferrari, and so forth, and the curious miracles procured by the faith of many in Pius IX and Pius X during the life time of those pious popes, but a multitude of strange mystics, holy friars or nuns, levitations and long fasts, visions and prophecies, well attested and often convincing. I confess that I have made no particular study of these matters. Some of the happenings might be explicable as natural phenomena. But God's intervention ought not to be astonishing to any Theist; and Christians are taught that a very little faith will remove a mountain into the sea.[1]

[1] Disbelief in miracles as even possible, is usually made possible by ignorance of the evidence. Hume, for example, may have read parts of the Gospels, and have heard of some Jansenist *convulsionnaires*, but it is very unlikely that he knew anything about sworn evidence or pilgrimages or contemporary lives of Saints. So he was able to expatiate on the weakness of human testimony and its incapability to establish anything unusual. It does not seem to have struck him that such fallibility in human observation and human witness would a fortiori be incapable of establishing the invariability of laws of sequence and connexion.

The curious barrenness of sixth-century Italy may be put down, apart from the conscientious criticism of sources by St. Gregory, to the depopulation and misery caused by barbarian invasions, and also to the Arian domination. But the devout Pope found enough matter to feed the devotion of his times.

St. Gregory was probably born not long before 540, and I hope to show that St. Benedict probably lived later than 550. Their lives overlapped for fifteen years, more or less. I assume therefore that the former is a good witness as well as a careful witness when he speaks of the celebrity of the latter.

The first incident related is nearly 100 years back, and may be regarded by some as on the verge of legend (*Dial.* II. 1.): St. Benedict leaves Rome, and stops with his nurse at Enfide; the miraculous mending of a sieve ' was known to all in that place, and was wondered at so much that the inhabitants hung up the sieve in the Church porch, in order that those who were present and those who should come after might all recognise from what perfection this boy had started by the grace of his conversion. For many years it hung there before the eyes of all, and was hanging above the Church door up to these days of the Lombards '. Benedict flies from admiration, and is hidden in a cave by the monk Romanus, who gives him the monastic habit, and feeds him by a cord from above. Now comes the important passage:

' When however Almighty God willed both Romanus to cease this work, and that the life of Benedict should be shown as an example to men, so that it might shine as a lamp placed upon a lampstand, SO AS TO LIGHT ALL WHO ARE IN THE HOUSE OF GOD, the Lord appeared to a certain priest,' etc. Gregory says nothing like this of any of the abbots or priests or popes whose miracles he records: of all these saintly personages Benedict alone is set on a candle-stick to light the whole Church. Of others two or three mentions are made; to Benedict a whole book is devoted, and a few other references besides.

The solitary is found by the priest by revelation, he is discovered by shepherds, whom he instructs 'so that his name became known to all in the vicinity', and 'from that time many people used to visit him' bringing him the necessaries of life.

When his temptation had been cured by rolling in thorns, 'after this many began to leave the world and to hasten to his teaching' (c. 2), and by the praise of his admirable life his name became famous (c. 3), so that the monks of a neighbouring monastery persuaded him against his will to become their Abbot.

According to ecclesiastical rule he must have been appointed by some authority, presumably the bishop. By the latter he will have been solemnly blessed according to custom.[1] St. Bernard in a later age became Abbot at 22; St. Benedict was probably not much older. After his failure to reform his monks, he returned to his solitude, where he increased in signs and wonders, *uirtutibus signisque*. 'Many were congregated at that spot to the service of Almighty God,' so that he built twelve monasteries, each having twelve monks. He appointed a *Pater* for each,—further on these superiors are called *praepositi*,—while he himself remained at the Sacro Speco with a few chosen disciples. He was now Abbot of a group of thirteen cells and 150 monks; his former blessing by the bishop giving him the necessary authority and position. Religious nobles (*nobiles et religiosi*) from Rome now came in numbers to visit him and offered their sons as monks.

---

[1] For references to the blessing of an Abbot inter missarum sollemnia, see p. 60, note.

There is no reason to doubt this history. Benedict was first famous as a wonder-worker and then as a saint and as the Abbot of a swiftly growing community about 500-15. When he migrated to Montecassino,—hardly much earlier than 520,—he began afresh with a few monks, building the monastery by their work. He was now twice as far from Rome, 86 miles, but in a very conspicuous site above the chief road from Rome to the South. His miracles increase, and his fame, now that he is in a more frequented spot; he becomes known as a prophet (c. 12), and is reputed to have raised the dead more than once.

Now I find it frequently assumed in modern fashion that St. Benedict's fame was mostly posthumous, resting upon the swift diffusion of his Rule; and that his Rule was admired and propagated on account of the admirable order of his monastery and its high reputation for moderation and strict observance. For these views St. Gregory gives little support. We are told nothing of the reputation of Montecassino; only that Benedict at Subiaco became a *magister uirtutum*, and his rule is referred to incidentally (c. 12, *mos cellae, de usu Regulae*, cp. *S. Reg.* c.51), at a time when it was scarcely likely to exist in writing. His celebrity is ascribed to his miracles, whence also came his reputation for sanctity and wisdom.

Any other view will be modern conjecture, with no serious support from our only authority, and none at all from the conditions of the sixth century.

The modern attitude towards miracles is an unfortunate obstacle to historical study. For example, the twelfth century was the age of St. Bernard, not because the incomparable sermons of the saint to his monks in the Chapterhouse moved the Church to reform and the laity to embrace the Crusade, nor even because the undoubted reputation for observance of his monastery impressed all Europe;

but because he was a thaumaturgus to a very remarkable though not unprecedented degree.[1] Yet historians are inclined to slur over his miracles, which are unfashionable things, and thus to leave his influence unexplained. For such negligence there can be neither excuse nor pardon. The sixth book of the *Vita prima* of St. Bernard gives for a short period the miracles done day by day, as written down then and there by eye-witnesses. The first part is by Hermann bishop of Constance, Eberhard his chaplain, an Abbot Baldwin, the well-known Abbot Frowin of Engelberg, the famous monks of Clairvaux, Gerard and Gaufrid, Philip archdeacon of Laon and two clerics, Otto and Franco; each writes down in turn what he has witnessed, in one line or ten or more, as the case may be, so that on one day a dozen or three dozen cures are noted down as distinct and certain, and though sometimes the crowds and the shouting prevented sight and hearing of more.[2] St. Benedict was not a saint of the active life like St. Bernard, and opportunities for continual miracles like this were lacking. But it is clear from St. Gregory's account that he was the chief wonder-worker of his day, a second Martin, an anticipated Curé d'Ars or Don Bosco.

If I insist upon this point, it is because it must be the starting point when we investigate the century of St. Benedict. If we wish to see ' St. Benedict in his century ' we must know what was his relation to his century. It seems certain

---

[1] The thaumaturgus who works miracles almost by a habit is rare among saints; yet in every century there will at least be a few, or more than a few. But St. Bernard belongs to the very small number who have worked signs and wonders by the hundred, like St. Vincent Ferrar, the Dominican, or Blessed Salvator of Horta, a Franciscan lay-brother.

[2] A good sixth-century parallel is the second Book of the *Vita S. Caesarii*, where the priest Messianus and the deacon Stephen relate what they have seen of the Saint, either separately, or together with the three bishops, Cyprian of Toulon, Firmin of Uzès and Viventius (of an unknown see, present at Council of Orléans, 541). The want of sequence in the book shows its composite character. A number of miracles are related, with many details, and witnesses are mentioned.

that he was a great celebrity, in Italy certainly, and probably beyond. And his fame was from his miracles and his prophetic gifts. From these were inferred his sanctity and his wisdom. From these also came his success in assembling monks in at least three monasteries, monks of good family in monasteries of good report.

CHAPTER II

FOUR possible answers: 1. For Montecassino. 2. For St. Benedict's three or more foundations, as though he were the founder of an Order. 3. For certain Abbots who wished to reform their monasteries. 4. As a Rule for all Italy—No. 1 being impossible, No. 2 suggests that St. Benedict's own monasteries were not observant—But No. 3 is nearer the truth, as the Rule is for many places, provinces and climates—But this evidence carries us beyond No. 3 to a wider sphere—St. Benedict's hesitations contrasted with his air of authority lead us to examine the claims of the Rule—It is the Mistress, to be obeyed by Abbot as well as monks—The doctrine of the authority of the Rule is St. Benedict's great innovation. Sancta Regula.— The cenobitic life defined by 'Rule and Abbot'—The Rule is a minimum because absolute, and intended for all monks— Its chronological position between Dionysius Exiguus and Justinian—The rule is a code, a summary of the experience of three centuries.

FOR whom is the rule intended? Why did St. Benedict write it? Several alternative answers are at first sight possible.

1. It was written as a description of the observance of Montecassino, for the use of future generations of Abbots and monks in that place. This is quite impossible, for the Rule explicitly contemplates various places. Consequently this solution is modified by most writers on the Rule thus:

2. It is intended besides for St. Benedict's other foundation at Terracina, and for other unknown abbeys which he may have founded, or intended to found. This very common view regards St. Benedict as the 'founder of a religious Order', like St. Francis or St. Dominic, or the three Cistercian founders, propagating this new Order by new foundations. This conception, however, does not seem to be older than the twelfth century. The traditional Benedictine method is of reform, not foundation, by applying the Rule, or new Constitutions, to existing monasteries. This was the method of Charlemagne and St. Benedict of Aniane, of the Cluniacs, and even of Bec. This was the means of propagating the reforms later of St. Justina of Padua or of Bursfeld, or of SS. Vannes et Hydulphe, or of St. Maur. Only the destruction of the monasteries in Germany and France caused the modern congregations of Solesmes and of Beuron to proceed by the method of new foundations, as the Cistercians did, and the orders of Friars of the thirteenth century, and the Jesuits, and the hundred and one more recent congregations.

3. We arrive thus at another possibility, that St. Benedict's Rule was intended to be applied to existing monasteries rather than to new foundations. This is, of course, what actually happened, when, in the course of the seventh century (and we may assume, to a great extent in the sixth), the Western monasteries received the Rule of St. Benedict. The fact that the Rule was exactly adapted to this method, and was easily and smoothly assimilated by the older monasteries, suggests that it had actually been intended for this particular use. Thus we infer as our third alternative that the Rule is the answer to a question addressed to St. Benedict BY VARIOUS ABBOTS, HIS FRIENDS AND ADMIRERS: ' How can we reform our monasteries,—how can we govern them in regularity and discipline? '

4. The Rule eventually becomes practically universal in the West. Did St. Benedict look forward to this? And if he did, was it by prophetic inspiration? OR DID HE ACTUALLY INTEND NOTHING LESS, and had he a rational assurance that his intention would be carried out? This is a bold suggestion, but logic suggests that we should entertain it as a possibility. But then, who can have suggested to St. Benedict the idea of writing a universal Rule, or have persuaded him that such a notion could be carried into effect? Surely only an Emperor or a Pope.

I confess that for many years I used to hold No. 2, without much thought, modifying it with the idea that St. Benedict contemplated the possibility of some other Abbot admiring his rule and adopting it. But gradually some years ago I found myself driven to the conclusion that No. 3 was the true solution, for St. Benedict was certainly writing for other monasteries than his own. But it is a sloppy method to go by general impressions, however well one may have the Rule by heart. We must take in detail the evidence of the Rule itself, which we shall find to be abundant.

A. No. 1 and No. 2. The Rule contains a code of punishments in five chapters (23–27), followed by two chapters on the expulsion of the contumacious, and the receiving back of those who leave of their own accord (28–9); later on there is a chapter on satisfaction for faults (44), and penances for light faults are given in 43, 45–6. Expulsion is elsewhere referred to (58 *fin.*), even of priests (62) or of the praepositus (65 *fin.*). Excommunication is threatened, major or minor, for various faults, and ' regular discipline', which includes whipping, is continually recurring. Apart from the Prologue, the Instruments of Good Works, and the three great monastic virtues, together with the chapters on the division of the Psalms for the week, the Holy Rule strikes the casual reader as a sort of Paenitentiale, full of recurring punishments and threats. The two chapters of advice to the Abbot (2 and 64) do something to mitigate this impression, for the Abbot is to mingle *terroribus blandimenta*, and he is to show the kindliness of a father as well as the *dirus magistri affectus*. But the general idea we get of the monastery which is supposed by solution No. 1 to be described, is of a house containing many *indisciplinati* and *inquieti*, continually repressed by excommunications and even the cat, some expelled, even a Prior (*saepius contigit*) who causes scandal, others leaving after their vows,—it is not necessary to complete the picture. I think we are bound rather to hold that Montecassino and Subiaco were models for other monasteries, and that the Rule as one naturally reads it is not a description of the sort of discipline St. Benedict habitually had to put in practice.[1]

B. No. 3. But the meaning of all this code is at once apparent if we take it as an answer to an Abbot's question: ' How can I introduce regularity into my monastery, and preserve it there '. St. Benedict replies by giving a short code of coercive legislation, mostly moral—excommunication *ab oratorio* and *a mensa*, reproofs, exhortations and sympathy—and by adding references to these punishments in all the cases which arise in subsequent chapters. He gives elaborate advice as to the Abbot's own action in his duty of government, or rather of reform; for both c. 2 and c. 64 deal with the reform of his flock and of individual

---

[1] Not that St. Benedict's monks were faultless. We hear of one (*Dial.* II, 19) who retained some *mappulae* given him by neighbouring nuns, without permission. A boy monk went to see his parents without getting the Saint's blessing (*ib.* 24), and another monk wanted to run away from the monastery, and his excited imagination frightened him back (*ib.* 25).

Earlier, in one of the cells at Subiaco (not under the Saint's own eye) a monk used to be drawn away from the choir office by a black devil, visible to the Saint, who did not chastise him, but simply ' uirga percussit ', and the devil returned no more. Other Saints, in particular St. Ignatius Loyola by good testimony, chased away the devil by a blow with a stick.

sheep much more than with ordinary government. The Abbot may even fail in his attempts to reform, as St. Benedict did in his first monastery; but if he has given all diligence to his ' unquiet and disobedient flock ',[1] he will not be held answerable for their spiritual sickness.

C. An example may be given. The chapter on poverty (33) does not begin by saying that all things are to be in common and that each individual must possess nothing, and then afterwards continue by saying that any contravention of rule must be severely punished. Conversely it begins violently: ' Above all this vice *must be extirpated* radically from the monastery, that anyone should dare to give or receive anything without the Abbot's order ';— then comes the principle,—lastly the threats: ' If anyone is found to delight in this most wicked vice, he shall be admonished once and again; if he does not amend his ways, he shall be subjected to punishment '. Now the first words seem absolutely to *assume* that religious poverty is not yet strictly observed in the monastery, so that monks have objects without special leave. It is to be introduced, by the vigorous extirpation of the opposite vice. This chapter is not meant for Montecassino, but for the instruction of Abbots elsewhere.[2]

D. No. 4. We have apparently been driven to solution No. 3, which seems to be made quite certain by very obvious

---

[1] Cap. 2: Si inquieto uel in oboedienti gregi pastoris fuerit omnis diligentia attributa, et morbidis earum actibus uniuersa fuerit cura exhibita . . . . ipsi uero contemnentes spreuerunt me '.

[2] Of course it is quite easy to reply that ' hoc uitium radicitus amputandum est ' is the apodosis of a suppressed protasis ' if such a vice should happen to grow up '. If that had been in St. Benedict's mind, surely the whole framework of the chapter would have been different. I do not forget c. 2: ' neque dissimulet peccata delinquentium, sed *mox ut coeperint oriri* radicitus ea ut praeualet amputet '. I simply think that in c. 33 the idea of ' ut coeperint oriri ' is conspicuously absent. The last sentence, ' Quod si quisquam huic nequissimo uitio deprehensus fuerit delectari ' refers to a time subsequent to the promulgation by the Abbot of the strict observance which has just been enjoined.

arguments. The Rule is meant for monasteries both large and small:

c. 21. Si *maior* fuerit congregatio . . .
c. 31. Si congregatio *maior* fuerit . . .
c. 57. Artifices si sunt in monasterio.

and in different places and conditions:

c. 40. Quod si aut *loci necessitas*, uel labor, aut ardor aestatis amplius poposcerit (uini).
ibid. Ubi autem *necessitas loci* exposcit, ut nec supra scripta mensura inueniri possit, sed multo minus, aut ex toto nihil.

These two passages suppose first a place where more wine is wanted, and secondly a place where little or none can be got, probably where there are no vineyards.

c. 48. Si autem *necessitas loci* aut paupertas exegerit ut ad fruges recolligendas per se occupentur,

One place may have a great deal of harvesting, and the monastery may be too poor to pay for help to the *coloni* at harvest time, if it can even be got.

c. 41. Si labores agrorum non habent . . . si operas in agris habuerint.
c. 55. Vestimenta fratribus secundum *locorum qualitatem* ubi habitant, uel aerum temperiem dentur, quia in *frigidis regionibus* amplius indigetur, *in calidis* uero minus . . . Nos tamen mediocribus locis sufficere credimus. . .

For ' moderate ' climates a thick cowl for winter and a thin or worn one for summer. But St. Benedict assumes that his Rule is also for ' cold ' and ' hot ' provinces: the colour and coarseness do not matter:

ibid. 'sed quales inueniri possunt *in prouincia qua degunt*'.

The Rule therefore is meant for various provinces: not merely Nursia, Valeria, Campania, but for cold or hot

climates, for which St. Benedict does not venture to legis-
late for want of experience. An Englishman will find
Subiaco and Montecassino very cold in winter and very
hot in summer. But St. Benedict evidently counts them
as ' mediocres ', since we may presume that his legislation
is from experience. Consequently the ' hot ' provinces
must be the South, beyond Naples,—Sicily and perhaps
even Spain or Africa. The ' cold ' provinces are north
of the Apennines, and perhaps even beyond Italy.[1] In
c. 61 we have ' de longinquis prouinciis '.

c. 64. in notitia episcopi *ad cuius dioecesim pertinet locus* ipse.

It is a matter of course that the monasteries legislated for
must be in different dioceses.

c. 65. (maxime in illis locis ubi ab eodem sacerdote uel ab
eis abbatibus qui abbatem ordinant, ab ipsis etiam et praepositus
ordinatur) . . . Quod si aut *locus expetit,* aut congregatio
petierit.

It is clear, therefore, that the Rule is intended, deliberately
and carefully adapted and intended, by St. Benedict for
many places, various provinces, contrasting climates. Does
this prove No. 3? I think it proves too much, a great deal
too much.

For No. 3 stated that St. Benedict wrote for various
Abbots, his friends and admirers,—two or three? or half
a dozen? But the Rule contemplates many places, other
provinces, unaccustomed climates, and suggests too large
a selection of widely distributed Abbots, if the Rule was
asked for by Abbots for themselves only.

---

[1] I have been at Bologna just after a fall of snow about four feet deep: the
river at Parma had nearly two-inch ice except in the rapid parts. The winter
at Milan or Turin is short but very severe, though in summer Milan is as hot
or hotter than Naples. All over Italy the difference between winter and
summer is considerable; whereas in England the distinction is often scarcely
perceptible, except from the leaves on or not on the trees.

E. Next let us note the hesitations of St. Benedict:

c. 39. Sufficere *credimus* ad refectionem cotidianam . . . cocta duo pulmentaria,

c. 40. et ideo *cum aliqua scrupulositate a nobis* mensura uictus aliorum constituitur . . . *credimus* heminam uini per singulos sufficere per diem.

c. 48. ideoque hac dispositione *credimus* utraque tempora ordinari:

c. 55. nos tamen mediocribus locis sufficere *credimus.*

c. 65. Ideo nos *uidimus* expedire, propter pacis caritatisque custodiam, in abbatis pendere arbitrio ordinationem monasterii sui.

In these passages the writer seems to say: ' I am obliged to lay down the law, and this is my opinion, this is what I have thought out.' Now this hesitation contrasts rather strangely with the authoritative character of most of the legislation in the Rule; and it evidently arises precisely from the fact that whatever decision St. Benedict arrives at has to be observed:—it is an absolute law, unless he himself modifies it, as in c. 40, by allowing for exceptional cases, or in c. 55, by refusing to make rules for unfamiliar climates.

The best-known example of this is the most important: At the end of c. 18, after the very careful division of all the Psalms between the day and night offices of the week, the legislator humbly hesitates and says:

' Especially we call attention to this point: if anyone should happen to be displeased with this distribution of the Psalms, *let him arrange it otherwise* if he judges it better so ';

So far there is uncertainty. The ' anyone ' obviously means ' any Abbot of another monastery '. St. Benedict gives a definite permission to vary his arrangement. But (and the ' but ' is important) there is a condition:

' *Provided that* he should *at any rate* take care of this, that every week the whole number of 150 Psalms shall be said, and shall be always begun over again on Sunday at the Night Office; because those monks exhibit too lazy a service of their devotion who sing less than the Psalter together with the usual Canticles in the circle of the week ', etc.

The condition is absolute : an Abbot is free to modify the arrangement, but not the quantity.

F. This last point leads us to consider the passages where the authority of the Rule is mentioned.

c. 3. *In omnibus* igitur omnes MAGISTRAM sequantur REGULAM, neque ab ea temere declinetur a *quoquam*.

ibid. Ipse tamen Abba cum timore Dei et *obseruatione* REGULAE omnia faciat.

c. 64. (Ordinatus autem Abba) . . . et *praecipue* ut PRAE-SENTEM REGULAM *in omnibus* conseruet, ut dum bene ministrauerit, audiat a Domino quod seruus bonus, etc.[1]

Nothing could be much stronger than these injunctions. The Rule is the Mistress ; all must obey it in every point. The Abbot has enormous discretion outside the Rule ; but where the Rule comes in he is allowed none whatever. In c. 64 he is given a great quantity of good advice as to moderation and discretion, but all leads up to the final ' he must observe in all points *this present Rule* ',[2] as to which he has no dispensing power. For his observance and enforcement of the Rule he will be rewarded as the good steward in Matt. xxiv. 47.

G. This Rule is precisely that to which the monk binds himself. A novice, after two months, during which

[1] Other mentions of the Rule must be compared. Though pity for the aged and children is sure to be felt, this fact must not prevent the Rule from regarding them: '*Regulae auctoritas* eis prospiciat ' c. 27, and they are not to suffer from its severe application (*districtio Regulae*). No one is to speak after Compline: this is called *haec taciturnitatis Regula*, the word being applied to a particular command of the Rule (c. 42). Similarly in c. 62, a priest is bound to keep ' Regulam decanis uel praepositis constitutam '.

[2] I do not understand how Abbot Butler in his edition of the Rule (2d. ed. p. 214, in the *Index rerum*, s.v. Regula) puts down this expression *praesentem Regulam* under the heading ' praescriptio particularis '. This sixty-fourth chapter is not a ' rule', but good advice; and ' this present Rule ' can mean nothing else but the whole Rule, as in c. 3.

he begins to feel at home, is to have the Rule read to him right through, with the injunction :

' This is the LAW under which you wish to fight ; if you can observe it, enter : but if you cannot, depart freely '. After six months THE SAME RULE is read to him, and again after four months. If he embraces it the third time he is to be received into the Community, ' Knowing however that BY THE LAW OF THE RULE it is ordered that from that day he is not allowed to leave the monastery, nor to shake THE YOKE OF THE RULE *from his neck* (c. 58).

If a priest enters, ' he must know that he has to observe all the DISCIPLINE OF THE RULE, without any relaxation. Clerics must equally promise the OBSERVANCE OF THE RULE and their stability (c. 60). If a monk is ordained ' Priest ' he must not forget THE OBEDIENCE AND DISCIPLINE OF THE RULE ; nay, if he will not be submissive and OBEY THE RULE, he is to be cast out of the monastery (c. 62). The same is true even of the Prior (Praepositus) : ' the more he is set above others, the more carefully he must *observe* THE PRECEPTS OF THE RULE. If he *despises* THE HOLY RULE, he shall be admonished until four times, then he is to be punished ; and if that does not amend him, he is to be deposed (c. 65).

Here we encounter the astonishing expression *contemptor* SANCTAE *Regulae*. We find the same in c. 23. ' If a brother be contumacious or disobedient, or in anything opposed to the Holy Rule ', *contrarius existens* SANCTAE *Regulae*.

H. This Holy Rule is to be read over and over again, not to the novices merely, but to all the monks, so that no one can excuse himself by ignorance if he breaks it :

' HANC autem REGULAM saepius uolumus in Congregatione legi, ne quis fratrum se de ignorantia excuset ', c. 66 *fin*.[1]

[1]It has often been pointed out that these words at the end of chapter 66 must mean that the Rule originally ended at this point. The following

This doctrine of 'the Rule' is very extraordinary.   There had been nothing like it in the East, except the institutions of St. Pachomius, which had a great vogue during his own lifetime and in Egypt.   St. Basil's admonitions scarcely touch practical matters, and do not form a Rule in St. Benedict's sense.   The same is obviously true of the Western literature, Cassian and Rufinus, St. Augustine and the renderings of the *Verba Seniorum*.   The monastic tradition was exemplified by St. Antony, St. Martin, St. Augustine and St. Benedict himself, (and dozens of others),—A GREAT ASCETIC OR BISHOP ROUND WHOM DISCIPLES GATHER. We know of no written law for Lerins, any more than for Marseille and Tours.   St. Fulgentius wrote no Rule, nor did Eugippius.   St. Caesarius did write one for virgins ; and he elaborated it, together with one for monks, after the model of St. Benedict.

---

seven chapters, 67-73, are therefore an afterthought. But the addition was made before the Rule was published to the world (as in the case of St. John xxi) since there is no textual disturbance in any manuscript whatever. Traube's strange conjecture that Simplicius added these chapters is obviously unacceptable; they are in exactly the same style as the rest. Besides, the Rule was published forty years at least before Simplicius became Abbot (see p. 136).

I am sorry I can see no meaning in Abbot Butler's contention that *hanc Regulam* in this passage refers to a ' particular Rule ' that the monks are not to leave the enclosure. No such Rule has preceded: the precept is to read *hanc Regulam* in the community, that is, publicly. If what has preceded is meant, then the monastery is to have read to it frequently that ' The monastery is so to be constituted, if possible ', that it has water, a mill, a garden, etc. It would be rather ridiculous to read this out frequently. Abbot Butler means apparently the end of this paragraph: but it is impossible to ' read ' publicly a final clause without the main clause: ' ut non sit necessitas monachis uagandi foras', and a final clause is not a ' regula '; nor does this particular clause state a ' rule ' that monks are never to go out,—there existed no such rule, except for nuns,—only that there ought to be no necessity for them to do so. Or does Abbot Butler mean that the last words of all, ' omnino non expedit animabus eorum ', are to be read? But then there is no antecedent to *eorum*. Abbot Butler is aware that in every Benedictine monastery the Holy Rule *saepius legitur*, and this has been invariably done from time immemorial, whereas it has never been the custom, nor could have been, to read this one paragraph frequently, by itself, about water and mill and garden, still less the subordinate clauses appended to it, which could not be read by themselves. St. Benedict means that not only the novices should repeatedly hear the Rule read, but that the professed monks should hear it again and again.

Writers on St. Benedict have tried to find a special characteristic of his monastic teaching; but a formidable difficulty lies in the fact that his Rule is too well balanced to have any obvious character, except the negative one of 'discretion',—which means that it has no particular extravagances or impracticabilities. Many have seized upon 'stability' as an epoch-making innovation. But the *Gyrovagi* of whom St. Benedict speaks were admired by no one; and the days when fervent disciples migrated from one celebrated hermit to another had passed away even in the East. It is not clear that 'stability', in any sense of the word, was an innovation.[1]

To me, I confess, this is St. Benedict's characteristic, his startling innovation, his lasting contribution to monachism: command instead of counsel. *Magistra Regula*, *Sancta Regula*, the Sovereign Rule, the Sacrosanct Rule above the Abbot,—obeyed absolutely by the monks, the Deans, the Prior, the Priest, and *praecipue* by the Pater monasterii. No doubt monastic life is a 'counsel', resting on the 'evangelical counsels', 'counsels of perfection'; but when solemnly promised it becomes an obligation, a law. In that case it is desirable to know exactly what the obligation is, and how far it reaches—to possess a Rule.

The Easterns, with myriads of monks, had been satisfied with the general idea of 'leaving the world' and 'seeking God', and this remains the basis of monastic vocation (of course) in the West also.[2] But St. Benedict insists on 'the Rule', a perfectly definite form of life, to be thoroughly understood by the novice, to be promised by

[1] See pp. 121–4.
[2] And this idea discriminates clearly between a ' monastic vocation ' and a vocation to one of the religious orders or congregations. Something more definite is needed for a Jesuit, a Dominican, a Brother of St. John of God, a Salesian, a Redemptorist. A Benedictine novice ought not to be able to say vaguely he wishes to give himself to God, and to be unable to explain any further.

him to God, and then to be observed exactly. The novice knows what he is in for—*scit ad quod ingreditur.* There is nothing new to be sprung upon him later. The Abbot cannot alter the Rule.

The Rule and the Abbot (who administers and applies it) are essential to the cenobitic life, says St. Benedict; they are its distinctive properties, as opposed to Hermits and Sarabaites and Gyrovages: St. Benedict's definition is given at the beginning of the first chapter of the Holy Rule. It is cut and dried, short, plain:

Primum (genus) coenobitarum, hoc est monasteriale, MILITANS SUB REGULA UEL ABBATE.

Vel means 'and', as very frequently in the Rule. The military idea is always to the fore. The definition is entirely new, and it is epoch-making.

But if this new definition and the conception of a Sovereign Rule constitute an astonishing innovation, the writing of this Rule—necessary to the theory—is more astonishing still. ST. BENEDICT boldly COMPOSES the Rule that is needed: he calls it 'the Mistress', 'the Holy': it is adaptable for the various provinces, conditions, climates: Abbots are to adhere to its sanctions: no one may rashly turn aside from its definite line:

And he explains candidly why he wrote it: 'We have written this Rule in order that observing it in monasteries we may show that we have to some extent both decency of morals and a beginning of monasticity'.[1] He goes on to say that for the perfection of monastic life the necessary instructions will be found in the teachings of the Holy Fathers (St. Augustine is obviously meant in the first place, St. Jerome also), in the Old and New Testaments, the

---

[1] For an apology for the neologism ' monasticity ', see p. 224. The Latin of c. 73, the end of the Rule, runs thus: ' REGULAM HANC descripsimus, ut hanc obseruantes in monasteriis, aliquatenus uel honestatem morum aut initium conuersationis nos demonstremus habere '.

Collations and Institutes of Cassian, the lives of the Fathers (by Sulpicius Severus, or in translations by St. Jerome, Rufinus, Dionysius Exiguus and others), and the Rule of 'our holy Father Basil'. This explains the title St. Benedict has given to this final chapter : 'That in this Rule is not set down the observance of all justice', *De hoc quod non 'cmnis iustitiae obseruatio' in hac sit Regula constituta*. This is not modesty, it is a plain statement of fact. No doubt 'all justice' is contained in the Instruments of Good Works, and the highest perfection is taught in the chapter on Humility ; but essentially the Holy Rule is within the reach of every monk, and he must observe it ; and the Abbot must not demand more, though he may advise more : but several hours a day are set apart for the study of the books which lead to higher individual perfection.

Consequently St. Benedict can continue with the nothing less than amazing words which end this chapter and the Rule :

'WHOSOEVER THOU ART, therefore, who hastenest to the heavenly country, *quisquis ergo ad patriam caelestem festinas*, with the help of Christ carry out perfectly this tiny Rule for beginners, *hanc minimam inchoationis Regulam descriptam adiuuante Christo perfice*, and then thou shalt in time arrive with God's protection at the greater summits of knowledge and virtues which we have just mentioned '.[1]

The modesty is obvious : St. Benedict refuses to write another book of advice for higher perfection, since so many are to hand. But there is an assumption of authority behind : 'Whosoever', *quisquis*. This is the way, walk ye in it. We turn back from the explicit to the incipit, and there we find the same assurance, authority, exclusiveness : '*Ad te nunc mihi sermo dirigitur*, QUISQUIS abrenuntians propriis uoluntatibus, Domino Christo uero Regi militaturus,

[1] The reference is to Matt. iii, 15: *implere omnem iustitiam*.

oboedientiae fortissima atque praeclara arma sumis' (*Prologue*). These words are simple enough, if merely addressed to any postulant, *quisquis*, who knocked at the door of Montecassino. But now we know that the Rule is for many provinces and climates, neither the Prologue nor the last Chapter is limited in its address : they appear to be spoken to monks in general, or at least postulants in general, and QUISQUIS becomes in both places universal. Similarly *in monasteriis* becomes universal in application (73. 'Regulam hanc descripsimus, ut hanc obseruantes *in monasteriis* . . .)

These considerations throw light on the singularly majestic words which open the Prologue :

'*Incipit prologus Regulae* MONASTERIORUM'.

'Obsculta, o fili, UERBA MAGISTRI, et inclina aurem cordis tui, et admonitionem PII PATRIS libenter excipe et efficaciter comple, ut *ad Eum* per oboedientiae laborem redeas, a quo per inoboedientiae desidiam recesseras. Ad te ergo nunc MIHI SERMO dirigitur, quisquis', etc.

It has always been a crux whether to take MAGISTER and PIUS PATER to mean St. Benedict, or God ; whether, that is, they go with *ad Eum* or with *mihi sermo*. I am inclined (with Abbot Butler and others) to take them of St. Benedict, both because *mihi sermo*[1] seems to be the same as the *uerba Magistri*, and because this authoritative pronouncement agrees with the Epilogue and with the commanding manner of the Rule.

I see no way of escaping the conclusion that our solution No. 4 has to be accepted : the reason why the Rule of St. Benedict became with such ease the Rule for many provinces and circumstances throughout the West, and the only monastic Rule of the West, is not because accidentally a

---

[1]*Mihi* is an ' ethical ' dative, like Horace's ' Quid mihi Celsus agit ' in the grammars. Dom Martène follows St. Peter Damian in holding that the Holy Ghost is meant by *Magister*, as otherwise the humble St. Benedict would be guilty of intolerable presumption.

Rule for a few Abbeys was found to be applicable elsewhere, but because *the Rule was written with the definite
purpose of providing a single Rule for all Western monasteries.*

I did not start out to reach this conclusion. I started
out to prove No. 3. The facts when massed together gave
me a shock.

We have seen several instances of St Benedict's hesitations, we have seen his moderation and modesty in the
Epilogue. They contrast with his imperious orders, but
they are explained by them. It is just because he knows
that his will is to be law, and because he insists that his
will is to be law, that he is afraid of being too definite where
circumstances vary, and of being too exacting where his
Rule must apply to many.

We have still a passage to add : the end of the Prologue :
'We have, therefore, to initiate a school of Divine Service',
'Constituenda est ergo NOBIS dominici schola seruitii'.
Why must he do so? Are there not plenty of monasteries
about all the provinces of the Empire which are excellent
schools of holiness? What of Aequitius and his monasteries in Valeria? of Eugippius at Naples, of Fulgentius
in Sardinia or Africa, of Caesarius in Narbonensis, Ennodius
at Pavia? What of Marinus at Lerins, still flourishing,
and the traditions of Marseille and Tours, of Vercelli and
Milan? Is everything to be begun over again? 'Sunt
doctrinae sanctorum Patrum' ! what is this new 'school'
and why *must* Benedict, who has never been a monk, constitute it, to the overthrow of all the running concerns,
which get on so well with a holy Abbot, without a Rule?

The question is suggestive. For an answer we may turn
to the movement of the times.

From the days of the Twelve Tables the Republic was
ruled by an accumulation of successive laws and of in-
numerable treatises upon them. It needed a thousand

years[1] before Theodosius II produced his code, anti-quating most of the laws, reducing the rest to order, but leaving the legists. This was in 438. In 529 Justinian produces a new code; but he does much more; his lieu-tenants, under Trebonian's hasty guidance, sum up the principles of jurisprudence into the 'Institutes', and extract the pith of the vast tomes of the lawyers into the Digest, a work of surprising scope, performed in a sur-prising hurry, just after the writing of the Holy Rule.

The ecclesiastical law of the West (that is, of the Roman ' Patriarchate ', so-called by the Easterns, with the ex-clusion of its Greek-speaking lands, Macedonia, Greece, etc., and of Latin Africa) consisted mainly of Papal Decre-tals, together with the Nicene canons, approved by the Popes. Bishops were supposed to make themselves ac-quainted with these frequent Decretals or Constitutions and to communicate them to one another.[2] These decretals were in the form of letters addressed to some Metropolitan, just as imperial laws were addressed to some great functionary, but they were obligatory on the rest of Europe. A collection of these and of canons of councils was much needed. The Scythian monk Diony-sius Exiguus, to whom we owe the Christian era now in use, made a collection and translation of Greek councils at the request of a certain Brother Laurentius and of the bishop of Salona (Spalato) in Dalmatia. After the death of St. Gelasius (496) he settled in Rome, and there made a collection of Papal decretals from 385 to 496, including one of Pope Anastasius (496-8). The book was presum-ably published soon after that year. This was at the

---

[1] The ' codes ' of Gregorius and Hermogenius were apparently private ventures at the end of the third century.

[2] St. Siricius is very explicit on this in his famous letter of 385 to Himerius of Tarragona; so are later Popes. A good example of this is St. Innocent to St. Victricius of Rouen in 404. On the government of the Western Church by the Popes, see my *Studies on the Early Papacy*, ch. I.

request of Julianus,[1] Priest of the title of St. Anastasia at Rome. The dedicatory letter to him is mainly concerned with the virtues of his late master, Gelasius, and implies that this learned, holy, practical and legally-minded Pope had wished for such a work; for it is clearly meant that it is because Julian is his disciple that he has urged Dionysius to undertake this publication.

Later on, when the troubled reign of Symmachus is over, and Hormisdas sits (July 514) in the chair of Peter, this great Pope, in controversy for the next four years with the Acacianizing Emperor Anastasius, finds that the Greeks misinterpret or misquote the councils. He therefore bids Dionysius prepare him a copy of the Greek councils with Greek and Latin in parallel columns on the same page.[2] It is probably from this date at the latest (514-18) that the collections of Dionysius came to be habitually used by the Roman Church, as Cassiodorus (*Instit. Div. litt.* 23) tells us they were about 552 : ' quos hodie usu celeberrimo Ecclesia Romana complectitur '.[3]

Hormisdas also re-issued the *Decretum Gelasianum*, with its celebrated index of forbidden books, and list of recommended ones, but with some significant alterations (made after 519) : the council of Constantinople 381, which he

[1] This Roman priest Julianus is present at the Council of Symmachus of 499; his name is given twice over in MSS. (58 and 65, Mommen's *Cassiod. Variae*, p. 402), and again (*ibid.* p. 414) he signs in full: Julianus presbyter tituli Anastasiae subscripsi ' (twice! 50 and 61); he is also present at the Council of 502 (p. 443; Thiel, pp. 644, 653, 684). There were perhaps two Julians; but both cannot have had the title of St. Anastasia at one time.

[2] We learn this from Dionysius's dedicatory letter to the Pope, preserved in a single MS. in a very corrupt form (Maassen, *Gesch. der Quellen des Canon. Rechts*, p. 964). ' Your veneration, being unable to endure the arrogance of those who boast that they are specialists in the Greek canons, and when asked about any ecclesiastical decree reply as though from some mysterious oracle, has deigned to order by that authority in which you excel other bishops, that I shall with all diligence strive that the Latin should not disagree with the Greek, and should append them side by side on each page, divided by a line into equal portions', etc. A single copy is meant, not an edition, as Maassen and others have assumed.

[3] He is really thinking of his experience before he left the world, *c.* 542.

found was reckoned as oecumenical in the East (see the words of his legates who speak of four councils Ep. 76.4, and 98.2, though until now Rome had only counted three,) and other councils included by Dionysius in his collection.[1] This brings us to about 520.

The labour on the Code of Justinian begins in 530. About in the middle of this decade was published the Rule of St. Benedict, since I hope to prove in the next chapter but one that it was used by Justinian for the first time in 531, and by St. Caesarius in Gaul about 532. The Holy Rule is a very elaborate mosaic, and must have needed a considerable time to compose. I presume, therefore, that it was begun before the death of the great Hormisdas, August 6th, 523, and finished about 526 at latest.

Now its position between the Code of Dionysius and that of Justinian is notable. Justinian became virtual ruler with his uncle, Justin I, in 518; he became Augustus in 527 at the age of 45. In February of the next year he announced to the Senate his intention of correcting and abridging the Gregorian, Hermogenian and Theodosian codes with the addition of subsequent laws, and named the committee. He must have had the idea in his mind before he was Emperor, and the code was ready in April, 529.[2] The enormous labour of the Digest was completed between December, 530, and December, 533; the Institutes were finished a month earlier. Thus St. Benedict's Rule is midway between Dionysius and Justinian. Collections of laws were in the air.

But the parallel is closer with Justinian than with Dionysius. The latter put together a number of councils, and such important decretals as he could find, into collections; and a monastic parallel to this would be the *Codex*

---

[1] See my article against Dobschütz, *Revue Bénéd.*, April, 1913, vol. 30, pp. 191-3.
[2] It contains laws, however, up to November, 534.

Regularum of St. Benedict of Aniane at the beginning of
the ninth century. But a sylloge of contradictory Rules
would be useless as legislation, and the reformer of Aniane
was fain to make a harmony of these disparate elements,
by turning them into a sort of commentary on the Rule
of St. Benedict, in his second work, the *Concordia Regularum.*
Justinian's code omitted the laws that were antiquated or
revoked, and gave extracts from the others, appending his
own most recent ones at length. Similarly, in the Digest,
he gave the pith of the commentators in short extracts,
and in the Institutes he summarised their principles.

Abbot Butler's edition of the Holy Rule enables us to
compare it with this work done by Trebonian for the
Emperor. In the second edition (1927) he gives no less
than 347 references to probable sources of the Rule,
without counting a few quotations giving only illustrations.
(I should deduct 19 of St. Caesarius, leaving 328.) Of
these, 46 are regarded by Abbot Butler as verbal quotations; but in many of the other passages the borrowing
of the sense is even more impressive. It is impossible
that Abbot Butler's diligence should have been able to
garner every stray passage used in the Rule, and it is
extremely probable that we do not possess all its sources.
A good many chapters appear to be St. Benedict's very
own, with no ' sources '. But the greater number are a
cento from former Rules and books of piety.

I give a list of the chief authorities used by St. Benedict,
adding the number of resemblances noted by Abbot
Butler. The verbal quotations are given in brackets :

Cassian 110 (10); Augustine 42 (9); Jerome 14 (4);
Basil 22 (4); Regula Macarii 14 (2); Regulae Serapionis,
Macarii, Papnutii, etc. 11 (1); Regula Pachomii 28;
Vita Pachomii 2 (1); Regula Orientalis 10; Rufinus,

Historia Monachorum 15 (3); Verba Seniorum 12 (1);
Vita Antonii 2 (1); Orsiesius 4. Of the Fathers: St.
Cyprian 7 (1); St. Ambrose 6; St. Leo 3 (3).

There are a few more besides, such as tags from the
Acts of Martyrs. Every part of Holy Scripture is quoted
or alluded to. The whole Rule is only about fifty pages
of ordinary print.

For example, the Prologue is founded on St. Augustine,
with bits of Jerome and the Vitae Patrum and Cassian
as usual; the rest is largely from the Psalms. Yet the
whole is curiously personal and unlike the authorities.
Chapter 1 is from Jerome through Cassian, enlarged from
Augustine, with expressions apparently from the Vitae
Patrum and Rufinus: but the important definition
' militans sub Regula uel Abbate ' is apparently pure
Benedict. Ch. 2 on the Abbot is, as we shall see, founded
on the Collections of Dionysius, as well as from common
sense and experience, together with much from Scripture,
but set down by one who has a great deal of monastic
literature by heart, so that some of the doctrine and many
of the expressions are paralleled in sources.[1] Ch. 3 seems
to be original. Ch. 4 (Instruments) has probably a
source unknown to us.[2] Ch. 5 is traditional teaching in
traditional language, chiefly Cassian, Pachomius and the
Dialogue of Sulpicius Severus; the simplicity and direct-

[1] See pp. 41, 42.
[2] The ' Instruments of Good Works ' are found without the rest of the Rule
in a good many MSS., and it has been conjectured that they existed in this
separate form before St. Benedict, and that he incorporated them in his
Rule. This seems quite inconceivable. St. Benedict studied with care a
great number of previous writers, for whom he had a profound veneration;
but he never adopted their words, he entirely re-wrote them when he borrowed
their teaching, and coincidences of more than two or three consecutive words
are rare. The ' Instruments ' in the MSS. referred to are borrowed straight
out of the Holy Rule. As to sources of the ' Instruments ', I merely refer to
the excellent discussion by Abbot Butler in the *Journal of Theol. Studies*, Jan.
1911 (vol. XII, n° 46), pp. 261-8.

ness is St. Benedict, but also Cassianesque. The sources of Ch. 6 are unknown. Ch. 7 of the ' steps ' of Humility, is from Cassian, but much enlarged, with expressions borrowed from others. And so forth.

The Holy Rule thus reminds us of Justinian's code, who quotes predecessors in brief, and adds long laws of his own; it is still more like the Digest and the Institutes combined: like the Institutes it is an ' introduction ' (to monastic observance), like the Digest it uses the words (or at least the ideas) of former jurists. Of course it is far more original than either, especially in what it omits.

St. Basil's Rules are mainly ascetical. Cassian relates practical details, but is chiefly concerned with the moral virtues and prayer. St. Benedict's Rule is practical: it deals with the Divine Office, the distribution of the day, the punishment of faults, the government of the Abbey and of the monks, the officials, the reading and work, the guest-house, the kitchens, the infirmary. He does indeed discourse on three virtues, because they are necessary to the order of the establishment,—obedience, its foundation in humility, and the love of silence; he also has a short chapter on attention to the Divine Office. ' Poverty ' is mentioned as the absence of a vice against obedience; it does not appear as a virtue. Mortification, especially spiritual mortification, comes under humility. For the virtues in general we are referred to Holy Scripture, to Cassian and to the Fathers.

It is remarkable that the language is strikingly legal. St. Benedict may have begun to read law at Rome; but this is most unlikely, as he left his studies *scienter nescius et sapienter indoctus*, despising *litterarum studia*, which would be completed before law was undertaken. It would rather appear that in order to compose the Rule he must have consulted the imperial laws concerning monks and clerics.

But was he not even more likely to consult the canons of councils on the same subject, and the decretals of the Popes? Very few of the imperial laws about ecclesiastical matters have been preserved to us by Justinian in his code, for he prefers his own. There is little concerning monks in the code of Theodosius.

It was necessary for any Abbot to have some general knowledge of both imperial and ecclesiastical legislation. But a code of laws for monks, intended for many provinces, must needs be founded on a study of the subject, sufficient to avoid any clashing.

Hence it seems *a priori* possible if not probable that St. Benedict, who had made so thorough and penetrating a study of all the monastic literature available, would not omit to make himself acquainted at first hand with the authoritative sources of civil law and Church law regarding monasteries and monks, especially the latter. We have to ask ourselves, therefore, whether there are any traces in the Holy Rule of a knowledge of civil laws, and still more of the Dionysian canon law.

CHAPTER III

ST. BENEDICT quotes the translations of Dionysius—How digestion takes place during sleep—The legal style of the Holy Rule derived from civil laws and from Dionysius—St. Benedict has taken over the formulas and vocabularies of the Dionysian collections, and applies to monks what was laid down for clerics —He applies to Abbots what the Papal decretals said of bishops and their flocks.

DIONYSIUS EXIGUUS was a famous person in his day. The learning with which he calculated the Christian era was remarkable enough ; still more remarkable is the fact that it was officially accepted throughout the East as well as the West. As was said above, his collections of canon law were officially used by the Papal chancery. He was tutor in Dialectics to that young man of high birth and great talents, Cassiodorus. He lived at Rome as an Abbot from about 498 till after 526. St. Benedict could not but know him well by name.

It has, in fact, been shown by Abbot Butler that he quotes the translation by Dionysius of the life of St. Pachomius :

Vita Pachomii, 13 : Constituit praepositos qui sibi *ad lucrandas animas*, quae ad eum quotidie confluebant, adiutores existerent.

S. Reg. 58, 12 : et senior eis (uenientibus ad conuersationem) talis deputetur qui aptus sit *ad lucrandas animas*, qui super eos omnino curiose intendat.

I think St. Benedict knew also Dionysius's translation of the Invention of the head of St. John the Baptist, for his two churches at Montecassino were dedicated to St. John and St. Martin, the latter the most celebrated Father of monks in the West, the former the patron (one would think) of solitaries rather than of cenobites. But the preface of Abbot Dionysius, addressed to another Abbot, Gaudentius, seems to explain why St. Benedict regarded the Baptist as the Patron of monks. It was a divinely ordered coincidence, says the Abbot, that monks should have discovered the head of the saint, and that an exiguous monk should publish the story for Roman ears :

' Nec hoc sine diuino nutu gestum esse perspicio: et idem sanctus Iohannes, praeuius Domini ueritatis praeco, prophetarum culmen omnium, INSTITUTORQUE MONACHORUM, sicut primitus se monachis ostendit, qui sacratissimum caput eius de domo Herodis quondam regis impii sustulerunt, dein ablatum Emesae,[1] de multis ignoratum temporibus, item monachis se declarauit: ita nunc officio monachorum, quamuis humilium, hanc de se Romanis historiam manifestare dignatus est '. (P.L. 67, col. 417).

Here St. John the Baptist is definitely the founder of monasticism, his disciples being the first monks.[2]

Further, it is very likely Dionysius who induced St. Benedict to speak of 'our Holy Father St. Basil' (*S. Reg.* 73 : 'sed et Regula sancti Patris nostri Basilii'), an expression astonishing in a Western mouth. But it is St. Basil's own brother, Gregory of Nyssa, who seems to have suggested the phrase, for we find in the Prologue to his Supplement to

---

[1] Migne's text has *Emesenae*. I presume we ought to read *Emesenae ciuitati*.

[2] Dionysius therefore ignores the Carmelite view that St. John was not a monk but a friar: that the Carmelites founded by St. Elias were (like Benedictines) separate communities without a common head, in the days of the schools of the Prophets and of Pythagoras (the author of the multiplication table) and of other celebrated friars, but that the Baptist united them and became the first General of the order.

St. Basil's Hexäemeron, '*De creatione hominis*', which Dionysius translated : 'uere ad imaginem Dei conditus formatusque Basilius, communis Pater noster atque præceptor'.

One has often wondered where St. Benedict found his notion of digestion going on during sleep, so that it is best not to rise until it is completed : 'octaua hora surgendum est, ut modice amplius de media nocte pausetur, et iam digesti surgant' (*S. Reg.* 8). Perhaps St. Gregory Nyssen provides us with a reply. He has a long chapter on the necessity of sleep, and a dissertation on its uses which is not easy to follow; but his view that sleep is necessary for digestion is plain in Dionysius's translation : I quote one sentence : 'Necessaria uero est corpori quies, ut sine impedimento quoque cibus in omnia membra per occulta eidem itinera diffundatur, nulla intentionis obice meabilem praecludente transgressum'.[1] It would seem that St. Benedict's practical mind studied this elaborate piece of science, and determined that monks ought to have sufficient time allowed them for the work of digestion in sleep.[2]

[1] A little more may be added in a note: ' Nam sicut ex infusa imbribus terra, cum radiis solis fota fuerit, uapores quidam caliginosi de profundis eius finibus extrahuntur, similiter et in nostra fit terra: cum cibus intrinsecus congenitoque calore decoquitur, uapor quidam naturaliter, utpote aereus, ad superna contendit, et ueluti fumus per rimas parietis penetrans ad capitis loca peruenit, inde per dictos adnexus sensibus exhalatur. *Unde necesse est tunc sensus otium gerere*, uaporum transgressione detentos. Oculi sopiti sunt, et palpebrarum obductione ueluti quodam mechanicae artis aequo pondere conteguntur: ipsis quoque uaporibus et auditus obstruitur, et quasi quodam ostio auribus imposito a sua naturali operatione feriatur. *Haec autem talis passio somnus dicitur*, uacantibus in corpore sensibus et iuxta naturalem motum nihil prorsus agentibus, *ut digestiones escarum exitu faciliore proueniant*, et suos meatus ipsa exhalatione transcurrant. Quapropter si coangustentur his exhalationibus ea loca quae circa sensus sunt, et *quadam somnus occupatione tardetur*, uapore complentur' , etc. The Saint then gives an explanation and a scientific description of the phenomenon of yawning. (P.L. 67, col. 366, cap. 14, and P.G. 44, col. 168, cap. 13.)

[2] *De creat. hom.* 20 fin., col. 580, supplies another resemblance:

Persuadet autem *serpens* ut edatur, ut per hoc mortis machinetur ingressum; cum *suasione ipsa* praeualuit, lethale consilium tribuens, et colori quodam fallaci eumdem fructum,

cp. *S. Reg.* Prol. 71. Qui malignum diabolum aliqua suadentem sibi *cum ipsa suasione* sua a conspectibus cordis sui respuens, deduxit ad nihilum.

We have now some justification for comparing the Holy
Rule with the canonical collections of Dionysius. The
obviously legal *Si quis* followed by a penalty is naturally
very frequent in laws. I give instances from laws prior to
Justinian in a note. There are seven instances in the Rule;
but then there are eight in the Rule of St. Pachomius.
There are 22 in the collections of canons of councils and of
decretals by Dionysius. St. Benedict is particularly fond
of *quod si* (31 times). This is only twice found in Pachomius
but nine times in Dionysius, and often in laws.

St. Benedict is very fond of *forte* (*nisi forte*, *aut forte*, etc.),
21 times; Dionysius 7; Pachomius twice.[1]

Particularly remarkable is St. Benedict's fondness for
praesumo. I have not noticed it in Pachomius,[2] nor in the
civil laws, which use 'si quis temptauerit' or 'ausus fuerit';
these expressions occur occasionally in canon law as well.
But *praesumere* and *praesumptio* are common in canon law
(14 times), and are used just as by St. Benedict, who in-
creases the number to 32 times![3] We may presume, if we
wish, connexion from resemblance.

---

[1] See note at end of Chapter.
[2] But in *Reg. Patrum* I (Serapion, etc.) c. 7.
[3] *S. Reg.*

3[10]	et non praesumant
3[19]	neque praesumat quisquam
3[21]	quod si praesumpserit
20[2]	non praesumimus, nisi
26[1]	si quis frater praesumpserit
31[31]	a quibus eum prohibuerit, non praesumat
33[2]	ne quis praesumat
33[13]	nec quisquam suum aliquid dicat aut praesumat
38[19]	nec praesumat ibi aliquis
43[27]	nec praesumant sociari choro
43[43]	et ne quis praesumat
43[45]	(quicquam cibi aut potus praesumere)
44[14]	uel aliud quid non praesumat
47[7]	cantare . . . et legere non praesumat
51[3]	non praesumat foris manducare
54[6]	non praesumat suscipere illud
54[12]	qui autem aliter praesumpserit
57[10]	ne aliquam fraudem praesumant
60[10]	nullatenus aliqua praesumat

We can similarly parallel St. Benedict's *si contempserit,*
inuentus (or *repertus*) *fuerit, si contigerit.*[1]   To such likenesses

62[56]	nec quicquam praesumat
62[17]	quod si aliter praesumpserit
63[36]	nec praesumat iunior
67[11]	nec praesumat quisquam
67[14]	quod si quis praesumpserit
67[15]	similiter et qui praesumpserit
69 *tit*	ut in monasterio non praesumat alter
69[2]	ne quauis occasione praesumat
69[6]	nec quolibet modo id a monachis praesumatur
70 *tit*	ut non praesumat passim aliquis
70[10]	qui praesumit aliquatenus
49[23]	praesumptioni deputabitur et uanae gloriae
70[1]	omnis praesumptionis occasio

Compare the collections of Dionysius:

Can. App.	38 (39)	nec ei liceat ex his aliquid omnino praesumere
Can. Nic.	16	si quis autem . . . praesumpserit
Can. Antioch.	9	amplius autem nihil agere praesumat
	11 *tit*	de episcopis et clericis qui . . . praesumunt
Can. Sard.	17	nullus debet praesumere ut
Innoc. Decentio *praef.*		traditiones antiquas humana praesumptione corruptas
Innoc. Victricio	10	quod si quis forte praesumpserit
Leo	1	contra constituta canonum et ecclesiasticam disciplinam praesumpta uel commissa
	31	quod a te cognouimus esse praesumptum
	36	nihil permittimus te ignorante praesumi
	28	temeritas praesumptionis
	6	aut a praesumptionis usurpatione reuocemus
Innoc. Victricio (pref. before 9).		multa non praesumenda praesumunt
Exuperio (pref. before 21).		usurpatione praesumpta
	46	usque adhuc habere praesumptum
	56	non posse praesumere
Zosimus I.		aspirare praesumeret . . . contra praecepta Patrum crediderant praesumendum.
Cp. Reg. Patrum 1 13		quod si praesumpserit talia facere

[1] A. S. Reg. 71[19] quod qui *contempserit* facere, cp. *Can. Ap.* 15 si uocatus
ab episcopo redire *contempserit.* B. S.R. 21[11] si ex eis . . . *repertus fuerit*
reprehensibilis. 48[46] si, quod absit, *repertus fuerit.* 55[35] si cui *inuentum*
fuerit. 61[15] quod si superfluus aut uitiosus *inuentus fuerit.* 65[42] si *repertus*
fuerit uitiosus. Cp. *Can. Chalced.* 18 si qui ergo clerici aut monachi *reperti*
fuerint. Can. Laod. 35 (138) si quis igitur *inuentus fuerit. Can. Nic.* ut si
quis *inuentus fuerit.* C. S.R. 6[1] *saepius* quidem *contingit* ut. cp. *Conc. Sard.*
sed quoniam *saepe contingit* ut. S.R. 11[33] quod *si contigerit. Can. Ant.* 23 ut
si contigerit. Can. Ancyr. aut ex aliqua occasione *contigerit,* and in the Code.
D. On the other hand with S.R. 34[12] quod *si deprehensus fuerit,* we may
compare civil laws: Code I. 3. 14 (A.D. 400) *si* . . . *fuerit deprehensus,* X 12 1
(380) quisquis . . . *deprehensus fuerit* et punitus, III 24 1 in aliqua culpa
seu crimine *fuerit deprehensus,* etc. Also the Rule of St. Pachomius 166 *si*
deprehensus fuerit aliquis.

of style one may add *rationabilis causa, necessitatis excusatio*
and the use of *occasio*,[1] all connected with the legal style.
So with correction, as *deiciatur, amputandum, contentiosus,
obedire*, etc.[2] *Vitio suo* for 'by his own fault' is to
be noticed.[3]

Contumax (S.R. 23[1], 71[20]) is a legal word, cp. Code III 23, 2 for example.
St. Benedict is very fond of *sciat* or *sciens;* so is the Code, e.g. III 27, 2, X 16[12],
and 25, 3, etc. I quote the sort of frequent sentences that remind one of the
Rule: 'capitali sententia subiugandam'; 'condemnatione plectentur';
'cruciatibus esse subdendum'; 'modis omnibus prohibemus'; 'prius
habita aestimatione'; 'ut his saltem horis atque temporibus quibus religiosos
uiros a turbulenta obseruatione praetorii uacare contigerit'; 'hoc nihilominus obseruando'; 'ita ut pro arbitrio uiri reuerentissimi'; 'post unius
uero anni spatium'; 'si quis in hoc genus sacrilegii proruperit'; 'qui
proteruo ausu temptauerit'.

[1]A. S.R. 2[50] *nisi* alia *rationabilis causa* existat. *Can. Ap. nisi* forte quis
eum *rationabilis causa* compellat. *ib.* 9 aut *causam* dicat, ut si *rationabilis* fuerit,
ueniam consequatur (cp. S.R. 24[14] usque dum satisfactione congrua ueniam
consequatur). B. S.R. 55[41] ut omnis auferatur *necessitatis excusatio. Can.
Chalc.* 25 nisi forte *necessitas inexcusabilis.* C. S.R. 62[7] nec *occasione* sacerdotii.
69[7] grauissima *occasio* scandalorum. 70[1] omnis praesumptionis *occasio.*
cp. *Can. Ap.* 38 nec eorum *occasione* ecclesiae negotia depraedentur. 24 (*bis*)
and 39 sub *occasione* (rerum, etc.) *Can. Ancyr.* aut ex aliqua *occasione* contigerit.
Bonif. 3 purgandi se *occasione* non utitur. So in the Code frequently, e.g.
occasione militiae, sub cuiuscumque priuilegii *occasione*, etc. It seems hardly
necessary to refer to certain legal expressions in the Rule: 58[43] de qua
promissione sua faciat petitionem . . . quam petitionem *manu sua scribat*,
aut certe . . . signum faciat. (The religious profession was valid in law,
of course.) 58[59] aut facta solemniter donatione conferat monasterio nihil
sibi *reseruans* ex omnibus; 59[6] de rebus autem suis aut *in praesenti petitione
promittant sub iureiurando* (common expression in law) . . . faciant . . .
donationem, reseruato sibi, si ita uoluerint, *usufructu.*

[2]A. S.R. 21[13] si emendare noluerit, *deiciatur.* 65[47] quod si neque sic correxerit,
deiciatur. cp. *Can. Ap.* 7 sin aliter, *deiciantur*, 6 *deiciatur*, 28 *deici* ab officio suo
praecipimus. 30 *deiciatur* et ipse. *Can. Nic. deiciatur* a clero. B. S.R 2[4]
radicitus ea ut praeualet *amputet.* 33[1] radicitus *amputandum* est. 55[23]
amputari debet. 37 radicitus *amputetur.* 64[35] cum caritate ea *amputet.* cp.
Can. Nic. consuetudinem omnimodis *amputari* quae praeter regulam in quibusdam partibus uidetur admissa. S. Leo 2 diligentius *amputentur.* 49 quaedam
uero penitus *amputanda.* Also *Reg. Patrum* I (*Serap. Macar. Paphn.*). 7 *ampu-
tandae* sunt primo ab huiuscemodi diuitiae saeculi; et si quis pauper . . .
habet et ipse diuitias quas *amputare* debet. C. S.R. 71[10] quod si quis *contentiosus* repperitur, corripiatur. cp. *Can. Ant.* 1 et de ecclesia pellendos
censemus, si tamen *contentiosi* aduersus ea quae bene sunt decreta perstiterint;
(cp. S.R. 65[52] de monasterio pellatur, 71[20] expellatur). D. si tamen talis
fuerit eius contumacia, ut subdi aut *oboedire* Regulae *nolit.* cp. *Can. Ant.* nec
consentire *nec obedire uoluerit.*

[3]S.R. 29[1] frater qui *proprio uitio* egreditur de monasterio. 43[34] qui per
neglegentiam suam aut uitio.
    Can. Ant. 18. non *suo uitio*, sed quod
         ib. non tamen *eius uitio* perpetratam.

Certain uses of words are merely noticeable as of the same date,—*sociari, sociandus, conuentus.*[1]

The titles of the chapters of the Rule frequently remind us of those of the canons of Dionysius, especially the six which begin *De his qui.* The Rule is in fact mainly a series of monastic ' canons '.

Dionysius actually translates κανών by *regula*, instead of preserving the Greek word ; and κανονικός he often renders by *regularis*. The result of this is a curious likeness to St. Benedict's wording. Is it accidental, or has the Saint borrowed half-consciously from the canons and the decretals?

The canons speak of clerics as those who are *sub regula* :

Can. Nic.	16	quicumque *sub regula* prorsus existunt.
	17	quoniam multi *sub regula* constituti.
Can. Ant.	6	omnes qui *sub regula* esse monstrantur.
S. Reg.	1 [3]	coenobitarum (genus) . . . militans *sub Regula* uel abbate.

This parallel between clergy and monks occurs often :

Can. Ant.	11	episcopus aut presbyter aut quilibet *regulae subiectus* ecclesiae.
S. Reg.	60[11]	(sacerdos) sciens se *disciplinae regulari subditum.*
	58[35]	excutere collum *de sub iugo regulae.*

---

[1]α. S.R. 61[17] *sociari* corpori monasterii. 60[17] si quis . . . monasterio *sociari* uoluerit. 61[21] suscipiatur congregationi *sociandus.* cp. S. Leo 2 sacri altaris ministerio *sociandus.* Code I, 3, 20 (434) bona . . . ecclesiae uel monasterio . . . omnifariam *socientur.* I 46 2 (416) scholae agentum in rebus *societur*, etc. Also S.R. 43[27] *sociari* choro psallentium. 53[8] sic sibi *socientur* in pace [52]nullatenus *societur* neque conloquatur. cp. *Can. Sard.* 17 nullus debet praesumere ut eum communione *societ.* Code I, 3, 20 bona . . . monasterio *socientur.* β. S.R. 13[28] ut *conuenti* per ipsius orationis sponsionem. Here *conuenti* is the past participle passive of *conuenire*, to summon: ' being urged to do so by the very promise in the prayer.' This would have been too obvious to state, were it not for the inconceivable note in the index to Wölfflin's edition of the Rule, p. 76: ' conuenti=conuentuales? 13, 23, cp. 20. 9 '. I therefore compare for this very common word *Can. Sard.* 5 quod si *conuentus* litteris tacuerit. *Bonif.* 3 *Conuentus* autem dicitur euitasse et adesse minime uoluisse (' when summoned ').

This subjection to ' regular discipline ' is recurrent, but
Dionysius prefers ' canonical ' in some cases :

Can. Nic.	5	sententia *regularis* obtineat, ut
Can. Chalc.	9	canonicis correptionibus subiacebit
	25	correctione ecclesiasticae subiacebit
	24	canonum sententiis subiacebunt
S. Reg.	48[48]	correptioni *regulari* subiaceat
	62[6]	disciplinae *regulari* subdendum
	67[14]	uindictae *regulari* subiaceat

Compare also the ' holy rule ' :

Can. Ant.	1 omni extrinsecus honore priuari quem *SANCTA* *regula* et sacerdotium Dei promeruit.
S. Reg.	23[3], 65[44] contrarius, contemptor, Sanctae *Regulae*.

It would seem from all this evidence that St. Benedict's
style and vocabulary were considerably influenced by the
study of the canons and decretals collected by Dionysius,
and very likely also by some acquaintance with the civil
laws concerning clerics and monks. But it seems still more
clear that he borrowed matter as well as words from these
venerable councils and papal constitutions. There is a
remarkable parallel between the rules for bishops and
clergy, and the rules made by St. Benedict for monks ; and
especially in chapters for which Abbot Butler has not been
able to suggest sources. Let us first take a passage about
deference to seniors, remembering St. Benedict's method,
—to borrow from Augustine or Cassian or Pachomius freely,
modifying the sense, and retaining very few, sometimes
none, of the actual words :

S. Reg. 63[35] Transeunte maiore minor surgat et det ei locum
sedendi; nec praesumat iunior consedere, nisi ei praecipiat
senior suus: ut fiat quod scriptum est: ' Honore inuicem
praeuenientes '.

The parallel with the council of Nicaea (repeated by that of Laodicea) supplied a precedent more venerable even than any of the recommendations of ancient hermits :

Can. Nic. 18 sed *nec sedere* in medio presbyterorum diaconis liceat; quia si hoc fiat, *praeter regulam et ordinem* probatur existere.
Can. Laod. 20 (123) quod non oporteat diaconum coram presbytero sedere, sed *iussione presbyteri sedeat.* Similiter autem et diaconis *honor habeatur* ab obsequentibus.

This resemblance suggests a comparison of the preceding clauses :

Can. Nic. ibid. Peruenit ad sanctum magnumque concilium quod in quibusdam locis et ciuitatibus presbiteris gratiam sacrae communionis diaconi porrigant: quod *nec regula* nec consuetudo permittit . . . Haec igitur omnia resecentur, et in sua diaconi mensura permaneant, *scientes* quod episcoporum quidem ministri sint, presbiteris autem inferiores probentur *per ordinem :* ergo post presbiteros *gratiam communionis accipiant,* aut episcopo eis aut presbitero porrigente. sed nec sedere, etc.
S. Reg. 63[8] ergo *secundum ordines* quos constituerit (abbas), uel quos habuerint ipsi fratres, *sic accedant* ad Pacem, *ad Communionem,* ad psalmum inponendum, in choro standum, *etc.*

The excommunication of the Rule, whether from the Divine Office or from the common table, is taken by St. Benedict from the Regulae Patrum and from Cassian. But he may have been influenced by the words used of ecclesiastical excommunication. For example, the following passage is borrowed in substance from Cassian *Inst.* II 16, but it is parallel to two canons :

S. Reg. 26. Si quis frater praesumpserit sine iussione abbatis fratri excommunicato quolibet modo se iungere, aut loqui cum eo, uel mandatum ei dirigere, similem sortiatur excommunicationis uindictam.

Cass. Inst. II 16. quisquis orationi eius, antequam recipiatur
a seniore . . . communicare *praesumpserit,* complicem se dam-
nationis eius efficiat . . . cum illo uel confabulationis uel
orationis communione miscendo.

Can. Ap. 12. Si quis cum damnato clerico ueluti cum clerico
simul orauerit, et iste damnetur.

Can. Ant. 2. *cum excommunicatis* autem *non esse communicandum.*[1]

But these assimilations of monks to priests and deacons
and clerics are less noticeable than the assimilation of
abbots to bishops, as pastors of souls. But first compare
the relation of bishops to metropolitans :

Can. Ap.	35	nihil amplius praeter eius (primi) consci-entiam gerant
Can. Ant.	9	*sollicitudinem* totius prouinciae *gerere* . . . et nihil amplius praeter eum ceteros episcopos agere, secundum antiquam a patribus nostris regulam constitutam, nisi ea tantum. . . . amplius autem nihil agere praesumat
S. Leo.	36	ita nihil permittimus te ignorante praesumi.[2] (to the Bishop of Thessalonica, Papal legate for Eastern Illyricum, over the metropolitans and bishops).
S. Reg.	21[4]	qui sollicitudinem gerant super decanias suas in omnibus, secundum mandata Dei et praecepta abbatis sui.
	27[13]	magnopere enim debet sollicitudinem gerere abbas. . . .
	65[36]	qui tamen praepositus illa agat cum reue-rentia quae ab abbate suo ei iniuncta fuerint, nihil contra abbatis uoluntatem aut ordinationem faciens.

More important are the references to *pastor* and *oues,*

[1] For mere wording compare S. Reg. 25[2] ‘ *suspendatur* a mensa simul ab
oratorio ’, with *Can. Ap.* 13 ‘ si quis clericus a communione *suspensus.*

[2] Compare, a few lines earlier, St. Leo's expression ‘ cum *in locum eius* alius
fuerit *subrogandus* ’ with S.R. 65[49] ‘ et alius qui dignus est *in loco eius* subro-
getur ’.

whether *sanae* or *morbidae* ; *regere animas sibi creditas* or *commissas*, for which, as well as for himself the ruler must *reddere rationem.*

Can. Ap. 39 (40). Presbiteri et diaconi praeter episcopum nihil agere pertemptent, nam Domini populus *ipsi commissus est*, et pro animabus eorum hic redditurus *est rationem.*

Can. Ap. 40. si enim *animae hominum* praetiosae illi *sunt creditae.*

Can. Ant. 24. iudicio et potestate pontificis, *cui commissus est* populus et *animae* quae intra ecclesiam congregantur.

S. Innoc. Victricio praef. (after 8). ut de cetero sollicitudo sit unicuique sacerdoti in sua ecclesia curam huiusmodi habere, . . . ne alicuius *morbidae ouis* afflatu conscientia nostra contaminata uioletur. . . .

Illud certe tuam debet mentem uehementius excitare, ut ab omne labe saeculi istius *ante Dei conspectum securus inueniaris ; cui multum enim creditur, plus ab eo exigitur* usura poenarum. Ergo quoniam *non pro nobis tantum,* sed pro populo Christi cogimur *praestare rationem,* disciplina deifica populum erudire debemus.

S. Innoc. 49 (Laurentio) Tuum est, frater carissime, quae praecepta sunt non segnius agere, ne *plebem tibi creditam* dissimulatione[1] *deperdas,* et incipias *Deo de perditis reddere rationem.*

Leo (Italis). 5 (p. 280). In consortium uos nostrae *sollicitudinis* aduocamus, ut uigilantia pastorali, . . . *commissis uobis gregibus diligentius* consulatis; ne is qui . . . *per nostram curam a nostris ouibus morbus* abicitur, etc.

6 (281). ne *sanctum gregem sua contagione* polluerent, . . . Aliter enim nobis *commissos regere* non possumus, nisi hos qui sunt perditores et perditi, zelo fidei dominicae persequamur, et *a sanis* mentibus, ne pestis haec latius diuulgetur, seueritate qua possumus *abscindamus.*

. . . Ut enim habebit a Deo dignae remunerationis praemium, *qui diligentius,* quod ad salutem *commissae sibi plebis* proficiat, *fuerit exsecutus,* ita *ante tribunal Domini* de reatu negligentiae se non poterit excusare, quicumque plebem suam contra sacrilegae persuasionis auctores noluerit custodire.

Leo (Januario). 14: congratulantes tibi, quod ad custodiam *gregis Christi pastoralem curam uigilanter exequeris,* ne lupi qui sub

---

[1] Compare S.R. 2[73] neque *dissimulet* peccata delinquentium.

specie ouium subintrarunt bestiali saeuitia simplices quosque dilacerent, et non solum ipsi *nulla correctione proficiant,* sed etiam ea quae sunt *sana* corrumpant.

Si quisquam . . . se utcumque haereticae communionis *contagione* macularit, resipiscens, in communione catholica sine professione *legitimae satisfactionis* habeatur.

Leo. 14. cum persecutionum saeuitiam suppleant et *dissimilitudines morum,* et *contumaciae inobedientium,* et malignarum tela linguarum. . . .

Quis ab insidiis luporum custodiet oues, si pastorum cura non uigilet? . . .

Constanter tenenda est iustitia, et benigne praestanda clementia. *Odio habeantur peccata, non homines.*[1] Corripiantur tumidi, *tolerentur infirmi,* et quod *seuerius castigari* necesse est, non saeuientis plectatur animo sed medentis.

Leo 31. quia etsi plerumque existunt inter *negligentes uel desides fratres* quae oporteat maiore auctoritate curari, sic tamen *adhibenda est correctio,* ut *semper salua sit dilectio.* . . . plus tamen erga corrigendos agat beneuolentia quam seueritas, plus cohortatio quam commotio, plus charitas quam potestas . . . dum *dominari* magis quam *consulere* subditis placet, honor inflat superbiam, et quod prouisum est ad concordiam, tendit ad noxam.

S. R. 2[12] memor semper abbas quia doctrina suae uel discipulorum oboedientiae, utrarumque rerum *in tremendo iudicio Dei* facienda erit *discussio.* Sciatque abbas culpae pastoris incumbere, quicquid in ouibus pater familias utilitatis minus potuerit inuenire.

2[18] si inquieto uel inobedienti gregi *pastoris fuerit omnis diligentia attributa,* et *morbidis* earum actibus uniuersa fuerit cura exhibita, *pastor eorum* in iudicio Domini absolutus, dicat. . . .

2[89] *regere animas* et multorum seruire moribus.

2[94] ut non solum detrimenta *gregis sibi commissi* non patiatur,[2] uerum in augmentatione boni gregis gaudeat.

---

[1] This proverb occurs in many forms: St. Leo: *Odio habeantur peccata non homines ;* St. Benedict: *Oderit uitia, diligat fratres.* St. Gregory, Ep. XI. 9, vol II. p. 269[2]: *ut personam diligas, et uitia persequaris.* Abbot Butler on *S. Reg.* 64[28] cites Aug. Serm. 49, 5: *Dilige hominem, oderis uitium ; De Civ. Dei,* XIV. 6: *oderit uitium. amet hominem ;* Ep. 211, 11 ('Rule' of St. Aug.): *cum dilectione hominum et odio uitiorum ;* and Caesarius, (ad Virg. 22). I suppose St. Benedict is thinking of the 'Rule' of St. Augustine; but he also knew the passage of St. Leo.

[2] Compare *Can. Ap.* 39 (40) nec ecclesia detrimentum patiatur.

2[97] ante omnia, ne dissimulans aut paruipendens salutem animarum sibi commissarum, . . .

2[100] sed semper cogitet quia *animas* suscepit *regendas,* de quibus et *rationem redditurus est.*

2[107] sciatque quia qui suscipit *animas regendas* paret se *ad rationem reddendam.*

2[111] in die iudicii ipsarum omnium animarum *est redditurus Domino rationem,* sine dubio *addita et suae animae.* Et ita timens semper futuram *discussionem*[1] *pastoris* de *creditis ouibus* . . .

3[23] Ipse tamen Abba cum timore Dei et obseruatione Regulae omnia faciat, sciens se procul dubio de omnibus iudiciis suis aequissimo iudici Deo *rationem redditurum.*

27[13] Magnopere enim debet *sollicitudinem gerere* abbas et omni sagacitate et industria curare, ne aliquam de *ouibus sibi creditis* perdat. Nouerit enim se *infirmarum curam suscepisse animarum,* non *super sanas* tyrannidem. . . . *Et Pastoris* boni pium imitetur exemplum.

28[7] tunc abbas faciat quod sapiens *medicus ;* si exhibuit fomenta, si unguenta exhortationum, si medicamina Scripturarum sanctarum, si ad ultimum ustionem excommunicationis uel plagarum uirgae . . . quod si nec isto modo sanatus fuerit, tunc iam utatur abbas ferro abscisionis . . . ne una *ouis morbida* omnem gregem *contagiet.*

31[18] (cellararius) sciens sine dubio quia pro his omnibus in die iudicii *rationem redditurus est.*

63[4] Qui abbas non conturbet *gregem sibi commissum,* nec quasi libera utens potestate iniuste disponat aliquid; sed cogitet semper quia de omnibus iudiciis et operibus suis *redditurus est Domino rationem.*

64[20] Ordinatus autem abbas cogitet semper quale opus suscepit, et *cui redditurus est rationem* uilicationis suae, (sciatque sibi oportere prodesse magis quam praeesse). Oportet ergo eum esse doctum in lege diuina, ut sciat, et sit unde proferat noua et uetera; castum, sobrium, misericordem; et semper superexaltet misericordiam iudicio, ut idem ipse consequatur. *Oderit uitia, diligat fratres.* In ipsa autem correptione prudenter agat . . .

---

[1] This use of *discussio* in 2[15] and 2[114] is paralleled in Dionysius: *Can. Ancyr.* 15 (35) *discutiatur* et uita eorum; *S. Celest.* 19 nec *discussionem* nostram effugere poterunt; *S. Leo* 2 huius *discussionis* curam.

65[53] Cogitet tamen abbas se de omnibus iudiciis suis Deo *reddere rationem*, ne forte inuidiae aut zeli flamma urat animam.

These long lists of quotations need some study; but the connexion can hardly be doubted. St. Benedict has studied and assimilated without citing, as usual.[1]

One may also compare the *uoluntas abbatis*, so prominent in the Rule:

S. Reg.	49[21]	ut cum eius fiat oratione et uoluntate
	49[24]	ergo cum uoluntate abbatis omnia agenda sunt
	65[39]	nihil contra abbatis uoluntatem et ordinationem faciens.
Can. Ant.	22	nisi forte cum consilio et uoluntate regionis episcopi.
	24	quae etiam dispensanda sunt iudicio et potestate pontificis.

One or two other points[2] are at least illustrative:

S. Reg.	22[2]	lectisternia *pro modo conuersationis*, secundum dispensationem abbatis sui accipiant.
Can. Ancyr.	5(6)	*modum conuersionis* (*conuersationis* should be read) eorum probantes.

[1] Some adaptations of bishops to cellarers are curious, as examples of wording.
Can. Ap. 38 (39) *omnium* negotiorum ecclesiasticorum *curam* episcopus *habeat*, et ea tamquam Deo contemplante *dispenset*.
S. Reg. 31[6] *Curam* gerat de *omnibus*. [16] cum omni sollicitudine curam gerat. [30] omnia . . . habeat sub cura sua.
Can. Ant. 9. amplius autem nihil agere praesumat.
S. Reg. 31[30] a quibus eum prohibuerit non praesumat.
Can. Ap. 35 nec quae sunt *necessaria subministrentur* eis, et nihil amplius praeter eius conscientiam gerant.
S. Reg. 31[7] sine iussione abbatis nihil faciat. and so forth.
[2] Compare also:
55[3] in frigidis regionibus *amplius* indigetur, in calidis uero minus. Haec ergo consideratio *penes* abbatem est.
Can. Ancyr. 2 quod si forte . . . uoluerint eis aliquid *amplius* tribuere uel adimere, *penes* ipsos erit potestas. (ch. S. Reg. 40[10] quod si aut loci necessitas . . . amplius poposcerit, in arbitrio prioris consistat).
S. Reg. 21[2] elegantur de ipsis fratres *boni testimonii* et sanctae conuersationis.
S. Leo. 33 etiamsi *bonae* uita *testimonio* fulciatur.

S. Reg.	48[53]	si quis uero ita *neglegens et desidiosus* fuerit.
S. Leo.	31	*neglegentes uel desides* fratres
	14	desides neglegentesque rectores.
S. Reg.	7[31]	si *timorem Dei* sibi *ante oculos* semper ponens
Can. Nic.	16	neque *timorem Dei prae oculis* habentes, nec agnoscentes ecclesiasticam regulam[1]
S. Reg.	61[34]	*commendaticiae litterae.*

These are regulated in *Can. Ap.* 13 and 34; *Can. Ant.* 10; *Can. Chalc.* 11; *Can. Sardic.* 9.

It seems to me clear that the famous Chapter 2, *Qualis debeat abbas esse*, and the other passages on the same subject are largely based on the canons and decretals I have compared, especially on the superb letters of St. Leo, whose sermons on Lent were certainly used for ch. 49. The beautiful advice to Rusticus (14) and to Anastasius of Thessalonica (31) would strike any reader as much by the sympathetic charity and wisdom they show as by their exquisite wording, unsurpassed in Latin literature except by Cyprian.

---

[1] But this canon is referring to the Psalm ' non est timor Dei ante oculos eorum.

ADDITIONAL NOTE TO CHAPTER III

THE LEGAL STYLE IN THE HOLY RULE

S. Reg. 23[1]   si quis frater contumax
       24[4]   si quis tamen frater in leuioribus
       26[1]   si quis frater praesumpserit
       28[1]   si quis frater frequenter correptus
       31[9]   si quis frater ab eo
       32[9]   si quis autem sordide
       45[1]   si quis dum pronuntiat
       46[1]   si quis dum in labore
       59[1]   si quis forte de nobilibus
       60[1]   si quis de ordine sacerdotum
       61[1]   si quis monachus peregrinus
       62[1]   si quis Abbas

S. Reg. 18[63]   ut si cui forte
       35[10]   uel si qui
       55[35]   et si cui inuentum fuerit
       61[7]   si qua sane
       68[1]   si cui fratri

Next compare the codex Justinianus (selections at random):

I   3[48]   (531)   si quis ad declinandam legem Falcidiam
      3[50]   (531)   si quis in conscribendo instrumento
      3[12]   (398)   si quis curialis
      3[20]   (434)   si quis presbyter aut diaconus
      3[5]   (364)   si quis . . . ausus fuerit
      3[10]   si quis in hoc genus sacrilegii proruperit
      2[5]   (412)   si quis contrauenerit
II   26[6]   (c. 320) si quis aduersus
III   28[33] (529)   si quis suo testamento

	28³⁴	(531)	si quis filium suum
IX	38¹	(409)	si quis posthac
IX	49⁷	(369)	si quis intra prouinciam
	49⁹	(396)	si quis posthac
	49³¹		ut si quas
	49¹⁷	(416)	ut si quis
	49²²	(445)	si qua per calumniam postulatio
III	28³⁵	(531)	ut si quis a patre
IX	39²	(451)	si qui latrones

So also in the collection of Dionysius:

Can. Ap.	3.	Si quis episcopus aut presbiter, (and 8, etc.)
	12.	Si quis cum damnato clerico
	13.	Si quis clericus aut laicus
	15.	Si quis presbiter aut diaconus
	32.	Si quis presbiter
	31.	Si quis episcopus (37, etc.)
Conc. Nic.	1.	Si quis a medicis
		si quis autem (and 16, 18, 19)
	15.	si quis uero (and 19)
Conc. Ancyr.	19.	si cuius uxor
Conc. Neocaes.	4.	si quis proposuerit
	12.	si quis in aegritudine
Gangrense	1.	si quis *begins every canon*, (1-20).
Conc. Antioch.	1.	si quis autem . . . temptauerit.
	2.	si uero quis
	4.	si quis episcopus (and 11, 14, 15, 16, 17, 1ᵇ)
	6.	si quis a proprio
	10.	si quis autem (and 22)
Laodicea	35.	si quis igitur
Chalcedon	2.	si quis episcopus
	14.	si quis autem
	18.	si qui ergo clerici

But St. Pachomius indulges in the same habit:

22.	Si quis dormitauerit sedens
32.	Si quis ad comedendum
49.	Si quis accesserit
52.	Si quis ante ostium steterit
69.	Si quis remanserit

83. Si quis de altera domo
86. Si quis ambulauerit
105. Si quis fratrum laesus fuerit
131. Si quis aliquid perdiderit
149. Si quis tulerit rem non suam
171. Si quis promiserit
183. Si quis absque conscientia duorum
187. Si quis de foris uenerit
190. Si quis ex fratribus
192. Si quis ab his quae praecepta sunt

St. Benedict is particularly fond of *quod si :*

Prol.[39] quod si
2[51] quod si ita . . . uisum fuerit
3[21] quod si praesumpserit
28[5] quod si nec ita correxerit
28[16] quod si nec isto modo
29[5] quod si denuo
33[14] quod si quisquam
34[12] quod si deprehensus fuerit
39[10] quod si cenaturi sunt
39[12] quod si labor forte
40[10] quod si aut loci necessitas
42[20] quod si inuentus fuerit quisquam
43[7] quod si quis
51[5] quod si aliter fecerit
54[5] quod si etiam
54[8] quod si iusserit suscipi
57[3] quod si aliquis ex eis
61[15] quod si superfluus
61[19] quod si non fuerit
62[17] quod si aliter praesumpserit
62[20] quod si nec sic emendauerit
64[8] quod si etiam
65[31] quod si aut locus expetit
65[47] quod si neque sic correxerit
65[50] quod si et postea
67[13] quod si quis praesumpserit
68[4] quod si omnino
68[9] quod si post

69[7] quod si quis haec transgressus fuerit
71[9] quod si quis contentiosus repperitur

So St. Pachomius:

31 quod si quis uel locutus
51 quod si uoluerint
    quod si ad uesperam uenerint
54 quod si necessitas impulerit
63 quod si ipse qui ductor est
71 quod si sicca non fuerint
147 quod si perierit
176 quod si per ignorantiam

A few instances from the Code out of many:

I   3[28]   (468)   3 quod si testator
                          4 quod si in uico
I   3[4]   (361)   quod si clandestinis
I   3[5]   (364)   quod si . . . ausus fuerit
I   40[15]   (471?)   quod si quis aliquando
IX   42[3]   (369)   quod si ingenuorum
X   23[2]   (408)   quod si rector prouinciae
Conc. Nic.   13. quod si desperatus
Conc. Ancyr.   2. quod si quidam
                      17. quod si etiam
Conc. Neocaes.   2. quod si defecerit
Conc. Sardic.   3. quod si in aliqua prouincia
                          quod si aliquis episcopus
                       5. quod si conuentus litteris
                       7. quod si is qui
Innoc. Victricio 10. quod si quis forte

The legal use of *forte*, by St. Benedict:

11[30] nisi forte, quod absit
18[63] ut si cui forte
20[9]   nisi forte ex affectu
21[10] si ex eis aliqua forte quis inflatus superbia
22[11] ne forte per somnium
28[5]   aut forte, quod absit
38[21] nisi forte prior
38[25] et ne forte graue sit

39[4]   ut forte qui ex illo
39[13]   quod si labor forte
43[19]   erit forte talis
48[12]   aut forte qui uoluerit
51[4]   nisi forte ei ab abbate
52[7]   uult sibi forte secretius
53[22]   nisi forte praecipuus
54[10]   cui forte directum fuerat
57[12]   ne forte mortem
59[1]   si quis forte de nobilibus
60[12]   et si forte ordinationis
61[10]   ne forte pro hoc ipso
62[13]   et si forte electio

So in Dionysius's collections:

Can. Ap.	14.	nisi forte quis eum
Conc. Ancyr.	2.	quod si forte quidam
Conc. Antioch.	22.	nisi forte
Conc. Chalced.	25.	nisi forte
Conc. Sardic.	8.	nisi forte is qui
	11.	ne forte inuitatus est
Innoc. Victricio.	10.	quod si quis forte

CHAPTER IV

JUSTINIAN's love of ecclesiastical detail—He partially enforces the Benedictine method of election of Abbots in 530; it is retracted in 535, and more clearly laid down once more in 546—The Benedictine rule of a common dormitory quoted in 535, and with more detail in 539, and again in 546, St. Benedict's exception being then added—Other echoes of the Rule in these passages—The degrees of faults are explained by Justinian in 546, according to St. Benedict—Some further coincidences of imperial legislation with the Holy Rule—A note on *responsa*—The life of a monk according to Benedict and Justinian.

THE novels of Justinian, though concerned with police matters, are less readable than modern detective stories, and one is more likely to consult them by necessity than to peruse them for pleasure. But in January 1928 I happened to be reading through some of the Codex Civilis, and I was very much struck by the resemblance of the legislation of Justinian himself for monks with that of St. Benedict, and still more with the resemblance of the legal style to that of the Patriarch of monks. And on reading Novella 5, of 535, I began to think that St. Benedict must have used the imperial laws and have copied their language. In fact, they were sent to Italy by Justinian in 534; and the law of 535 will have been promulgated there.

But further examination brought me to a law of 546, just as close in its matter to St. Benedict. Now the Rule cannot well have been written as late as this. Consequently it seemed that the legal style of the Rule must merely show that St. Benedict was familiar with the imperial laws before the codex of 529, and had possibly studied law at Rome in the latter part of the preceding century.

On the other hand, the common date, 530, for the publication of the Rule rests on no authority whatever. It is just as likely that its date is 525 or earlier. Our second chapter has shown us that St. Benedict's Rule was meant for all Italy, at least; our first chapter has shown us that St. Benedict's fame at Rome as a wonderworker was great long before this. Justinian, who poked his nose into every kind of business, and especially ecclesiastical business, even before he became emperor in 527, was extremely likely to make himself acquainted with the new Rule, lately published near Rome itself as a norm for the West by the great Thaumaturgus of the day.

Besides, it should always be remembered that Justin and Justinian were not of the Eastern Church, were not Orientals, were not Byzantines, but Macedonians, born in the Roman 'Patriarchate' (in Eastern phrase). Their first move in 518 was towards reunion of the East with Rome. Justinian insisted that the Popes were the head of all bishops, even while he persecuted them. Zeno and Anastasius had been satisfied with the Empire of the East, and had no objection to being cut off from Roman communion. Italy was governed in their name by Heruli or Goths, and they had no hope of winning it back. But the pious Justinian was determined to destroy the Arian domination in Italy and Africa and Spain, and to recover the Empire of the world, with New Rome for its political capital and Old Rome for its religious centre. He aimed at nothing less from the commencement of his reign, and he had meditated his plans while his uncle was yet alive. And of all his multiple and detailed occupations theology was the dearest to his heart, dearer than the ordering of campaigns, the codification of the Jus Romanum, the composition of elaborate Novellae, the building of forts and palaces and churches. He was a theologian already in 519, and his last interests in 565 were the minutiae of Aphthartodocetism. He regulated the lives of the clergy and the monks. He venerated their aims, and reprobated their faults. He knew their laws and customs and ancient Rules. It was to be expected that a Western Rule would interest him particularly, and that he would apply some of its sober principles to the restless and often turbulent monachism of the East.

Let us take the proofs in order.

ELECTION OF ABBOT. A law of Nov. 17th, 530, in the Code, Bk. I, iii, 46 (47), says:

' We deem it needful to add to our sacred laws one which provides that religious Superiority should be from virtue and not from time; so that in pious monasteries and *asceteria*, on the death of the Abbot or Abbess (*hegumenos* or *hegumena*) it should by no means be the next or the second in order who succeeds, (for we are conscious that by nature we are not all made equally good or equally bad), but that one who is (fit for this office) by a good life and serious behaviour and assiduous observance, and is judged worthy *by the* WHOLE NUMBER *of the remaining monks* or *the* MAJORITY *of them*, and is elected with the Holy Gospels set in the midst, be called to the Superiority.

So that if the first after the defunct be a good man and worthy to rule over monks, he is to be preferred to the others; but if the next after him, similarly the vote for Superior is to be for him. But if neither of these appear worthy, then he who is fit, out of the whole number, *of whatever rank he be, shall be appointed Abbot* . . . And that this must be made *known to the Bishop of the place;* so that receiving information as to the elect, and giving his approval, he shall *promote* him to the rank of Abbot '. (The Patriarch and the bishops are to weigh such an election) ' remembering the judgment of God ', *if they allow* human passion to influence them, ' as *by their neglect* will ensue the cause of sins to many souls '. The law is to apply to nuns as well as monks.

We gather that there had been a practice that the oldest monk by profession—that is, the first in order after the Abbot—should be the Abbot's successor, unless, of course, quite obviously an impossible candidate; in this case, the next in order had a prescriptive right to the dignity. The bishop appointed and ordained according to this custom, and the monks had no voice. This is now abolished.

The source of this 'addition' to the imperial laws about monasteries might be common sense, or it might be the Rule of St. Benedict. I cannot think of any third view, for no other rule or homily is explicit on the subject.

There are some resemblances to St. Benedict's *Sancta Regula*, c. LXIV, and they are notable, though the adoption of his views is incomplete.

α. The bishop still appoints and ordains; so St. B. *constituere, ordinare*, are the words.[1] But now the monks

[1] I pointed out in 1919 (Downside Rev. vol. 38, p. 87) that *eligere* means to choose, and *constituere* to appoint. Abbot Butler accepted this in the second edition of *Benedictine Monachism* (1924, p. 408), and sums up his view in the second edition of his annotated Rule (*Regula Monasteriorum*, p. 117,) in a note to c. LXIV: ' non erat electio canonica, sed manifestatio desideriorum monachorum, uel praesentatio nominis, ut dicitur: constitutio uel ordinatio abbatis erat penes episcopum uel uicinos abbates '. I agree with this, except that I suppose that while *constituere* means ' appoint ', *ordinare* here (and c. LXV) more probably means the solemn ' blessing '. St. Gregory the Great, some years later, is quite clear on this subject: often he appoints an abbot himself, but the abbot has thereafter to be ' ordained ' by the bishop of the place. I cite two interesting passages. Ep. IX 20 (Ewald, vol. II. p. 54, 27), to an Abbot named Urbicus: ' Acceptis ergo scriptis nostris, fratrem et coepiscopum nostrum Victorem (*of Palermo*) ad Lucuscani monasterium tua dilectio inuitet, quatenus ipse illic *Missarum solemnia celebrare* et praedictum Domitium auctore Deo *abbatem ordinare* debeat '. And Ep. III 23 (I p. 181, 20): ' ut suprascripto Secundino remoto (ab) abbatis officio, Theodosium quem *congregatio ipsa* sibi *petiit ordinari*, in monasterio S. Martini *solemniter* per eum cuius interest facias *ordinari*.' The Pope seems uncertain to whose diocese the monastery belonged. It was probably at Alatri. It is interesting to know that the blessing of an Abbot was already performed ' solemniter ' and during the Bishop's Mass. Elsewhere in the Rule *ordinare* has the two usual meanings, to ' order ', and to ' ordain ' sacramentally. St. Gregory's *formulae* usually belong to a much earlier date, and we may be sure that the blessing of an Abbot was an old custom in his time.

are to elect anyone they please, as with St. Benedict, and to present him to the Bishop.

β. Seniority is not to be considered in election : compare τὸν ἐκ πάντων ἐπιτήδειον οἱουδήποτε ἂν εἴη βαθμοῦ with St. B. ' etiamsi ultimus fuerit in ordine congregationis, and ' uitae merito et sapientiae doctrina elegatur '.

γ. Γνώριμα δὲ ταῦτα γίνεσθαι τῷ κατὰ τόπον θεοφιλεστάτῳ ἐπισκόπῳ reminds one of ' in notitia episcopi ad cuius dioecesim pertinet locus ipse. Again οἷα τῆς αὐτῶν ἀμελείας πολλαῖς ψυχαῖς ἁμαρτημάτων αἰτίας παρεχομένης is like ' sicut e diuerso peccatum si neglegant '.

So far, then, we gather that this law against appointment by seniority may have insisted on election by the monks either because it was a sensible reform, or because it was suggested by the Rule of St. Benedict.   The resemblance to the latter is incomplete as to the system, but details are curiously parallel.

2. A law of March 20th, 535 de Monachis (Novellae, V. cap. 9) purports to repeat the law of the code.   The older of the two Latin versions of the Novellae is called the authentica or official, and is certainly contemporary ; its text is corrupt, and has many omissions, some by homoeoteleuton.   But it was probably the authoritative translation for Latin-speaking countries.

' Ordinationem uero abbatum, si quando contigerit egere monasterium abbate, non per ordinem reuerendissimorum fieri monachorum, nec omnino eum qui post primum est, mox abbatem fieri, nec qui post illum secundus est, neque tertium aut reliquos (hoc quod etiam lex nostra alia dicit) ', and so forth, ' Sed procedat quidem secundum gradum praecedentis inspectio; qui uero prior mox inter numeratos optimus apparuerit, is abbas sit, et ordinem simul et uirtutem suffragantem habens '.

This law de monachis necessarily speaks of the appointment of abbots, but only in c. 9, the last chapter.   It

claims to be reinforcing the law of the code we have
already discussed. But it does not mention election by
the other monks, and speaks as though the bishop alone
could choose; and he is obliged to choose the highest in
rank who is suitable. This is neither according to the
Code nor to St. Benedict, but evidently perpetuates the
state of things before 530.

3. We are therefore not surprised that the matter is
taken up anew in the law of May 1st, 546 (Novella 123,
'De sanctissimis et Deo amabilibus et reuerentissimis
episcopis et clericis et monachis'), c. 34:

'Jubemus igitur abbatem aut archimandritam in unoquoque
monasterio ordinari non omnino secundum gradum monachorum,
sed <quem> *omnes monachi*, <*uel*> *melioris opinionis* eligant (ἀλλ᾽ ὃν
πάντες οἱ μοναχοὶ ἢ οἱ καλλίονος ὑπολήψεως ὄντες ἐπιλέξονται)
propositis sanctis euangeliis,[1] dicentes quia neque propter
amicitiam aut aliam quamlibet gratiam, sed scientes eum et
fide rectum et uita castum et gubernatione dignum, et *qui
possit monachorum disciplinam et omnem monasterii statum utiliter
custodire*, eum elegerunt; sanctissimum autem episcopum, sub
quo monasterium constitutum est, eum qui ita electus est
omnibus modis abbatem ordinare.'

It seems clear that the Novella of 535 had wilfully mis-
interpreted the law of 530 in the Code, in order to reintro-
duce the older habit of the eldest monk being (if suitable)
appointed Abbot by the Bishop. Now in 546 there is a
reversion to the law of the Code. But its source being
known to have been the Rule of St. Benedict, the Rule
is also consulted. It is seen that the Code had wrongly
understood the manner of election, as being by unanimity
or majority of votes; for the Rule says *quem siue omnis
concors congregatio . . . siue etiam pars quamuis parua congre-*

---

[1] St. Gregory's expression (frequent in the 9th book of his letters) is *mediis
sacrosanctis euangeliis*, in the case of courts of justice held by his officers. Also
in a formula Bk. XIII 49.

gationis saniore consilio elegerit. This is now correctly interpreted as meaning ' either by a vote of all the monks in session, or by the election being committed to a number however small who will use a sounder judgment '.[1] Hence the decree of 546 corrects not only the bad law of 535, but the original law of 530 in the code, and says the election is to be by all the monks or else by οἱ καλλίονος ὑπολήψεως ὄντες. Thus the only difference from St. Benedict's law is removed.

I have italicised some words on account of the parallel with St. Benedict's ' *sed domui Dei dignum constituant dispensatorem* '.

I take it that the similarities in the law of 530 are strongly confirmed by the greater resemblances in 546, and that the source in both cases is S. Reg. LXIV.

THE COMMON DORMITORY. Another law of St. Benedict has forcibly struck Justinian, S. Regula, c. 22, *Quomodo dormiant monachi*, which insists that the monks shall sleep together, the younger being together with their elders. Justinian notes that this is proper for cenobites, that it is good for discipline, and especially for chastity (a point which St. Benedict commonly avoids mentioning). This peculiarity of our Holy Rule is enforced by three laws, those of the years 535, 539 and 546.

1. Nov. V of 535, c.3. ' Volumus enim nullum monasterium sub dicione nostra constitutum, siue plurimorum hominum est, siue paucorum, monachos qui ibi sunt diuisos ab alterutris esse et propriis habitationibus uti, sed communiter quidem

---

[1] At least St. Benedict may mean this, viz. election by *compromissio*. But I am quite ready to admit that both St. Benedict and Justinian may mean simply this: the Bishop (or Abbots of neighbouring monasteries) who have the right of appointment shall consider the result of the election, for it may be that a majority of bad monks has elected an accomplice of their lax behaviour, while a minority of sounder judgement has chosen a worthy candidate; in this case the latter is to be appointed and ' ordained '. This seems an equally good explanation. Anyhow, Justinian and Benedict meant the same, whichever method it was.

eos comedere sancimus, *dormire uero* OMNES IN COMMUNI, unoquoque
quidem *in quadam* PROPRIA STRATURA iacente, *in domo uero una*
collocatos, aut *si forte non sufficit* AD MULTITUDINEM *monachorum
domus una*, in duas forsitan aut plures, non tamen seorsum et
apud semetipsos, sed in communi testes alterutri sint honestatis
et castitatis, et neque ipsum somnum desidiosum habeant, sed
meditantem bonum ornatum (εὐκοσμίαν) propter increpationem
respicientium.

Nisi tamen quidam eorum in contemplatione et perfectione
degentes, uitam remotam habeant in hospitio, quos uocare
anachoritas (id est, discedentes) et hesychastas (id est quiescentes)
consueuerunt, tamquam a communione (τῆς κοινότητος) ad
meliora acceptos: alioquin alios quibuscumque inter multitudinem conuersatio est, *in his quae uocantur coenobia* (id est,
in communi uita) esse uolumus.

Sic enim zelus eis ad uirtutem crescit, et maxime *inuenibus, si
cum senioribus constituantur :* fiet enim seniorum conuersatio
iuuentutis educatio perfecta.

Et sic sint *in coenobiis suo proprio abbati oboedientes*, et traditam
sibi conuersationem inculpabiliter obseruantes.

2.   The law of 539 repeats the same instructions, with
further detail and some severity.   Private cells are forbidden more distinctly.

Nov. 133. ' Quomodo oportet monachos uiuere '. *Praef.* . . .
sequimur etenim *sacras regulas et antiquos patres* qui haec sanxerunt,
quia nihil segne (ἄβατον) fit ad quaestionem imperio, communem omnium sollicitudinem ex Deo suscipienti.

Dudum (ἤδη) quidem scripsimus constitutionem uolentem
in multitudine existentes monachos in commune degere *secundum
quod appellatur coenobiorum schema*, et neque propria habere
habitacula, neque substantias congregare, neque uitam sine
testimonio <habere>, sed communiter quidem eos comedere,
dormire uero omnes in commune, et honestam sectari uitam,
et testes esse ornatus (κοσμιότητος) alterutris, et iuuenes quidem
uereri canitiem haec respicientium (τὴν πολιάν τῶν ταῦτα
ἐποπτευόντων), et ex studio etiam uigilias assumere, *ut ne quid
facinoris ueluti per somnum fiat*, neque turpis uideatur aliis, sed
unusquisque suam honestatem etiam dormiendo custodiat.

c. 1. Quibusdam uero nobis nuntiatis, quae digna et maiori cautela legis egebant, recte ad praesentem uenimus sanctionem, ad illius perfectionem et supplementum, per quam sancimus, nullum penitus licentiam habere habitare appellatam cellulam, nisi solus fuerit <in monasterio uno forte aut> duobus utens ministris, et continentem et quietam degat uitam.

Sed omnino cum sint plurimi uiri, una sit eorum conuersatio, et orantium et quae naturae sunt facientium, quatenus inculpabiles et inaccusabiles consistant; et communiter quidem, sicut dictum est, comedere, *communiter quoque dormire.*

*Et si quidem tanta sit multitudo quanta in uno habitaculo capiatur—*alioquin duo forsan aut tria habitacula esse quae capiant eos.

Nullum tamen omnino proprium habere, sed in commune uiuere noctibus et diebus, ut noctes eis eandem habeant quam dies obseruationem. Non enim dormiunt omnes semper; sed palam est quia alii quidem in somno sunt, alii uero uigilant, et *omnino sunt*[1] *quidam dormientes inspicientes.*

Si autem aliqua habitacula sunt in quolibet monasterio sub tua (*i.e. the Patriarch Menas*) constitutorum sanctitate, siue in hac magna ciuitate, siue in eius per circuitum habitaculis siue a nobis ipsis aedificatis siue ab aliis, seorsum habitationem habentia aliquorum monachorum, haec omnibus modis, aperiesque eis alterutr [is] <visum> [ubi celebrentur *om*] <et cuncti uidebunt actiones aliorum>. Quid enim formidabunt hoc agentes, semel <se> ipsos dicantes Deo et abrenuntiantes publicae comessationi?

Et hoc quidem ita ualere nunc et in futurum omne uolumus tempus, nullo (sicut dictum est) habente habitaculum seorsum, sed congregandis omnibus et inspicientibus quae [ab] alterutris aguntur. Certum enim est quia talia studebunt ea constituere qualia omnino inculpabilia manent. [Et] si quis apparuerit tantum impudens, ut audeat temptare praeuaricari quod sancitum est, monasterii praesul haec examinet.'

3. In 546, in the longer constitution as to bishops, clergy and monks, the same rule is enforced :

Nov. 123, c.36. In omnibus autem monasteriis, quae coenobia dicuntur, iubemus *secundum monachicos canones* in uno habitaculo

---

[1] Read *erunt*, the Greek being ἔσονται.

omnes <habitare et communiter ali, et simili modo *in uno habita-culo omnes*> *separatim dormire*, ut mutuum alterutris testimonium castae conuersationis praebeant; nisi quidam tamen ex eis aut propter longaeuam in monasterio conuersationem, quiete uolentes uiuere, *aut senectutis atque corporis infirmitatis causa, in remotis cellulis intra monasterium constitutis degant;* hoc autem cum conscientia *et uoluntate abbatis* fieri.

<His omnibus> in monasteriis et asceteriis feminarum <seruatis>.

A comparison of these three laws with St. Benedict's 22nd chapter is suggested by the words I have italicised above. S. Reg. c. 22 : ' Singuli *per singula lecta* dormiant . . . Si potest fieri, *omnes in uno loco dormiant ; sin autem multitudo non sinit,* deni aut uiceni *cum senioribus qui super eos solliciti sint,* pausent.'

These are the principal points : Each has his own bed (once called *stratura*, cp. c. 53 ' lecti strati sufficienter '). All sleep in one place. If the ' multitude ' is too great, they may be divided. The seniors to be very careful of the others.

Again, ' *Adulescentes fratres iuxta se non habeant lectos, sed permixti cum senioribus* '. This is dwelt upon by Justinian at length, as a great benefit to the juniors. Cap. 63 of the Rule may also be compared.

A more general consideration is the determination of Justinian that the monks should be ' cenobites ', just as St. Benedict dismisses all other classes, c. 1, ' His ergo omissis, ad coenobitarum fortissimum genus disponendum adiuuante Domino ueniamus '. The Emperor tolerates only a very few solitaries in a monastery, thus abolishing an ancient custom, as far as possible. The words ' et sic sint *in coenobiis proprio abbati oboedientes* ' cannot but re-mind us of the Rule, c. 6 : ' *in coenobiis* degentes, *abbatem sibi praeesse* desiderant '.

In the law of 546 it has been observed that in the earlier laws an exception had been forgotten which St. Benedict had made, and the words are added: ' aut senectutis atque corporis *infirmitatis* causa, *in remotis cellulis* intra monasterium constitutis degant ' ; as in the Rule, c. 36 : ' Quibus fratribus *infirmis* sit *cella super se* deputata '.

Certain likenesses of wording suggest that the Latin version, though corrupted by many omissions and badly worded, is equally original with the Greek. It is therefore possible to draw attention to the curious translation of ἵνα μή τι πάρεργον μηδὲ ἐξ ὕπνου γένηται (' that some accident should not occur through sleep '), a very vague remark. But the *uersio authentica* has ' ut ne quid *facinoris* ueluti per somnum fiat ', and the explanation is found in St. Benedict's warning in this very chapter : ' Vestiti dormiant, et cincti cingulis aut funibus, ut *cultellos* suos ad latus suum non habeant dum dormiunt, ne forte *per somnum uulnerent dormientem* ', the danger is that a sleeping monk may seize his knife and stick it into his neighbour.[1] This suggests to Justinian that some accident (or ' extravagance ') or some *facinus* may happen.

Other echoes of the Rule[2] are possible : 'Sic enim *zelus ad uirtutem* crescit', which reminds us of the '*zelus* bonus quem debent monachi habere', described in c. 72, a 'rivalry' in mutual charity and observance.

Nullum tamen omnino proprium habere is like c. 33 : 'neque aliquid *habere proprium, nullam omnino rem*' . . . 'omniaque omnibus sint communia'.

[1] This explanation is not necessitated by the true reading *uulnerent*, as the subject may be *cultelli ;* but then we should probably have to read *dormientes* with the MSS. which have *uulnerentur*. The readings *uulnerentur* and *dormientes* may be as old as the *Regula Magistri*, who explains, like all later commentators: ' Bracili fratrem in nocte uti ideo prohibemus, ne dum se regyrat per somnum oppressus, exiens per thecam mucro cultelli carni eius figatur '. The Magister uses *bracile* for *zona*. But I think Justinian may be considered a witness to the older readings *uulnerent* and *dormientem*.

[2] Again, ' cum conscientia et uoluntate abbatis ' reminds us of the four places where St. Benedict speaks of *uoluntas abbatis*, S. Reg. LXII, LXV, and especially XLIX: ' Abbati suo suggerat, et cum eius fiat oratione et uoluntate . . . Ergo *cum uoluntate Abbatis* omnia agenda sunt '.

We may also observe that the Novella 133, Præf., of 539, declares 'sequimur etenim sacras regulas et antiquos patres', and that of 546 (123, c. 36) has 'secundum monachicos canones'. What *regula*, κανών, is meant? St. Basil has nothing, I think, on any subject so material as a common dormitory. The Greek has θείοις κανόσι, not ἱεροῖς; so imperial decrees are not meant. But St. Benedict's *Sancta Regula* fits exactly, and the reference to 'ancient Fathers' may perhaps be his, *Reg.* 73: '*Regulam hanc descripsimus . . . ceterum . . . sunt doctrinae sanctorum Patrum*'. Canons of councils can hardly be referred to; and none are extant on this point. St. Benedict's Rule seems the only alternative.

THE DEGREES OF FAULTS. In Novella 133, of 546, 'Quomodo oportet *monachos uiuere*', the cenobitic principle laid down makes discipline necessary, and a gradation of guilt in faults is therefore described.

1. c. 4. Quia uero nihil quod sancitur nisi custodiam habeat competentem poterit servari decenter, sancimus per tempus uniuscuiusque monasterii praesulem frequenter inspicere et perscrutari uniuscuiusque conuersationem et disciplinam, et *sicubi aliquid paruum fiat* contra quam decet, hoc repente corrigere et non sinere maius fieri lapsum,[1] et perire animam ad salutem conuersationis fugientem . . .

(Cp. *S. Regula* XXIV: 'Si quis tamen frater *in leuioribus culpis* inuenitur, a mensae participatione priuetur, and XLIV fin.)

2. c. 5. . . . Si quis autem deliquerit (nam multa sunt humana, et nullus poterit naturam sic retinere ut non peccet nihil: hoc enim proprium est solum Dei),[2] hunc, *si quidem mediocre peccatum est*, et monere et *suspendere* (καθείργειν) et *paenitentiae ei dare tempus*, ut meliorem ordinem sumens mox

[1] Cp. *S. Reg.* c. II: 'peccata . . . mox ut coeperint oriri radicitus ea, ut praeualeat, amputet.'
[2] Cp. Matt. XIX 17.

reuertatur ad semetipsum, et non quos iam posuit amittat labores.

(Cp. *S. Reg.* XXV: 'Is autem frater, *qui grauioris culpae noxa tenetur, suspendatur* a mensa simul ab oratorio . . . solus sit ad opus sibi iniunctum, *persistens in paenitentiae luctu.*)

3. c. 5: 'Si uero *maioris culpae sit modus, secundum commissum, et medelam correctionis esse,* et rursus admonitionem uehementiorem et paenitentiam fortem (μετάνοιαν ἰσχυράν) exigere.

(*S. Reg.* XXVIII: 'Si quis frater frequenter correptus pro qualibet culpa' . . . XXIV: '*Secundum modum culpae, et excommunicationis uel disciplinae* mensura debet extendi'.)

4. c. 5: ' Et si quidem ualuerit istis modis amouere lapsum suscipiendum (read 'saluare labi incipientem, σῶσαι τὸν ὀλισθαίνειν ἀρχόμενον) (hoc autem et in mulieribus conuersis (ασκαύσων) et in uiris dicimus) grates agere magno Deo, cum et in caelo fiat gaudium angelicis uirtutibus quando aliquis saluus fit peccatorum; si uero potiores *ultra medicinam* (κρεῖττον ἢ κατὰ θεραπείαν) causae fiant, tunc etiam expelli a monasterio, quatenus dans semetipsum ex melioribus ad peiora, ipse suis malis potiatur solus, *et non per eius malum etiam alii uiolentur, sicuti* MORBOSORUM et incurabiliter *languentium iumentorum* '.

(Cp. *Reg.* XXVIII: 'tunc Abbas faciat quod sapiens medicus: si exhibuit fomenta, si unguenta adhortationum, *si medicamina* Scripturam . . . Tunc iam utatur ferro abscissionis . . . ne una *ouis morbida omnem gregem contagiet.*)

The correspondence is not exact as to the degrees between Justinian and St. Benedict; but in view of the other likenesses in this Novella to the Holy Rule, this distinction of three classes of fault is not likely to be independent; and therefore the parallels *suspendere, modus culpae, ultra medicinam, ouis morbida* are worthy of consideration. We know of no other rule whence the pious and methodical and somewhat finicking Emperor could have borrowed this idea of degrees of blame, just as we know no other source for the laws about abbatial elections and common dormitories.

Some Lesser Coincidences

A. *Slave and free.* Justinian often legislates in these laws as to the entrance of slaves into religious life, and as to the result for them of their failure in it. But in one place he notes the equality of free and slave, after St. Paul, just as St. Benedict does :

Nov. V, 2: ' Hinc autem nobis etiam de singulis monachis cogitandum est, quo conuenit fieri modo, et utrum liberos solum aut etiam forte seruos; eo quod omnes similiter diuina suscipit gratia, praedicans palam quia, quantum ad Dei cultum, *non est* masculus neque femina, neque *liber neque seruus : omnes enim in Christo unam* mercedem percipere. Sancimus ergo sequentes regulas', etc.

Cp. *S. Reg.* c.II : 'Quia, *siue seruus siue liber, omnes in Christo unum sumus*, (Gal. III 28) et sub uno Domino aequalem seruitutis militiam baiulamus : quia non est apud Deum personarum acceptio (Rom. II 11).

The Greek of Justinian has no *mercedem percipere*, but translates St. Benedict's (Vulgate and Old Latin) *unum sumus* by ἓν εἰκότως νομίζεσθαι, whereas St. Paul wrote πάντες γὰρ ὑμεῖς εἷς ἐστε. Justinian is not likely to have known any MS. reading ἕν for εἷς, which spoils the sense.[1] He seems, therefore, to be using a Latin source.

B. *Monk becomes Priest.* In Nov. V 8 we read :

' Si quis autem monachicam profitentium conuersationem meruerit clerici ordinationem, maneat etiam sic puram seruans conuersationem (ἄσκησιν), etc.

We may be reminded somewhat of S. Reg. LXII : 'Nec occasione sacerdotii obliuiscatur Regulae oboedientiam et disciplinam, sed magis ac magis in Deum proficiat'. But Justinian includes minor as well as major orders.

---

[1] The bilingual F G read ἕν, having borrowed it from the Latin. The first hand of ℵ wrote εστε εν and was corrected.

C. *The monk and his body.*   In Nov. LXXVI, *praef.* it is said :

‘ Et quoniam nostrae pietatis lex uult eos qui se monasteriis dedicant, seu uiros seu mulieres, antequam ingrediantur in monasterium eo quo uoluerint modo quae sua sunt disponere, nec posse postquam ingrediuntur in monasterium ulterius agere quicquam de propriis, utpote domini rerum non existentes ulterius (eo quod sanciuerimus nos huiusmodi uiros et mulieres *cum corpore et anima* ipso ingressu ad monasterium *dedicare se suasque substantias*, et siquidem discesserint, manere etiam sic eorum substantias ad monasterium, eo quod domini harum ulterius non existent)’, etc.

This short Novella is an interpretation dealing with a particular case, and therefore recites the previous legislation in its preface. The law referred to is Nov. V, *De monachis*, chapters 4–7, which deal with the whole law regarding religious poverty. But here we have the curious addition, that the monk ‘ dedicates his body and soul ’, as well as his substance. We get an ancient interpretation for the words of S. Reg. XXXIII : ‘ neque aliquid habere proprium, nullam omnino rem . . . quippe quibus *nec corpora sua nec uoluntates* licet habere in propria uoluntate (or potestate), and again LVIII, of the profession of a novice : ‘ Res si quas habet, aut eroget prius pauperibus, aut facta *sollemniter donatione*[1] *conferat monasterio*, nihil sibi reseruans ex omnibus : quippe qui ex illo die *nec proprii corporis potestatem* se habiturum sciat ’ The reference is of course to obedience, by which body and will are given up to the will of the Abbot and Rule.[2]

[1] This is previous to the extension to Italy of the legislation of Novella V, according to which a solemn donation is unnecessary. For (cap. 5) goods are to be disposed of before entrance, because otherwise they go to the monastery: ‘ Ingredientem namque simul secuntur omnino res, *licet non expressim quia introduxit eas dixerit*, et non erit dominus earum ulterius ullo modo ’.
[2] The index to Abbot Butler’s edition of the Rule has under *corpus :* ‘ corporis potestas (castitas) LVIII 62 ’. But we find ‘ nec corpora sua nec uoluntates ’ in cap. 33.

D. In Nov. 133, after the strict directions to open out any private cells to the view of all, (quoted above), we find mention of the porters : C.1 :

‘ Volumus enim uehementiorem quam nunc est fieri obseruationem; et primum quidem non plurimos esse in monasterium ingressus, sed unum aut secundum forte, et adstare *senes*[1] castos et testimonii boni ex omnibus, qui neque reuerentissimis monachis concedant sine abbatis uoluntate deserere monasterium, sed intus eos detineant . . . nec alios quosdam introire in monasterium noctibus et diebus sinant . . . ’

We may compare S. Reg. c. LXVI, *de Ostiariis Monasterii :* ‘ Ad portam monasterii ponatur *senex* sapiens, qui sciat *accipere responsum* et *reddere,* et cuius maturitas eum non sinat uagari . . . ut uenientes semper praesentem inueniant a quo *responsum accipiant . . .* et cum omni mansuetudine timoris Dei *reddat responsum* festinanter cum feruore caritatis ’. I have quoted this, because of the reference to *responsa,* or messages; for according to the laws of Justinian every monastery must have ‘ representatives ’, ἀποκρισιάριοι, *responsarii,* to do their business outside; for earlier laws (e.g. of Justinian in 531, Code I, iii 52, renewing one of Leo of 471, Code I, iii 29) forbad monks to leave their enclosure, or walk in towns.[2]

---

[1] The plural agrees with St. Benedict’s title, *de ostiariis,* though the chapter itself has the singular *senex.*

[2] Nov. 133, c.V (of 539): ‘ Oportet autem unumquodque monasterium sub abbate constitutum, sicut praediximus, habere eos qui uocantur responsarii (ἀποκρισιαρίους), uiros senes et iam monachicum certamen superantes et non facile corporales uiolentias passuros, qui eorum rebus et eorum occupentur utilitatibus. Et non solum si uirorum monasterium, sed si etiam mulierum contingat, esse duos aliquos aut tres uiros aut eunuchos, si possibile est, aut senes et castitatis testimonium habentes, qui causas agant (τὰ πράγματα αὐταῖς πράξουσι) et ineffabilem eis praebeant communionem, cum huius tempus fuerit.’ They are only to speak to the Abbess, or by means of the reverend portresses.

In Nov. 123 of 546 it is explained that these ἀποκρισιάριοι have to be in major orders, c. 36: ‘Feminis autem quemcumque ipsae elegerint siue presbyterum siue diaconum ad faciendum eis responsum (εἰς τὸ ποιεῖν

The passages quoted in a note show that these legal terms were regularly applied in monasteries. We are accustomed to the name *apocrisiarius* to mean a ' plenipotentiary ' or representative, nuncio, of the Pope in the East. But we seem to learn that St. Benedict is using the proper word, when he speaks of the porter ' giving and receiving *responsa*': he has to take upon himself the person of the speaker and repeat the message. It is not merely the duty of listening politely to a question, and giving a suitable answer. He is an ambassador between the world without and the monks within.

F.   I will conclude these comparisons by a general statement by Justinian as to the life of a monk, which strikingly sums up our Holy Rule. In the Nov. 133 ' quomodo oportet monachos uiuere', the last chapter gives this as a conclusion, after ordering that if a monk is found in a tavern (taberna, καπήλειον), he is to be denounced to his Abbot, who shall expel him from the monastery (c. 6) :

' Oportet enim duplex hoc opus monachis esse, aut *diuinis uacare scripturis*, aut quae monachos deceant quae uocant *manuum opera* (ἄπερ καλεῖν εἰώθασιν ἐργόχειρα) meditari et operari: *mens enim frustra uacans* nihil bonorum parit '.

αὐταῖς τὰς ἀποκρίσεις) aut sacram communionem eis portandam, sanctissimus episcopus sub quo sunt deputet, quem rectae fidei et uitae bonae esse cognouerit.   Si uero qui ab eis electus est, non sit presbyter aut diaconus, dignum tamen huiusmodi ministerio episcopus iudicauerit, ordinationem ei imponat qua dignus esse uidebitur, et responsis, sicuti dictum est, monasterii distribuat, (ταῖς ἀποκρίσεσιν . . . τοῦ μοναστηρίου ἀπονέμετω), ita tamen ut neque sic electus ad responsa feminarum in monasterio maneat '.   And again c. 42: ' Prouidere autem sanctissimos locorum episcopos, ut neque monachi neque monachae circumeant ciuitates; sed si quod necessarium responsum (ἀπόκρισιν) habuerint, per proprios responsarios (ἀποκρισιαρίων) hoc agant, in suis manentes monasteriis '.

In purely legal matters *ad responsum* is a substantive, and means a representative, a person who represents another, the *locus classicus* for this use being a law of Anastasius of 492 (in Latin, of course) in the Code, XII 35, 18. For the ordinary sense, St. Gregory, Dial. II 12: ' Quoties *ad responsum* aliquod egrederentur fratres '.

St. Benedict says, c, 48 : ' *Otiositas* inimica est *animae;*
et ideo certis temporibus occupari debent fratres *in labore
manuum*, certis iterum horis *in lectione diuina* ',[1] and the
rest of the chapter divides up the day, according to the
season of the year, between these two duties of the monk.[2]

To sum up : We have three important pieces of legislation by Justinian, on Abbatial elections, on common
dormitories and on the gradations of punishment, which
might, individually, be due to common sense, but taken
together suggest that their source is the Rule of St. Benedict, as no obvious source for any of the three presents
itself, still less any other source for all the three.   This
prima facie argument is clenched by many curious resemblances, of which those which appeal to me most are the
minority vote, the danger of somnambulist crime, and the
avoidance of otiosity by reading and manual labour.

But if, as it seems, Justinian used the Rule of St. Benedict, he used it in the earliest of these laws, Nov. 17th, 530.
The Holy Rule will therefore date from 525, or not much
later.

[1] This characteristic of the Holy Rule is derived from St. Augustine, (*de
Opere Monachorum*, 29); but Justinian will not have taken it from that Father.
Among Greek writers, Evagrius Ponticus is specially strong on the benefits
of reading, ἀνάγνωσις.   In 539 Justinian was not yet under the influence
of Theodore Ascidas, yet he would hardly have consulted so hearty an Origen-
ist as Evagrius at any time.

[2] Novella 133, c. 2, is very interesting, though it has no particular connexion
with St. Benedict.   It tells how the monks who have no church are to go
to the Holy Sacrifice with the Abbot, and return, and read the Divine Scrip-
tures.   Four or five seniors are to be Priests or clergymen of other ranks.
These will speak to guests, and keep the younger within bounds.

CHAPTER V

THE two forms of the Rule of Caesarius ' ad Virgines '—The episcopal signatures to this Rule and to the Bull of Pope Hormisdas—The date of the recapitulation is that of the final edition, 534—The date of the Rule ' ad monachos ' in its latest form is probably the same—Abbot Tetradius—The additions of Caesarius from the Holy Rule examined. A note on ' Opus Dei '—Similarities in the legislation.

THE great metropolitan of Arles was a much older man than St. Benedict. The many points of resemblance between their Rules would *a priori* seem to be caused by borrowing on St. Benedict's part, and Abbot Butler has therefore tentatively included Caesarius among the sources of the Holy Rule. But I have long been under the impression that Caesarius was the borrower.

The parallels are not very striking; but several appear to have no common source, so that it is unlikely that all should be mere coincidences. The points are developed more thoroughly and logically in St. Benedict's Rule. This is no argument that he is posterior. It appears more likely that some of these likenesses are among the latest of the corrections made by St. Caesarius before his death, and therefore appear somewhat irregularly and sparsely. In this case they need not be new additions in each case, but elucidations of what was already suggested.

The rule of St. Caesarius *ad Virgines* has been published in two forms. The first of these, in the *Acta Sanctorum* for Jan. 12th, is the more complete; for the other, published by Holstenius in the Appendix to his *Codex Regularum* (reprinted by Migne, P.L. 67 1105) omits all the directions for the choir office. These directions are sometimes quoted as *Psalmodia Lirinensis*, since Caesarius says: 'Ordinem etiam quomodo psallere debeatis ex maxima parte secundum regulam monasterii Lirinensis in hoc libello iudicauimus inserendum'. In the middle of these directions are inserted some rules about fasting, which are preserved in the text of Holstenius. It does not seem likely that these rules of fasting had been in the earlier edition, and were afterwards incorporated into the liturgical directions when these were 'inserted'. I infer rather that the Holsten text is later, as having purposely omitted the liturgical directions. The Holsten text adds two chapters on the cellararia and the portress, both being taken straight out of the Rule of St. Benedict. Hence Holsten prefaces them by a note to this effect. Bollandus does not give them at all, having in their place the subscription 'Caesarius peccator regulam hanc sanctarum uirginum relegi ac subscripsi. Notaui sub die X Kalendas Iulii'.

Martène and Durand, apparently unacquainted with the edition of Bollandus, in a note to the edition of the letter of the Abbess Caesaria II to Radegundis, tell us they found an MS. of the Rule published by Holsten at Autun:

Hanc regulam cum aliis sanctorum Patrum regulis edidit Lucas Holstenius, eamque nos etiam reperimus in uetusto codice MS. Augustodunensis S. Martini monasterii, in cuius fine haec maxime notanda adiciuntur quae desunt in editis.

Caesarius peccator regulam hanc sanctarum uirginum rexit et scripsit sub die X calendas Julii Paulini consule tempore.

Simplicius peccator	consensit et signauit
Seuerus episcopus	consensi et signaui
Lupercianus episcopus	,, ,,
Johannes	,, ,,
Cyprianus episcopus	,, ,,
Montanus	,, ,,
Ferminus peccator	,, ,,

This is obviously the same subscription as that given by Bollandus, only *rexit et scripsit* is a mistake for *relegi et subscripsi*. But one would like to know whether it stood in the Autun MS. before or after the two chapters of the cellaress and portress.

After the subscription, Bollandus adds the Bull which St. Caesarius obtained from Pope Hormisdas, followed by the signatures of seven bishops who consented to it. The Bull must be before the death of Hormisdas in 523. The signatures may be a little later, probably 524. The approbation of the rule is *Paulino cos.*, i.e. 534. The two bishops, Simplicius and Firminus, who lived till 553-4, are not witnesses of the Bull. On the other hand Lupercianus of Fréjus is not a witness of the Rule: he succeeded Johannes about 527. If therefore the Johannes in each is the same, he is a bishop unknown in the contemporary councils. But the Johannes who countersigned the Bull is probably of Fréjus, in which case he signed before 527. Seuerus (his see is not known) was at three councils, 521, 524, 527, and is not heard of later. The only known Petrus of this date is of Saintes, 511. Consequently we may suppose the Pope's Bull was countersigned soon after its arrival, say 523-4. Anyhow it was before 534, since Contumeliosus was deposed in that year. The following table of dates

at which the bishops are known to have been living will
make the argument clear. :

Bollandus, signatures to Bull:

Marcellus	of Aire				533	
Johannes	of Fréjus		524			
Severus		521	524	527		
Cyprianus	of Toulon		524	527	529	541
Contumeliosus	of Reii		524	527		534 (dep.)
Montanus			524			
Petrus	of Saintes?	511				

Martène, signatures to Rule:

Simplicius	of Sénez					541	554
Severus		524					
Lupercianus	of Fréjus		527	529	536		
Johannes	[?]						
Cyprianus	of Toulon	524	527	529		541	
Montanus		524					
Ferminus	of Uzès					541	551 553

The order in the two editions is as follows :

		Bollandus		Holsten
1.	Rule	1—46 (47)	*Praef*	1—43
2.	Recapitulatio	48—60		1—11
3.	Election of Abbess	61		12
4.	and exhortation	62—5		13—14
5.	Psalterium Lerin. I.	66		
6.	De ieiunio	67		15
7.	Psalt. Lerin. II.	68—70		
8.	De conuinio, etc.	71—73		16—19
9.	Signature	*Signature*		
10.	Cellarer and portress		*Cellarer & portress*	
11.	Bull	*Bull*		
12.	Signatures	*Signatures*		

According to Bruno Krusch these various parts are not
in their right order, for he mistranslates *de infrascripta*

recapitulatione in c. 14 (65), making it mean 'the recapitulation written below *this*', whereas the recapitulation has preceded in both editions! Of course it means 'below the Rule', written immediately after the Rule'.

In Boll. the recapitulation is made to begin at 47 (c. 43), wrongly, for this is the end of the Rule, an address to the Abbess.

Then follows the recapitulation, its cap. 11 (Boll. 60) corresponding to cap. 42 (Boll. 45) of the Rule. Then comes an additional chapter (12, Boll. 61) on the election of an Abbess, followed by a long address to the nuns (c. 13-14, Boll. 62-5), which corresponds to the shorter address to the Abbess at the end of the Rule (c. 43, Boll. 47). The Rule had ended with the (metrical) clausula 'ad aeternam beatitudinem possitis feliciter peruenire'; this is actually quoted at the end of c. 13 (Boll. 63); but c. 14 (Boll. 64) has a still more solemn ending: an 'ascription' ending with *in saecula saeculorum, Amen*. This is obviously the real ending of the *recapitulatio*, which Caesarius wrote with his own hand.

It begins thus:

'Cum, Deo propitio, in exordio institutionis monasterii (in 512) uobis regulam fecimus, *multis tamen postea uicibus ibi aliquid addidimus uel minuimus:* pertractantes enim et probantes quid implere possitis, hoc nunc definiuimus, quod et rationi et possibilitati et sanctitati conueniebat . . . et ideo coram Deo et angelis eius contestamur ut nihil ultra mutetur aut minuatur.'

This is written after the death of Caesaria I, which occurred 'not long after' the council of 524 (*Vita S. Caes.* 57-8, ed. Krusch, p. 481). But the many changes made and tried and altered again imply more than twelve years (512-24), and are suitable to 534, the date of the approval by the seven bishops. As a fact the recapitulation and all that follows it seem to be continuous :

'. . . ut nihil ultra mutetur aut minuatur. Pro qua re, quascumque *schedas* prius fecerimus, uacuas esse uolumus; *hanc uero in qua manu mea Recapitulationem scripsi*, sine ulli deminutione rogo et moneo ut, Deo adiutore, feliciter impleatis.

. . . istam paruam *Recapitulationem, quam manu mea scripsi* fieri uolumus

c.14 (Boll. 64). Praecipue tamen *de infrascripta Recapitulatione*, quam manu mea scripsi [atque subscripsi] contestor ut nihil penitus minuatur.

ibid. Et si forte . . . fuerit aliqua de filiabus nostris tam pertinax animo, quae *huius regulae Recapitulationem* . . . implere contemnat.'

It seems obvious that all this recommendation of the Recap., whether at the beginning of it or after it, is all written at the same time : it is one piece beginning 'Cum Deo propitio' and ending 'in saecula saeculorum, Amen'.

As for '*scripsi et subscripsi*', we are forced to take them as epistolary perfects, for we have found *scripsi* twice before the *Recap.*, and *scripsi et subscripsi* after it. So we must translate 'which I am writing with my own hand' in the first two places, and 'which I am writing and signing with my own hand' in the last place.

No doubt the holy bishop intended to append his signature after *in saecula saeculorum*. But the *scheda* ('sheet', document) was not full; and he thinks of something else : 'Ordinem *etiam* quomodo psallere debeatis . . . *in hoc libello* indicauimus inserendum'. If *indicauimus* is right, then this 'Psalmodia Lirinensis' was not added by his own hand; but *iudicauimus* is more usual, and likely to be the true reading. Evidently *hic libellus* is the same as *haec scheda* in the preface to the Recapitulation. Again something is remembered : the *ordo conuiuii* is added, with a last exhortation to obedience, and a note about the side doors of the monastery. Then at last comes the signature, *Caesarius peccator*, June 22d 534, attested afterwards by seven bishops.

Thus it seems probable that the date of the final form of the Rule is also the date of the Recapitulation; even the original Rule itself was probably tinkered at the same time. If any one thinks the last three chapters only, or the Psalmodia also, were added in 534, at any rate the Recapitulation is later than the death of St. Caesaria, 524–5, and could scarcely have been used by St. Benedict. It is hardly likely to be much earlier than 530. But personally I think it reasonable to suppose that the whole was written in one *scheda* or *libellus* in 534.[1]

The date of the Rule *ad monachos* is more difficult to determine. It begins thus:

' Incipit in Christi nomine Regula, qualis debeat esse in monasterio ubi abbas est, quicumque fuerit '.[2]

' Here begins the Rule in the Name of Christ, as it should be in a monastery where there is an Abbot, whoever he may be '.

M. Malnory rightly says (S. Césaire, 1894, p. 252):

' It is not a mere abbot who comes to distribute to his community the fruit of his private experience: it is a metropolitan bishop, who is prescribing the law to be observed throughout the range of his episcopal (perhaps of his metropolitan) authority.' He points out that the council of Agde in 506 had submitted monasteries to

---

[1] We are told that before his death (*Vita S. Caesarii*, ed. Mabillon, II iv 34, ed. Krusch, II 47) he was carried to the convent, where Caesaria II ruled over more than 200 nuns, and exhorted them ' ut teneant Regulam quam ipse ante aliquot annos instituerat '. Here *aliquot* means eight years, 534-42.

[2] Maassen (*Quellen des canon. Rechts,* p. 605) gives the reading from MS. Paris B.N. (lat. 1564: ' In Christi nomine regula. Quale debeant in monasterio, ubi abba est, quicumque fuerit '.

episcopal power, and that in 554, shortly after the death of Caesarius the 5th council of his own Arles (can. 2) declared that every bishop could give to his monasteries the rule they had to follow. Caesarius's episcopate lasted from 502 to 542.

The interesting title of the rule was therefore quite wrongly interpreted by the *obseruatio critica* reproduced in P. L. 69, 1007, which takes *sacerdos* to mean 'priest'. The title runs as follows (Holst. II, p. 54):

'Incipit regula a sancto Tetradio presbytero, nepote beatae memoriae S. Caesarii episcopi Arelatensis, abbate, mea parua persona rogante transmissa, quam a suo supramemorato domino Caesario dixit ipse dictatam; quam dum esset sacerdos ipse per diuersa monasteria transmisit.[1]

It is clear that *sacerdos* has its ordinary meaning of 'bishop'. It is not necessary to take *dixit ipse* and *ipse transmisit* of the same person. If we did so, we should get the sense: 'I obtained the Rule from Tetradius, who was Priest and Abbot, and (later) while he was bishop he sent the Rule to divers monasteries'. But I prefer to think that Tetradius never became bishop,[2] and that the anonymous writer meant 'which Caesarius himself, while he was bishop, sent out to divers monasteries', as this exactly corresponds with the first words of the Rule, which are an episcopal injunction for all his abbeys to observe this Rule.

We thus get no definite date for the Rule, except that it was imposed by Caesarius upon the monasteries of his diocese, while he was bishop 502-42. It is much shorter

---

[1] The MS. just quoted from Maassen reads 'Incipit regula sancto Teridio presbytero . . . abbati' and 'transmittebat'.

[2] The sepulchral inscription of Tetradius was found at Autun, and is quoted by Krusch from Leblant, (M. G. Script. Mer. III, p. 448). He seems therefore to have been abbot at Arles, and to have died there. It would be difficult in consequence to identify him with one of the two or three contemporary Gallic bishops whose name was Tetradius.

than the Rule for Virgins, who were expected to need more detail. It may well be of the same date as the last edition of the nuns' Rule, as it contains the times of fasting and some directions for the office (shorter than the Psalmodia Lirinensis) ; now the corresponding directions in the nuns' Rule were the latest additions made by its author, so that the Rule for monks may also be as late as 534. More probably we have the latest form, and it had been written earlier and then somewhat improved.

The Rule for Virgins commences with a declaration that the nuns are never to leave the monastery until their death. This is repeated in the *Recapitulatio*; and the Rule *ad monachos* has a parallel commencement; both Rules have *usque ad mortem*; but for the nuns we find strict enclosure, *non egrediatur*, whereas for the monks there is merely *ibi perseueret*. Both these resemble St. Benedict's Rule, probably accidentally. But this law of enclosure struck Cyprian, the biographer of Caesarius, and St. Gregory of Tours.[1]

The most striking resemblances to St. Benedict are to his 58th chapter, *De disciplina suscipiendorum fratrum*.

S. Reg. 58[1] Nouiter ueniens quis ad conuersationem, non ei facilis tribuatur ingressus . . . et sit in cella hospitum paucis diebus. Postea sit in cella nouitiorum . . . et senior eis talis deputetur qui aptus sit ad lucrandas animas . . . post duorum mensium circulum legatur ei haec Regula per ordinem . . . et post sex mensium circulum legatur ei Regula . . . post quattuor menses iterum relegatur eadem Regula . . . Et si, habita secum deliberatione, promiserit se omnia custodire . . . tunc suscipiatur in congregatione, sciens et lege Regulae constitutum, quod ex illa die non liceat egredi de monasterio. . . .

Res si quas habet, aut eroget prius pauperibus, aut facta solemniter donatione conferat monasterio, nihil sibi reseruans ex omnibus.

[1] Vita, I, 35.

Compare with this :

Reg. S. Caes. ad Virg. 3. sed *uni ex senioribus* tradita, *annum integrum* in eo quo uenit habitu perseueret.

Recap. 8. quaecumque *ad conuers(at)ionem uenerit,* in *salutatorio* ei *frequentius Regula relegatur.* Et si prompta ac libera uoluntate professa fuerit *se omnia* Regulae instituta *completuram,* tamdiu ibi sit quamdiu abbatissae iustum ac rationabile uisum fuerit. Si uero Regulam dixerit se non posse complere, penitus non accipiatur.

Reg. ad Virg. c. i. usque ad mortem suam *de monasterio non egrediatur.*

S. Caes. Reg. ad monachos c. i. Vestimenta uero laica non ei mutentur, nisi antea de facultate sua chartas uenditionis faciat . . . Certe si non uult uendere, *donationis* chartas aut parentibus aut *monasterio* faciat,[1] dummodo liber sit, et nihil habeat proprium . . . quaecumque secum exhibuit abbati tradat; *nihil sibi reseruet.* . . .

Notice that the nuns have no *cella hospitum,* but only a *salutatorium* ; a parlour, but no guest-house. St. Benedict's chapter is logical and complete. It looks as if St. Caesarius had been struck by it, and had improved here and there some bits of his own Rules in accordance with it.

The *Psalmodia Lirinensis* begins 'Cum Dei adiutorio psallite sapienter' (cp. *S. Reg.* 19 7), and it ends thus :

'Si uero euenerit ut tardius ad uigilias consurgant, singulas paginas, aut quantum Abbatissae uisum fuerit, legant ; in cuius potestate erit, ut quando signum fecerit, qui legit sine mora consurgat, ut canonicus missarum numerus possit impleri.

---

[1] By the law of Justinian of 535 (*Nov.* 5, 5) a donation to the monastery became unnecessary: 'we decree this also, that one who desires to enter a monastery, *before he enters the monastery* has the right to use his possessions as he pleases. For when he enters, *all his possessions follow him, even if he has not expressly said that he takes them with him ;* and he shall be no longer the master of them in any way'. If he has given up to the fourth part of his goods to his children, they can claim no more. But if he has given them nothing, or less than a quarter, they can claim the quarter, even after he has entered the monastery. A wife left in the world will have her dowry, and whatever was settled upon her in case of her husband's death.

Pro qua re ipsae Vigiliae sic temperentur, ut quae sanae sunt post uigilias somno non opprimantur. Omni tempore post matutinos usque ad secundam horam legant, postea uero faciant opera sua '.

S. Caesarii Reg. ad monachos 14. Omni tempore usque ad tertiam legant; post Tertiam unusquisque sibi opera iniuncta faciat.

Cp. *S. Reg.* 11 [27]. Qui ordo uigiliarum omni tempore tam aestatis quam hiemis aequaliter in die dominico teneatur; *nisi forte, quod absit, tardius surgant,* aliquid de lectionibus breuiandum est aut responsoriis.

48 [23] A Kalendis autem Octobribus usque caput Quadragesimae, *usque in horam secundam plenam lectioni uacent : hora secunda agatur tertia,* et usque nonam omnes *in opus suum laborent* quod eis iniungitur.

S. Caes. Reg. ad mon. 2 [16]. Sint uobis omnia communia. Victum et uestimenta abbas ministret, quia sicut sancitum ut nihil proprium habeant, ita iustum est ut omnes quae necessaria fuerint a sancto abbate accipiant.'

Cp. *S. Reg.* 33 [8] *omnia uero necessaria a patre* sperare monasterii, nec quicquam liceat habere, quod abbas non dederit aut permiserit. *Omniaque omnibus sint communia,* ut scriptum est . . .

S. Caes. Reg. ad virg. 40. si uetera necessaria non habuerint, abbatissae refundant, pauperibus aut incipientibus uel iunioribus dispensanda.

Cp. *S. Reg.* 55 [17]. Accipientes noua, *uetera semper reddant* in praesenti, reponenda in uestiario *propter pauperes.*

There are other likenesses in the legislation : the sick only are to have baths (*Ad uirg.* 29, *lauacra, S. Reg.* 36 [14], *balneae*). St. Benedict's excommunication *a mensa* or *ab oratorio* recurs (*Ad uirg.* 10, 11), as *a communione uel a conuiuio* ; and compare 11. ' a communione orationis uel a mensa secundum qualitatem culpae sequestrabitur ' with *S. Reg.* 24 ' secundum modum culpae, et excommunicationis uel disciplinae mensura debet extendi '. Letters and *munuscula* are not to be received without leave (*Ad uirg.* 23, *Recap.* 6) as in *S. Reg.* 54. Flesh-meat is

forbidden except to the sick (*Ad mon.* 24, *Recap.* 17),
cp. *S. Reg.* 39 [22], etc.[1]

I note that the Rule for Virgins 10 uses the expression
opus Dei. The words presumably come from St. Benedict.
The next use is in the fifth book of the *Vitae Patrum*, IV.
57, the translation of which is said to have been by the
Roman deacon Pelagius, so famous in the dispute of the
Three Chapters; but it was interrupted by his elevation
to the Chair of Peter in 555, and continued by John,
afterwards John III. It is thus posterior to St. Benedict.
St. Gregory the Great follows St. Benedict in the habitual
use of *opus Dei*.[2]

It seems rather rash to suppose that St. Benedict's very
complete chapters on novices and on the hours of reading
and work were developed out of a number of widely-
spread suggestions in the two Rules of Caesarius, yet it
would be rash to deny that there is some relationship.

Again, the resemblances in the *Regula ad monachos* are not
very convincing if taken alone; whereas those in the

---

[1] In *Reg. ad uirg.* 10 we find: ' Quae signo tacto tardius *ad opus Dei* uel ad
opera uenerit, increpationi, ut dignum est, subiacebit. Quod si secundo aut
tertio admonita emendare noluerit, a communione uel a conuiuio separatur '.
This seems to be a summary of St. Benedict's lengthy chapter 43, whence is
borrowed his favourite expression *opus Dei*, which does not elsewhere occur
in Caesarius, I think.

[2] Epist. ed. Ewald, IV 18 p. 253 (Office 'ad corpus S. Pancratii '); X 18
vol. 11 p. 253 (' ibi opus Dei minime celebratur ' and ' opus Dei regulari
studeant institutione celebrare '); XI 54, II p. 329 (' monachos . . . opus
Dei celebrare '); X 13, II p. 247 (of a deacon to be made bishop, ' si in
opere Dei studium habuit uel psalmos nouit '). But once Gregory uses
the expression in a general sense of the conversion of pagan rustics in Sardinia,
—a ' work of God ',—IV 23, p. 258. On the other hand, *sacrum opus* is not
office but *Missarum solemnia* (VI 38 and 39, pp. 415 and 416), an interesting
distinction, since *sacer* is eminently used (*sacrum facere*) in this sense. Eugippius
uses *opus Dei* in the sense of ' divine worship '. *Vita S. Sever.* IV 5: ' Ciues
tantum *ab opere Dei* nec prospera nec aduersa retraherent '. *Ib.* XIII 3,
after a plague of locusts, the people came: ' Nec mora, omnibus in ecclesia
congregatio, unusquisque *in ordine suo psallebat ex more*. Omnis aetas et sexus,
qui etiam uoce non poterat, preces Deo fletibus offerebat . . . Omnibus
igitur huiuscemodi studiis occupatis, quidam pauperrimus, *opus Dei* deserens,
ad agrum . . . egressus est.' This man is then styled ' *sancti operis* temerator
atque contemptor '. The life of St. Severinus was written a good many years
before the Holy Rule. See also p. 97.

Regula ad uirgines are numerous and fairly close. Now it would be strange for a Roman Abbot to adapt to monks a rule written in Gaul for nuns! On the other hand, a Rule intended, as that of St. Benedict was, for many provinces, might be known in Gaul as early as at Byzantium, particularly to a Primate who was constantly in communication with Rome.

The Rules of St. Caesarius are almost as eclectic and composite as that of St Benedict, and we know that he retouched them again and again. St Caesarius himself tells us that he consulted other Rules:

Reg. ad uirg. Praef. ' quomodo in ipso monasterio uiuere debeatis *secundum statuta antiquorum patrum*'. ' Quia multa in monasteriis puellarum aut monachorum instituta distare uidentur, *eligimus pauca de pluribus*'.

He had therefore adapted for nuns what he found written for monks.

There seems good reason for thinking that St. Caesarius in 534 had a copy of the Rule of St. Benedict, and used it in the Recapitulatio, and even slightly corrected the Rule by it. In the Rule for monks, the passage in the first chapter about donation of goods may also have been an addition suggested by St. Benedict, whose Rule had been written about eight years before. It is impossible that St. Benedict should be the borrower; and independence seems almost equally impossible, at least in the case of the Rule for Virgins.

As to the two additional chapters on the cellararia and the *ostiaria*, no one is more likely than St. Caesarius himself to have appended them to his Rule. They are taken directly from St. Benedict.

CHAPTER VI.

CASSIODORUS AND THE HOLY RULE.

CASSIODORUS a pedant, but a promoter of the study of H. Scripture—All the other studies he recommends are to converge upon this principal one—Learned monks in Gaul and elsewhere before St. Benedict—The immense amount of reading enjoined by his Rule—Quotations of the Rule by Cassiodorus, especially of the steps of humility—The eight offices in Cassiodorus's Abbey, with Vespers by daylight and Compline as a choir office—The hymn for Sext quoted by Cassiodorus is the source of the Holy Rule, c. 16. The arrangements provided by Cassiodorus exactly coincide with the Holy Rule—He mentions no Rule, but presupposes one.

CASSIODORUS was claimed as a 'Benedictine' by mediaeval writers. Baronius would not admit this, and he was answered with more diffuseness than skill by Dom Garet. I have had to work a great deal at parts of Cassiodorus, and I was much surprised some years ago to find Abbot Butler (in *Benedictine Monachism*, ch. xx *init.*) culling from Dudden's *St. Gregory the Great* a description of Cassiodorus's monastic ideal, with the comment: 'That Cassiodorus was in any way beholden to St. Benedict is against all likelihood; Cassian appears to have been his authority on the monastic life'. For the setwo assertions no reason is given. One gathers that Abbot Butler thinks Cassiodorus's ideal was a life of study, while that of St. Benedict was a life of farm work. (See p. 107 and pp. 167–72.).

It must be admitted that Cassiodorus was more of a pedant than a scholar. The preciosity of his official style in the *Varia* is unprepossessing. His treatises are artificial; the metrical *clausulae* are awkward instead of natural; tricks like *ut arbitror* or *noscuntur*, not to speak of the pious *Deo iuuante* and *praestante Domino* are wearisome. But he is past middle age when he is 'happily converted', and he gives himself wholly to the foundation of his double monastery of hermits and cenobites. So little is his ideal the study of literature, that he is careful to provide caves for solitaries. He suggests no classical studies. Holy Scripture, and the commentaries on every part of it, and introductions by the Fathers, are assumed to be the staple of monastic reading. But for the appreciation of this sacred literature, and for correctness in copying, he thinks a cursory knowledge of Grammar, Logic and Rhetoric to be necessary;[1] this he provides in the second book of his *Institutiones* in a concentrated form; he adds music and geometry. He recommends a knowledge of geography also; but all is to centre round the Scriptural studies.

The 15th chapter of his *Inst. div. litt.* should be read.[2]

[1] The most notable words are these (*Inst.* c. 28): ' Verumtamen nec illud Patres sanctissimi decreuerent, ut *saecularium litterarum studia* respuantur, quia *exinde non minimum ad sacras Scripturas intelligendas sensus noster instruitur ;* si tamen, diuina gratia suffragante, notitia ipsarum rerum *sòbrie ac rationabiliter* inquiratur, ut non in ipsis habeamus spem prouectus nostri, sed per ipsa transeuntes, desideremus nobis a Patre luminum proficuam salutaremque sapientiam debere concedi '.

[2] Cassiodorus exemplifies in his Commentary on the Psalms his theory that the sciences of logic and rhetoric ought to be applied to Holy Scripture. In the Preface, c. 3, he defends this view, quoting St. Augustine and other Fathers. Dip at random into the book, and you find scheme and tropes explained: Ps. 61. 1 is an *epitrochasmos* (and we never had noticed it, though we say it so often!); Ps. 41. 17 is a *quinquepartite* syllogism, elaborately worked out; 43, 15 is an *anaphora* or *relatio ;* in 70 there is *ethopoeia ;* 33.5 exemplifies the third species of definition; in 34.8 we find *syncrisis ;* 22.1 has *synathroismos*, and so forth, on every page of the commentary : we are accustomed to hypallage, pleonasmos, synecdoche, climax, but epembasis, esotema, ethopoeia, coenonema, auxesis, ennoematice, syncrisis, diatyposis, antiplosis, polysyntheton, proanaphoresis, are less familiar, with many others. The pious student is certain that only by this scientific analysis can he arrive at the hidden

I doubt whether all this differs in theory from the monasticism of Africa, Italy and Gaul at this period. Only Cassiodorus is an enthusiast. He wishes his library to contain the best commentaries on every one of the books of Holy Scripture. He is also a pedant who wishes to preserve the older language and spelling, much as St. Sidonius Apollinaris did a century earlier, not to speak of another pedant, Ennodius. But he is not in the least a man of learning, a theologian, a brilliant writer, like the great African Abbot and Bishop, Fulgentius, who died before Cassiodorus left the world.

As for St. Benedict, we know his practical ideal from the rule he made after a careful study of earlier monastic writers. We also know that he dedicated the two churches at Montecassino to St. John the Baptist, hermit and preacher, and to St. Martin, the greatest of Western monks. St. Martin's monks made no baskets; they sold nothing; they did no manual labour, exercised no art *except that of copying books*. We infer that they did some reading.[1] They were evidently, at Marmoutier, not clerics; but they had a habit of becoming bishops. The fashion had been set by Augustine, and the African bishops were chosen from Tagaste or Hippo. Bishops came from Cassian's monastery; but the most famous are

---

wisdom, for the meaning is often very different from the sound: ' Simplicitas duplex, et sine dolo bilinguitas ', as he playfully expresses it (*Praef.* c. 3). At the end of the last Psalm he triumphantly exclaims: " Lo we have shown that the series of Psalms is filled full with grammar and etymologies, with schemata, with the art of rhetoric, with topica, with the art of dialectics, with music, with geometry, with astronomy, and with the expressions peculiar to the divine law." All the information crowded into the lists and diagrams (these should be seen in the Bamberg MS.) of the book *de Artibus ac disciplinis liberalium studiorum* is intended simply to assist the study of Scripture : *lectio diuina.*

[1] Sulpitius Severus, *Vita S. Martini* X: ' Ars ibi, *exceptis scriptoribus*, nulla habebatur: cui tamen operi minor aetas deputabatur: maiores orationi uacabant ' . . . ' Pluresque ex his postea episcopos uidimus. Quae enim esset ciuitas aut ecclesia, quae non sibi de Martini monasterio cuperet sacerdotem? '

the great prelates who issued from Lérins: Honoratus and Hilary, Faustus and Germanus and Eucherius, and so forth, and eventually Caesarius. Already in 432 the secular clergy of Gaul complained that they had no chance of succeeding to a see; and Pope St. Celestine wrote a sympathetic letter, saying that no monastery ought to be a seminary of bishops,[1]—he means less Lérins, I suppose, than Marmoutier. We know that the monasteries of Gaul were filled with learned monks and solitaries. We gather the same of Africa, though Fulgentius there had no peer. Of Italian monasteries we know less than of Gaul and Africa. In South Italy, however, we have at least the monastery of Nola, founded in the fourth century by a notable man of letters, St. Paulinus. In the first years of the sixth century, Abbot Eugippius of Naples was a great student of St. Augustine and of Holy Scripture, and the biographer of St. Severinus, the monastic Apostle of Pannonia. There may have been fewer monastic bishops in Italy than in Africa and Gaul. To Eusebius of Vercelli and Paulinus in the fourth century we may perhaps add the successor of St. Ambrose at Milan, Simplicianus, a correspondent and admirer of St. Augustine. In the fifth century at Pavia, St. Epiphanius and his biographer Ennodius both seem to have lived a monastic life. But there is no outstanding monastic figure in Italy between St. Jerome and St. Benedict, if we except the older contemporary of the latter, Aequitius, in Valeria.

Now there is a very obvious parallel between St. Benedict and Cassiodorus: both are concerned with the

---

[1] St. Celestine, Ep. 4, *ad episc. prov. Vienn. et Narbon.* no 7: 'Nec emeritis in suis ecclesiis clericis peregrini et extranei et qui antea ignorati sint, ad exclusionem eorum qui bene de suorum ciuium merentur testimonio, praeponantur: *ne nouum quoddam, de quo episcopi fiant, institutum uideatur collegium.* We gather that all these *peregrini et extranei* came from one place. The date of the letter is 428, when Lérins was only 18 years old: its multitude of bishops begins later, and St. Martin's disciples are probably meant.

instruction of their monks in sacred learning. St. Benedict orders reading for two hours a day and three in Lent, that is 730 hours plus 36, or 766 in the year. But much more reading was done on Sunday, say two hours more, —104. There was reading at meals, say half an hour at 365 + 305 days (allowing 60 days of fasts), or 335 hours. At Compline, say 10 minutes at least, or 60 hours. This totals 1,265 hours in the year, not counting the lessons at Matins for half the year.[1] I think 40 pages an hour is quick reading; but four pages is absurdly slow. At four pages an hour, the slowest monk would read 5,060 pages in a year, say twenty volumes, or four hundred in twenty years, eight hundred in forty years. A quick reader, at 30 pages an hour, would get through 37,950 pages a year, 150–180 volumes, 8,000–9,000 in fifty years.

The monastery library must have been very large, if the monks were numerous. The works enumerated by Cassiodorus would not suffice, unless there were many copies of each. I suppose 150 monks would not possess less than 3,000–4,000 volumes, small or large. There would be a great amount of copying, and a well-fitted scriptorium. St. Benedict does not mention things which were a matter of course. Writing books, rather than buying them, was certainly the custom in monasteries, and it is no more enjoined than the sweeping out of the dormitory and cloister.

There may have been monasteries in Italy where some of the monks could not read or write. This is unlikely, however, in any community where the office was said and sung in common, as it was by all cenobites. St. Benedict

---

[1] The length of an hour varied from equinox to equinox. I give St. Benedict's calculation above. Abbot Butler (in *Benedictine Monachism*, 2nd ed., pp. 279-81, in ch. XVII) supposes 2½ hours of reading in winter, on the average, and 3¾ in summer; in Lent about 3¾. This would make 200 hours per year more than my estimate.

thinks it possible that a novice at the date of his profession may not yet be able to write and sign his petition. But it is unlikely that any illiterate candidate would be received, unless young and capable of learning.

It is probable that neither Benedict nor Cassiodorus differed in theory from the habits of the more important monasteries. But the enormous amount of reading insisted upon by the former, and the completeness of the library of the latter must have distinguished them among their contemporaries.

It would be ridiculous *a priori* to doubt that Cassiodorus was acquainted with the Rule of St. Benedict. He must often have passed by Cassinum on his way from Ravenna and Rome to his properties in the South. He must often have heard the fame of the Wonder-worker, who had founded a group of cells at Sublacum and later a great Abbey on the conspicuous mountain. It would be parodoxical to doubt that the pious prime minister of the Arian Kings visited the Patriarch of monks as he passed. He must have done so. And he must certainly have consulted the Rule before founding his new monastery of Vivarium.

On the parallel passages collected by Abbot Amelli,[1] only one is recognised by Abbot Butler as convincing:

Regula XXVII : Et pastoris boni pium imitetur exemplum qui . . . abiit unam *ouem* quae errauerat quaerere ; cuius infirmitati in tantum compassus est, ut eam in sacris *humeris suis dignaretur* imponere, et sic *reportare* ad gregem.	Inst. cap. 32 : Oremus ergo, fr. k., quatenus qui humano generi tam magna largitus est ut *ouem* perditam *reportare suis humeris dignaretur.*

[1] In an appendix to his lecture, delivered at S. Calisto, Rome, 14th May, 1917 (printed at Grottaferrata), *Cassiodoro e la Volgata*, pp. 43-3.

This passage suggests that either Cassiodorus knew the Rule by heart, or else was looking it up when he wrote this chapter, which is addressed to the two Abbots of his double monastery. But there is much more than this.

In his comment on the first of the fifteen Gradual Psalms (*Expos. in Psalt.* Ps. 119, ed. Garet p. 429, P.L. 70, col. 901) he compares these fifteen steps upwards to steps of humility. I underline the coincidences with the Rule.

' Hinc quibusdam meritorum *gradibus ascendens, ad perfectam* atque aeternam Domini *peruenit caritatem,* quae in summo uirtutum fastigio noscitur collocata . . . ' And further on : ' Sed *gradus* iste *humilitatis est ascensus,* confessio peccatorum, sicut in octogesimo tertio psalmo dictum est : Ascensus in corde eius disponit in conualle lacrimarum. Sic enim istos gradus ascendere merebimur, si pro delictis nostris prostrati, Domino iugiter supplicemus. . . . Unde *scalam illam Jacob* pro parte aliqua his gradibus fortasse non immerito dicimus comparandam : illa enim et *ascendentes* habuit *et descendentes :* in istis uero *gradibus* beatorum solus ascensus est '.

The parallel of *Reg.* 7, *fin.* is striking :

' Ergo his omnibus *humilitatis gradibus ascensis,* monachus mox *ad caritatem* Dei *perueniet* illam, quae *perfecta* foris mittit timorem '.

This is from Cassian, Inst. IV 39 : ' humilitas uera . . . confestim te *ad caritatem* quae timorem non habet *gradu* excelsiore *per*ducet,' but the resemblance here to Cassiodorus is less. And Cassian has not twelve *gradus,* steps of humility, as St. Benedict has, but merely ten *indicia,* ' proofs ' of humility, which would not have suggested a comparison with the 15 steps of the Gradual Psalms ; nor does he mention Jacob's ladder, as St. Benedict does, *Reg.* VII *init.* ' Unde, fratres, si summae *humilitatis* uolumus culmen adtingere, et ad exaltationem caelestem, ad quam per praesentis uitae humilitatem ascenditur, uolumus uelociter peruenire, actibus nostris *ascendentibus scala illa* erigenda est, quae in somnio *Jacob* apparuit, per quam ei *descendentes et ascendentes* angeli monstrabantur '.

This uncontrovertible reference to the rule of St. Benedict is the more remarkable because it is in the commentary on the Psalms (chiefly based on St. Augustine), and not in connexion with monastic matters at all. It shows that Cassiodorus was very familiar with the Rule. And he echoes the same chapter again, *De anima* (p. 639, P.L. 70, col. 1306) : ' Ad te, sancte Domine, nemo se erigendo peruenit, quin potius humiliatus ascendit '. Cp. ' Scala illa *erigenda* est . . . scala uero ipsa *erecta* nostra est uita in saeculo, quae humiliato corde a Domino *erigatur* ad caelum '. Hence, by a trick of memory, Cassiodorus's curious use of *erigendo*, just as St. Luke in paraphrasing a passage of St. Matthew or St. Mark borrows a word, but uses it in a different sense.[1]

Thus we see that Cassiodorus borrows not from Cassian but from St. Benedict.[2]

On the words of Ps. 69, 1 ' Deus in adiutorium meum intende, Domine ad adiuuandum me festina ', Cassiodorus's comment naturally refers to a celebrated passage of Cassian : ' Sed non sequendus in omnibus generabiliter hunc locum facundissimus Cassianus, in decima Collatione plurima de eius utilitate disserens, tanto honore concelebrat, ut *quidquid* monachi assumpserint, sine huius

---

[1] List in Hawkins, *Horae Synopticae,* pp. 68–76.

[2] These certain borrowings throw light upon the less certain parallels given by Abbot Amelli, such as ' *sine aliquo murmure* praeceptis salutaribus oboedire ' (*Instit.* 31) with Reg. 5, *fin.,* si oboedit discipulus . . . in corde si murmurauerit, and elsewhere; ' *milites Christi* ' (*Instit.* 30) and *reuera milites Christi* (on Ps. 103. 17, p. 734) with St. Benedict's particular love of this metaphor for monks.

uersiculi *trina iteratione* non inchoent'. Now Cassian exemplifies the universal usefulness of this verse as an ejaculatory prayer by giving instances of all kinds of *temptations* in which it is to be employed, and he does not actually say (though he may be taken to imply) that it is to be recited before every action that monks take on (*assumpserint*). It is St. Benedict who says ' *quidquid inchoas bonum, ab eo perfici instantissima oratione deposcas* ' (*S. Reg. prol.*). And as for *trina iteratione*, it is entirely absent in Cassian (*Coll.* X. 10), and Cassiodorus has evidently in mind St. Benedict's thirty-fifth chapter, where the *septimanarii coquinae* before assuming office are to recite after Sunday Lauds ' Deus in adiutorium ' etc., ' Et hoc idem TERTIO repetatur ab omnibus '. Cassiodorus knows his Cassian less well than his Rule.

The use of the 33rd Psalm v. 12 in the Prologue of St. Benedict, is perhaps worth noting : Si uis habere ueram et *perpetuam uitam* . . . , where Cassiodorus's Commentary also inserts *perpetuam :* ' sed utinam sic *uitam perpetuam* quaereremus '.

Another likeness has escaped notice : S. *Reg. Prol.* ' non ilico pauore perterritus refugias *uiam* salutis, quae non est nisi ANGUSTO initio incipienda. Processu uero conuersationis et fidei, dilatato corde, inenarrabili dilectionis dulcedine *curritur uia mandatorum* Dei '. So Cassiodorus on Ps. 118, 32 : ' " uiam mandatorum tuorum cucurri, cum dilatares cor meum " ; ueritatis ordinem seruans, cucurrisse se dicit uiam mandatorum, quoniam cor suum a Domino asserit esse dilatatum. Non enim potuisset uel ambulare uel currere, nisi cor eius in latitudine scientiae fuisset extensum ; nam cum *uia mandatorum* eius legatur ANGUSTA, nisi *dilatato corde* non curritur.'[1]

---

[1] Cassian frequently speaks of ' pure ' prayer, and ' purity ' in prayer, and St. Benedict inherits from him this wording, S. *Reg.* 20: ' cum omni humilitate et *puritatis* devotione supplicandum est. Et non in multiloquio, sed *in*

For the monastic office (*Instit.* 30) Cassiodorus has *opus diuinum* (*S. Reg.* c.16, *titulus*, 195), which like *opus Dei* does not occur earlier than St. Benedict and St. Caesarius.[1]

This may remind us that the most original and peculiar part of the Holy Rule is the arrangement of the Offices and Psalms. Cassian had made up seven Offices in the day. But. St. Benedict introduced a new office, Compline, thus making eight hours, and he explains this twice over in the same chapter to make the propriety of his innovation clear: *S. Reg.* 16. 'Qualiter diuina opera per diem agantur. Ut ait Propheta: " Septies in die laudem dixi tibi ". Qui septenarius sacratus numerus *a nobis* sic implebitur, si Matutino, Primae, Tertiae, Sextae, Nonae, Vesperae, Completoriique tempore nostrae seruitutis officia persoluamus; quia de his diurnis horis dixit: " Septies in die laudem dixi tibi ". Nam de nocturnis Vigiliis idem ipse Propheta ait: " Media nocte surgebam ad confitendum tibi ".'

This is a definite refutation of Cassian, who in *Instit.* III 3 explains the day hours as corresponding to the first, third, sixth, ninth and eleventh in the parable of the Vineyard (Matt. XX 1-6), and then makes seven by the addition of the new Bethlehem 'second Mattins' (later called Prime) and the Night Office. St. Benedict declares that in Ps. 118, 164, the day hours alone are meant, *septies in die*, while verse 62 of the same Psalm, *nocte surgebam* gives the night office as eighth.

---

puritate cordis et *compunctione* lacrimarum nos *exaudiri* sciamus. Et ideo breuis debet esse et *pura oratio* '. It seems to be rather from St. Benedict than from Cassian that Cassiodorus has on Ps. 94, 6: ' Si tota *cordis puritate* deprecemur facile nos qui fecit reficiet ', and in Ps. 6, *introd.* ' Nam si *puro corde* petimus, cur dubitemus *exaudiri*, cum ab ipso et ad ipsum ueniamus instructi? Dona, Domine, in satisfactione nostra tota nos caritate *compungi*, qui nobis salutarem regulam praestitisti '.

[1] In Eugippius it is more general, for Mass or any service, see p. 86, note.

Hence Dom Suitbert Baümer (*Gesch. des Breviers*, p. 178), following a statement communicated to him by Mr. Edmund Bishop, asserts of the attempts to find Compline in earlier documents, such as St. Basil and Cassian : 'It seems to us, however, that these data, even if we may see in them a germ of Compline, do not prove its existence as an Office. To assume a veritable Compline before St. Benedict is unhistorical '.

St. Benedict concludes : 'Ergo his temporibus referamus laudes Creatori nostro " super iudicia iustitiae suae ", id est, Matutinis, Prima, Tertia, Sexta, Nona, Vespera, Completorio ; et nocte surgamus " ad confitendum ei".' Hence the common word *lucernaria* is dropped by St Benedict, for he has to shift that office somewhat earlier, and orders that it is so to be said 'ut lumen *lucernae* non indigeant reficientes, sed luce adhuc diei omnia consummentur' (41 *fin*). But the word *lucernaria* remained in rules derived from St. Benedict, as the *Regula Magistri* (often), St. Isidore's Rule, and the abstract of St. Benedict called the ' Second Rule of St. Augustine.'

If we accept the view of Dom Baümer and Mr. Bishop, we are obliged to suppose with the former (p. 179) that 'the Rule of St. Benedict was probably observed in Cassiodorus's monastery', as he has eight offices daily, including Compline:[1]

Comm. in Psalt. Praef. Psalmi sunt denique qui nobis gratas faciunt esse

(1)   *uigilias*, quando silenti nocte psallentibus choris humana uox erumpit in musicam, uerbisque arte *modulatis* . . .

[1] Mgr. Batiffol (Hist. du Brév. Romain, 3rd ed. 1911, p. 44) says: ' Il est possible que S. Bénoît n'ait fait que se conformer à un usage existant déjà, et dont témoigne son contemporain, qui ne fut pas vraisemblablement son disciple, Cassiodore '. But Mgr. Batiffol was probably not aware of Cassiodorus's quotations from the Rule of St. Benedict, which make his independence improbable, and had not noticed how St. Benedict feels the necessity of arguing (as I have shown) in favour of his seven day hours, because he feels he is making an innovation.

Cantus qui aures oblectat et animas instruit, fit uox una psallentium, et *cum angelis Dei*, quos audire non possumus, laudum uerba miscemus . . .

(2) Ipsi enim diem uenturum *matutina* exsultatione conciliant;

(3) Ipsi nobis *primam* diei horam dedicant,

(4) Ipsi nobis *tertiam* horam consecrant,

(5) Ipsi *sextam* in panis confractione laetificant,

(6) Ipsi nobis *nona* ieiunia resoluunt,

(7) Ipsi *diei postrema* concludunt,

(8) Ipsi *noctis aduentu*, ne mens nostra tenebratur efficiunt;

We notice first that the hours are eight in number :

Secondly, the *Vigiliae* are 'modulated', the word used in *S. Reg.* 11 : 'in quibus *Vigiliis* teneatur mensura : id est, *modulatis*, ut supra disposuimus, sex psalmis', etc. Elsewhere Cassiodorus has *Vigiliae nocturnae* (*Instit.* 30 ; in Ps. 76) : so St. Benedict 4 times. On Ps. 76, v. 4 Cassiodorus says : 'Dicit enim " oculos suos anticipasse Vigilias" ' quas in Dei laudibus solemniter exhibebat. Istas *USUS NOSTER* consueuit uocare *Nocturnos*', (So St. B., twice).

Thirdly, with *cum angelis* we may compare S. Reg. 19, presently to be quoted.

Fourthly, the most important point is that Vespers is a day hour, *diei postrema*, as for the first time in the Rule.

Fifthly, the place of the old Vespers is taken by Compline *noctis aduentu*.

We are told on Ps. 90 (*fin.*) that it is said at Compline : 'dicatur ergo a nobis post omnes actus diei *noctis aduentu*'. St. Benedict makes the three Psalms, 4, 90 and 113, invariable at Compline. He borrowed Ps. 90 from St. Basil, perhaps ; but Cassiodorus is obviously following St. Benedict directly.

In the comment on Ps. 118, v. 164, we again find the list of offices. But Dom Garet's edition of Cassiodorus is a very bad one, and the text is here corrupt :

Comm. Ps. 118, v. 164: ' Septies in die laudem dixi tibi, super iudicia iustitiae tuae '. Si ad litteram hunc numerum uelimus aduertere, *septem* illas significat uices quibus se *monachorum* pia deuotio consolatur, id est, Matutinis, <Prima>, Tertia, Sexta, Nona, Lucernaria, Completoriis, [Nocturnis]. Hoc et sancti Ambrosii hymnus in sextae horae decantatione testatur.'

I have inserted *Prima*, which must have been omitted by a scribe ; and I have bracketed *Nocturnis*, as a subsequent addition by another scribe to make up the number seven.[1] Obviously *Nocturni*, if mentioned at all, would have been the first office, not the last !

If anyone says these conjectures are too bold, (I should personally call them obvious,) the answer is to compare the absurd readings of Dom Garet in the *Institutio Divinarum Litterarum*, especially the exact parallel in the lists of Holy Scripture, cc. 12-14. Garet's list of the *antiqua translatio* is corrected not only by the Bamberg MS. (the 'codex archetypus') but by the codex Amiatinus ; we see that books are both omitted and inserted in Garet's text, and the same is the case (with different books) in many late MSS.[2]

The commentary on the Psalms was written principally for the use of Cassiodorus's own monastery, in order that his monks might understand what they sang. He expresses this beautifully in a passage to which Baümer refers (p. 180) :

' Hunc autem modum sanctae orationis (*first* oratio, *then* clamor) seruandum deuotissimus Christianus intelligat, ut

---

[1] Another (less important) reference to the office (secular) has not been noticed: on Ps. 70, v. 8: ' Sed huic bono addidit perpetuitatem; nam cum ponit *tota die*, numquid noctibus a laudibus Domini dicit esse cessandum, maxime cum se illo tempore laudibus Domini catholica consoletur ecclesia? Tunc enim *uespertini*, tunc *nocturni*, tunc *matutini* peraguntur, cum populus fidelis inuigilat.' But I wish to point out that *tota die* is assumed to mean ' day ' opposed to ' night ' (and not 24 hours) just as by St. Benedict. This confirms the conjecture that *nocturni* is an inept insertion in the passage just quoted in the text.

[2] See my article ' The Codex Amiatinus and Cassiodorus ' I, in *Rev.Bénéd.* April, 1926, p. 142, and note.

idipsum cogitet quod orat, ipsum respiciat mente cui supplicat, omnes superfluas cogitationes excludat, aliud non admittat extraneum: ne, ut ait quidam, purissimis fontibus apros immittere uideatur improuidos. Hinc etiam Sancti Ambrosii secundum Apostolum horae sextae roseus hymnus ille redoluit; ait enim:

> Orabo mente Dominum,
> Orabo simul spiritu;
> Ne vox sola Deo canat,
> Sensusque noster alibi
> Ductus aberret fluctuans,
> Vanis praeuentus casibus.

Tunc enim Deo accepta est oratio canentium, si *pura mens* idem gerat quod *explicat uox cantici*'.[1]   This is a roundabout way of expressing St. Benedict's admirable phrase (c. XIX): 'sic stemus ad psallendum, ut *mens nostra concordet uoci nostrae* '.

This hymn for Sext[2] is the same to which Cassiodorus referred in the passage previously quoted, where the second and third verses were meant:

1. Bis ternas horas explicans
    Diei, sol ingreditur,
    Ut sex idemque transigat
    Et noctis claudat aditum.

2. Nos ergo nunc confamuli,   *S. Reg.* 16
    Prophetae dicti memores   Ut ait Propheta,
    Soluamus ora in canticis
    Prece mixta Dauidicis

3. Ut *septies die*[m] uere   Septies in die laudem . . .
    Orantes cum psalterio
    *Laudes*que cantantes Deo
    Laeti *soluamus debitum.*   Nostrae seruitutis officia per-
                                       soluamus.

---

[1] We ought evidently to read *uox explicat cantici*, or the rhythm is wrong.
[2] In the ' Psalmodia Lirinensis ' arranged by St. Caesarius the Hymn for Sext is ' Jam Sexta sensim uoluitur ',

Cassiodorus attributes this hymn to St. Ambrose.[1] St. Benedict calls most hymns *Ambrosianum* (cc. ix, xii, xiii, xvii), but he does not use this word for the hymns of Terce, Sext and None. It is to be presumed that this hymn was sung or said daily at Sext at Vivarium; hence probably at Montecassino. We thus are induced to turn again to *S. Reg.* 16, just quoted; and we find such reminiscences of the hymn that it is surely inevitable that St. Benedict had it in mind : the word *Propheta* for the Psalmist is not unusual nor is the idea of *debitum soluere* ;[2] but when we find them in connection with the same text, Pss. 118, 164, and when we remember that St. Benedict (by the analogy of Cassiodorus) probably said the hymn daily, it is difficult to doubt that these lines were in St. Benedict's memory.

I am inclined to go further. The first verse of the hymn speaks of the six hours before midday, and the six hours after. To St. Benedict these are, we know, the twelve hours of daylight, and they are of variable length according to the season. Hence it was natural for him to conclude that St. Ambrose (if St. Benedict thought the hymn was his) took *Septies die* to mean 'seven times in the twelve hours of day'. And St. Benedict remembered that the hymn for Wednesday at Lauds, had :

Mentes manusque tollimus	S. Reg. 16 Nam de nocturnis
PROPHETA *sicut noctibus*	Vigiliis idem ipse *Propheta*
Nobis gerendum praecipit	ait: Media *nocte* surgebam ad
Paulusque gestis censuit.	confitendum tibi.

This seems to explain 'the same Prophet', when we

---

[1] It is given in the works of St. Ambrose, on the authority of Cassiodorus, and in Daniel's *Thesaurus Hymnologicus*, p. 22. But the reference to seven offices is probably later than St. Ambrose.

[2] Abbot Butler (*Reg. Monast.* 2nd ed.) *in loco* notes that the Gelasian Sacramentary (I, xxxvii) has the words ' *debitae seruitutis officio* '. Compare also S. Reg. c. 1., ' *seruitutis pensum . . . reddere* '.

should have expected 'the same Psalm'.[1]   It seems likely that these two hymns suggested to St. Benedict, or encouraged him, to explain the two verses, 164 and 62, of Psalm 118 as he does, and to increase the number of day offices to seven, besides the Nocturns.[2]

Now that it is established that Cassiodorus knew the Holy Rule so well that he quoted or paraphrased it by heart, and that he had the same offices in his monastery as those which St. Benedict was the first to ordain, we may examine the scanty data we possess as to the observance of the Abbey of Vivarium.   In the last five chapters of the *Instit. Div. Litt.* Cassiodorus gives some fragmentary advice to his monks and their two Abbots, *but assumes that they have a settled rule of life.*   Therefore we can gather but little as to their observance.

St. Benedict wrote for cenobites, *fortissimum genus;* but he had been an anchorite, and he contemplates such hermits as first undergoing a long probation in a monastery (c. 1).   So Cassiodorus provides places of retirement on Monte Castello surrounded by ancient walls (we cannot

[1] The hymn for Sunday Mattins, *Primo dierum omnium,* is attributed to St. Gregory the Great.   If it is later than St. Benedict, the second verse will be a reminiscence of St. Benedict's Rule, and not of the hymn for Sext, when it says: ' Pulsis procul torporibus Surgamus omnes ocius, Et *nocte* quaeramus Pium, Sicut *prophetam* nouimus '.

[2] We must also remember that the mere fact that Cassiodorus used a hymn at Sext (as he evidently did) again connects him with the Rule of St. Benedict. Dom Suitbert Baümer said (*Gesch. des Breviers,* p. 177) that ' of late years and with good ground ' it has been pretty universally recognised that it was St. Benedict who completed and rounded off the little hours with the *Deus in adiutorium,* Hymn, three Psalms, capitulum with versicle (or responsory) and collect.   (This sentence of Dom Baümer was put into its present form by the help of Edmund Bishop.)   We need not assume that before St. Benedict there was no hymn sung at the little hours; in fact it is probable that the hymn quoted was meant to be used at an office (at Milan), not merely as a private devotion at midday; and Caesarius sometimes had hymns at the little hours. But there is at least no proof that the hymn was an invariable part of the office before St. Benedict.   The Roman office seems originally to have had no hymns, if we judge from the fact that up to the present day it has none for Easter and its octave.   Dom Baümer says that even in the 8th century and the beginning of the 9th, Hymns were ' no integral part ' of the Roman Office (p. 256).

but remember the cyclopean wall at Montecassino) for hermits, but only after probation in the monastery by the river Pellena. He enlarges (it would seem) on St. Benedict's words. But he could have found the same in Cassian (*Inst.* V 36), 'in coenobiis primum diutissime commorantes,' and *Collat.* XVIII 4, 'prius in coenobiis instituti, iamque in actuali conuersatione perfecti, solitudinis elegere secreta'. And it is to Cassian that he refers in the words :

'Cassianum presbyterum, qui conscripsit de Institutione fidelium *monachorum* sedulo legite, et *libenter* audite. (*And, after a long parenthesis*) Cetera uero genera *monachorum* uehementer accusat. Sed uos, kmi fratres, Deo iuuante, eas partes eligite, quas salubriter cognoscitur ille laudasse'.

Here he seems to say : 'Follow Cassian's advice, and become cenobites,—following the *new Rule* of cenobites. For *libenter audite* reminds us of the first words of the Rule, *libenter excipe*. The *genera monachorum* are described by Cassian, after St. Jerome, and by St. Benedict after Cassian, adding a fourth, *gyrouagi*. Cassiodorus continues :

'Nam si uos in monasterio Viuariensi, sicut credere dignum est, diuina gratia suffragante, *coenobiorum consuetudo competenter erudiat*, et aliquid sublimius defaecatis animis optare contingat, habetis Montis Castelli secreta suauia, ubi uelut anachoritae, praestante Domino, feliciter esse possitis. Sunt enim remota et imitantia eremi loca, quando *muris pristinis* ambientibus probantur inclusa. Quapropter nobis aptum erit eligere *exercitatis iam* atque *probatissimis*, illud habitaculum, si prius in corde uestro fuerit praeparatus *ascensus*'.

Compare S. Reg. 1 : 'qui non conuersationis feruore nouicio, sed monasterii *probatione diuturna*, qui didicerunt contra diabolum multorum solacio *iam docti* pugnare ; et bene exstructi fraterna ex acie ad singularem pugnam eremi', etc. There is no contradiction here, at least, and some likeness.

St. Benedict recommends that a monastery should contain within it all that is necessary: 'id est, *aqua, molendinum, hortus,* uel *artes diuersae* intra monasterium exerceantur, ut non sit necessitas monachis uagandi foras', etc.

So Vivarium is described 'quando habetis *hortos* irriguos, et piscosi *amnis Pellenae fluenta* uicina . . . influit uobis arte moderatus, ubicumque necessarius iudicatur, et *hortis* uestris sufficiens et *mol[end]inis.*' Here the water, the garden and the mills are enumerated, almost as if to satisfy the requirements of the Rule. There is the sea also, and the fish pond or 'cloister of the fishes'. (The *artes diuersae* are partly spoken of in the preceding and following chapters.) Cassiodorus goes on:

'*Balnea* quoque congruenter *aegris* praeparata corporibus iussimus ædificari, ubi fontium perspicuitas decenter illabitur, quae et potui gratissima cognoscitur et lavacris'. Severus of Antioch and Fulgentius of Ruspe would have disapproved (see p. 117); but St. Benedict had said (c. 36); 'Balnearum usus infirmis quotiens expedit offeratur', after 'Infirmorum cura ante omnia et super omnia adhibenda est, ut sicut reuera Christo ita eis seruiatur'; so the baths have to be built.

The monastery is now so complete 'ut monasterium uestrum potius quæratur ab aliis, quam uos extranea loca iuste desiderare possitis'. But the monks must be spiritually detached from so much convenience: 'Verum haec, ut scitis, oblectamenta sunt praesentium rerum, non spes futura fidelium; istud transiturum, illud sine fine mansurum. Sed illic positi, ad illa potius desideria transferamus, quae nos faciant regnare cum Christo',— as in the last words of the Prologue to the Rule, 'ut et regno eius mereamur esse consortes',—a sentence of which the first part (*dilatato corde*) we heard above in the mouth of Cassiodorus.

Next come, in this c. 29, the words just quoted about Cassian, *sedulo legite et libenter audite*. So St. Benedict orders, and he has the Collations read daily at Compline (or edifying books), and in his last chapter specially recommends 'Collationes Patrum, et Instituta et Vitas eorum'. In order that these directions may be carried out without danger from Semipelagianism, a long parenthesis (evidently an afterthought) tells of the bowdlerised edition of Cassian prepared by the African bishop Victor of Tununum,—' a copy of this work will shortly', he hopes, ' be sent over from Africa '.

The 31st chapter deals entirely with the care of the sick, and the study of medicine and medical writers—' de monachis curam infirmorum habentibus '. He addresses the infirmarians with eloquence, and adds that they are ' ab illo *mercedem* recepturi, a quo possunt pro temporalibus aeterna retribui '. (So the Rule, c. 36 'quia de talibus copiosior *merces* acquiritur '). All this care may be due to St. Benedict's teaching that the sick are the first care in the monastery, ' ante omnia et super omnia ' (c. 36).

Of all manual labours Cassiodorus prefers the copying of books, c. 30 : ' Ego tamen fateor uotum meum, quod inter uos quaecumque possunt corporeo labore compleri, antiquariorum mihi studia (si tamen ueraciter scribunt!) non immerito forsitan plus placere '. He adds bookbinding, and has prepared a book full of designs for covers —if only it could be found, how interesting it would be. He has self-filling lamps for the Vigiliae nocturnae (this again implies that Vespers were said before sunset), and a sundial and a water clock, because ' it is well known ' (his favourite *cognoscitur* here seems a little comic to a Northerner) ' that on some days the brightness of the sun is absent '. Thus the soldiers of Christ will be roused as by trumpets to 'exercise the Divine work'. We see that the difficulty of calculating the time will be simplified, for St. Benedict had to say that 'the announcement of the hour of the work of God by day and night shall be the care of the Abbot'. Indeed, the computation of hours of varying length would need the ingenuity of Cassiodorus's friend, the famous Scythian monk, Dionysius the Little.

As to the arrangement of the day, we know only the two facts quoted above on p. 99 from the Preface to the *Comm. in Ps.*, 'ipsi *sextam* in panis confractione laetificant, ipsi nobis *nona* ieiunia resoluunt'. This merely tells us that the monks dined at mid-day, except on fast days of the rule, when they dined at None. But this was not necessarily a custom peculiar to St. Benedict's Rule (cc. 39, 41), though it corresponds with it exactly.

As for guests 'qui numquam desunt in monasterio' (*S. Reg.* 53), St. Benedict orders (*ibid*): 'Pauperum et peregrinorum maxime susceptioni cura sollicite exhibeatur, quia in ipsis magis Christus suscipitur; nam diuitum terror ipse sibi exigit honorem'. In accordance with this, Cassiodorus makes no mention of richer guests, but he says (*Inst.* c. 29): 'Inuitat siquidem uos locus Viuariensis monasterii *ad multa peregrinis et egentibus praeparanda*', and again (c. 32): 'Peregrinum igitur ante omnia suscipite, eleemosynam date, nudum uestite, esurienti panem frangite'.

As for manual work, St. Benedict says that on Sundays those who cannot spend the whole day in reading are to work (probably not garden work, 'servile work'): *S. Reg.* 48 [53], 'Si quis uero ita neglegens et desidiosus fuerit ut non uelit aut non possit meditare[1] aut legere, iniungatur

---

[1]*Meditare* (-ri) in the Holy Rule means to learn by heart; *S. Reg.* 8[5]: 'Quod uero restat post Vigilias, a fratribus qui psalterii uel lectionum aliquid indigent, *meditationi* inseruiatur. 48[53]: 'si quis uero ita neglegens et desidiosus fuerit ut non uelit aut non possit *meditare* aut legere, 58[10]: 'sit in cella nouiciorum, ubi *meditent* et manducent et dormiant.'

ei opus quod faciat, ut non uacet '.   Cassiodorus supposes
some monks will be incapable of becoming educated
and cultured men (*Inst.* 38) : ' Quod si alicui fratrum,
ut meminit Virgilius " Frigidus obstiterit circum prae-
cordia sanguis," ut *nec humanis nec diuinis litteris perfecte
possit erudiri,* aliqua tamen *scientiae mediocritate* suffultus, eligat
certe quod sequitur, " Rura mihi, et rigui placeant in
uallibus amnes ".   Quia *nec ipsum est a monachis alienum*
hortos colere, *agros exercere,* et pomorum fecunditate gratu-
lari ; legitur enim in psalmo centesimo uigesimo septimo :
" Labores manuum tuarum manducabis ; beatus es, et bene
tibi erit ".'   And he proceeds to recommend the best books
on gardening, on bee-keeping, pigeons and fish preserves.[1]

We are necessarily reminded of St. Benedict's words,
c. 48 : ' Si autem necessitas loci aut paupertas exegerit
ut ad fruges recolligendas PER SE occupentur, non contristentur ; quia *tunc uere monachi sunt,* si labore manuum
suarum uiuunt, sicut et patres nostri et apostoli.'

But St. Benedict never troubles to say what the ' daily
handiwork ' of the monks is likely to be.   In Egypt and
the East the ἐργόχειρα might be making baskets.   But
St. Benedict writes for many countries, and leaves the
matter open.   Cassiodorus's peculiarity is his personal
preference for copying Scripture and the Fathers.

From *Inst.* c. 32 I have already quoted reminiscences
of the rule.   I add two more :

----

[1] Cassiodorus follows this with regard to the novices: *Inst. diu. litt. prol.*
' Quocirca, si placet, hunc debemus lectionis ordinem custodire,
    ut primum, *tirones Christi,* postquam Psalmos didicerint, auctoritatem
diuinam in codicibus emendatis iugi exercitatione *meditentur,* donec illis fiat,
Domino praestante, notissima, ne uitia librariorum in impolitis mentibus
inolescant, quia difficile potest erui, quos *memoriae* sinibus radicatum constat
infigi.   Felix quidem anima, quae tanti muneris secretum *memoriae* sinibus,
Domino largiente, condiderit . . . Postquam ergo se milites Christi diuina
lectione compleuerint, et frequenti *meditatione* firmati, cognoscere coeperint
loca librorum opportune notata, . . . Mater est enim intelligentiae frequens
et intenta *meditatio*'.   In this last place ' consideration ' may be meant.
' ab studio legendi nullatenus abscedamus '.

Quapropter omnes, quos monasterii septa concludunt, tam *Patrum regulas* quam *praeceptoris proprii* iussa seruate, et *libenter* quae uobis salubriter imperantur *efficite*, quia magnae remunerationis est praemium *sine aliquo murmure* praeceptis salutaribus obedire. Vos autem, uiros sanctissimos Abbates Chalcedonium et Geruntium deprecor, ut sic *cuncta disponatis*, quatenus *gregem uobis creditum*, praestante Domino, ad beatitudinis dona perducere debeatis '.

Compare *S. Reg.* 3¹⁵: (Abbatem) *cuncta disponere;* 41¹⁰, Sic omnia temperet atque *disponat, qualiter* et animae saluentur, et quod faciunt fratres absque iusta *murmuratione* faciant; 63³: abbas non conturbet *gregem sibi commissum*, nec quasi libera utens potestate iniuste *disponat* aliquid; c. 2⁹⁴: detrimenta *gregis sibi commissi.*

A little further down :

' Et ideo futurae beatitudinis memores, *uitas Patrum,* confessiones fidelium, passiones martyrum, legite constanter,' etc.

Cassiodorus had already said of Cassian ' sedulo legite et libenter audite '. *Audite* refers to the reading of Cassian before Compline (S. Reg. 42), and *legite* to the recommendations of reading in private the Collations and Institutes, and *Vitae Patrum* in S. Reg. c. 73. Cassiodorus adds the Hieronymian Martyrology, and omits the Rule of St. Basil. But the latter was included above in the words *Patrum regulas.*

Note *quos monasterii septa concludunt ;* cp. *S. Reg.* 58 : ' ei ex illa die (*of profession*) non liceat egredi de monasterio' ; and 67, 15, ' *claustra monasterii* egredi '.

Lastly I wish to draw attention to the first words of the chapter, ' omnes . . . tam Patrum regulas quam praeceptoris proprii *iussa seruate*, et *libenter* quae uobis salubriter imperantur *efficite.*' Note the parallels with the last and the first chapter of the Rule. The last chapter says that beside *this Rule* (which is only a beginning) there are the *doctrines of the Holy Fathers* which lead men to perfection. Cassiodorus has ' tam *Patrum regulas* quam praeceptoris proprii *iussa* '. Who is this *praeceptor?* Does it mean the Abbot? And does *proprii* mean, ' your own, whether it happens to be Geruntius or Chalcedonius '? This is, in spite of the word *praeceptor*, perhaps the obvious meaning. But *proprius praeceptor* might well mean ' the author of your own Rule ', together with which you should observe the further recommendations of the Fathers. If so, the *proprius praeceptor* is none other than St. Benedict.

The reader will say this is exaggeration, and is calculated even to discredit my former conclusions. But note the parallel with the first words of St. Benedict's Rule:

Inst. 32	Prol. S. Reg.
tam Patrum regulas, quam *praeceptoris* proprii iussa seruate, et *libenter* quae uobis salubriter imperantur *efficite*.	OBSCULTA, o fili, *praecepta magistri*, et inclina aurem cordis tui, et admonitionem pii Patris *libenter* excipe et *efficaciter* comple, etc.

Praeceptor may come from *praecepta magistri*, while *iussa seruate* and *libenter efficite* might be a reminiscence of *libenter excipe* and *efficaciter comple*, slightly mixed.

However this may be, we have the strange situation, that Cassiodorus's monastery is remarkably like a Benedictine one, and that he has echoes of the Rule in his memory, *yet he never mentions St. Benedict !*

The only natural explanation is that the monks for whom he wrote took St. Benedict's rule for a matter of course. It had been read to them again and again when they were novices and frequently afterwards; they had chosen it as the Rule ' under which they desired to fight ', and they put it in practice daily.

CHAPTER VII

FERRANDUS AND FERREOLUS, TWO CRITICS

FERRANDUS seems to contrast the severe life of St. Fulgentius with the gentler norm laid down in the Holy Rule—Similarly he compares the monks of St. Fulgentius with the same norm—St. Fulgentius's ideal based on Cassian and on Egypt—Nearly half a century after the 'Vita Fulgentii', a Gallic bishop Ferreolus uses the Rule of St. Benedict in the Rule he composed for Uzès—As to stability he thinks St. Benedict too lax—The imperial laws and ecclesiastical canons had long since forbidden monks to return to the world, and had discouraged their migrating to other monasteries—Their donations to their first monastery could not be transferred to another—Examples from St. Gregory the Great.

IT will be interesting to contrast St. Benedict's modera-tion (or laxity, if you will,) with the biography of a con-temporary, St. Fulgentius, bishop of Ruspe in Africa, a great writer and theologian, and a monk from his youth up. He died in 533, and his life was written by one of his closest disciples (probably Ferrandus, the canonist and theologian) somewhat more than a year after the saint's death, and probably nearly twenty years before that of St. Benedict. The parallel is so close, that it seems almost certain that it is intentional, and that the writer was well acquainted with the Rule of St. Benedict, which he regards as a *minima inchoationis regula*, to use St. Benedict's own expression. North Africa and Sardinia (where the African bishops were long in exile) were in

close communication with Italy; Ferrandus himself was
a friend of Eugippius, the well-known Neapolitan Abbot,
while the Thaumaturgus of Montecassino dwelt on the
high road from Naples to Rome. Ferrandus could hardly
be ignorant of the famous monastery, which King Totila
himself was impelled to visit not long afterwards, and of
the more famous Rule.

Now Ferrandus tells us that St. Fulgentius, 'after
receiving the pontifical dignity, preserved the integrity
of his former profession,'—as in the great monastery he
had previously founded, and still more in the island he
fled to, in which 'ancient discipline'[1] was maintained
with great 'rigidness':

XVIII, 37: 'Nunquam denique pretiosa uestimenta quaesiuit,
aut *quotidiana ieiunia praetermisit,* aut conditos suauiter cibos
uel inter hospites manducauit, aut discumbendo saltem requiescere
et resoluere rigidum propositum uoluit; sed *una tantum uilissima
tunica, siue per aestatem siue per hiemem* patienter indutus, orario
quidem, sicut omnes episcopi, nunquam utebatur, pellico
cingulo tanquam monachus utebatur (*forte* cingebatur). Sic
studio humilitatis ambitionem uestium fugiebat, ut, nec ipsa
calceamenta suscipiens clericorum, aut *ultimis* (*scil.* uilissimis)
caligis in tempore hiemis, aut *caligulis* in tempore aestatis
uteretur. *Intra monasterium* sane interdum *soleas accipiebat,*
frequenter *nudis pedibus* ambulabat. Casulam pretiosam uel
superbi coloris nec ipse habuit, *nec monachos suos habere permisit.*
Subtus casulam nigello uel lactinio pallio circumdatus incessit.
Quando *temperies aeris* inuitabat, solo pallio intra monasterium
est coopertus. Scapulis uero nudis nunquam a nobis uisus
est, *nec deposito saltem cingulo somnum* petiuit. Suae autem con-
tinentiae, Deo teste, fidem gerens, *in qua tunica dormiebat, in
ipsa sacrificabat;* et tempore sacrificii, mutanda esse corda
potius quam uestimenta dicebat.

38. Huic beatissimo sacerdoti nullus aliquando extorsit
cuiuslibet generis carnes accipere, sed sola simplictor olera, ptisanas

---

[1] We read in XIV 29, ' in hoc monasterio rigidi propositi *disciplina antiqua*
seruatur '; it was bare rock, with no garden and scarcely any drinkable water.

et oua, quamdiu fuit iuuenis sine oleo; postquam uero senuit, superfuso oleo manducauit; ideo oleum persuasus accipere, ne caligo praeualens oculorum lectionis impediret officium. *A uino autem sanus semper abstinuit*'.

Now St. Benedict says the Abbot is always to dine with the guests : (c. 56 : ' Mensa abbatis cum hospitibus et peregrinis sit semper '). He is to break the ordinary monastic fast, for the sake of keeping them in countenance (c. 53 : ' Ieiunium a priore frangatur propter hospitem, nisi forte praecipuus sit dies ieiunii qui non possit violari '). But Fulgentius never omitted the daily monastic fast, nor ate dainties among the guests, or even reclined at table with them.

St. Benedict allows his monks two cowls, a thick one for winter, a thin one for summer, (c. 55 : ' cucullam in hieme uillosam, in aestate puram aut uetustam ',) and two tunics, one for day and one for night, and for the sake of washing (' duas tunicas et duas cucullas habere propter noctes et propter lavare ipsas res '). But St. Fulgentius wore the same cheap tunic both summer and winter, day and night ! When it was hot, he wore his cloak without a "chasuble" over it ; compare ' quando *temperies aeris* inuitabat ' with St. Benedict's ' Vestimenta . . . secundum locorum qualitatem uel *aerum temperiem* dentur '.

St. Benedict allows his monks shoes and stockings (' indumenta pedum, pedules et caligas '). St. Fulgentius wore cheap stockings (*caligae*) in winter, and socks (*caligulae*) in summer, and would not even wear those of the secular clergy. He even went further than the Cassinese monks, for within the monastery he sometimes wore sandals or went bare-foot.

St. Benedict says the monks are to sleep in their clothes, and girded (c. 22 : ' Vestiti dormiant, et cincti cingulis aut funibus '). St. Fulgentius wore the monk's girdle even at night.

St. Benedict forbids his monks, unless sick, to eat the flesh of quadrupeds. St. Fulgentius ate no meat at all, and lived on vegetables, eggs and herb broth.

St. Benedict allows a *hemina* of wine per day, and more, if necessary, ('licet legamus uinum omnino monachorum non esse', c. 40.) St. Fulgentius took a little wine in water when ill, and not otherwise.

If we suppose Ferrandus not to have St. Benedict in view, the parallel is indeed remarkable! It seems difficult to doubt that Ferrandus has in his mind the new (official or semi-official) Rule of St. Benedict, as a norm by which to judge the austerities and perfections of his hero. He goes on in the same vein to extol the bishop's government of his monks; again he seems to have the Holy Rule in view as a norm, with which he compares the monastery of his hero, in order to show how far he surpassed the *minima inchoationis Regula :*

XX 43 . . . 'illi monachi qui beatum Fulgentium seque-bantur, districtioris abstinentiae regulam custodientes, *nihil omnino proprium* possidebant, nec inter alios ciericos clericorum more uiuebant.'

XXVII 51: 'In quo (*sc.* monasterio Calaritanae ciuitatis) quadraginta et amplius fratribus congregatis, disciplinae *coenobialis* ordinem custodiuit illaesum, nemini dans licentiam professionis sanctae regulam praeterire, sed *principaliter* hoc ob-seruandum monachis tradens, ut nullus eorum quidquam *proprium* sibi uindicaret, sed essent *omnia omnibus communia.* Dicebat enim frequenter nec debere nec posse monachum iudicari, cui uoluntas habere priuatum *peculium* persuaserit . . . Dis-tribuebat sane ipse cum summa discretione seruis Dei *necessaria* uitae subsidia, singulorum uires *infirmitatesque considerans.* Verum-tamen quibuscumque *plus ceteris* consulebat, eos *humilitatem custodire* amplius admonebat, dicens eis, de substantia communi quisquis aliquid plus accipit, omnium fit debitor, quorum est illa substantia; porro debitorem sola iuuat *humilitas.* Sic efficiebat ne quis scandalum pateretur, quando uni *propter infirmitatem plus dare* uidebatur.   52.   Erat quoque ei nimia sollicitudo praeuenire cunctorum monachorum petitiones, ante tribuendo quidquid cuilibet uel necessitas uel ratio manifesta monstraret.   Si quis autem praesumpsisset priusquam acciperet petere, negabat ei continuo (!) etiamsi mereretur accipere, dicens monachos debere iis quae acceperint esse contentos.'

St. Benedict says the vice of ownership is above all (*praecipue*) to be rooted out (c. 33 : ' neque aliquid habere *proprium*, nullam omnino rem . . . sed *nihil omnino* . . . omnia uero *necessaria* a patre sperare monasterii . . . *omniaque omnibus sint communia*, ut scriptum est (Act. IV. 32)'. Ferrandus echoes the very words.   With his *peculium* also compare St. Benedict's *opus peculiare, uitium peculiare* (c. 55).

St. Benedict goes on to discuss ' si omnes aequaliter debent necessaria accipere ' (c. 34), and explains ' non dicimus ut personarum, quod absit, acceptio sit, sed *infirmitatum consideratio* . . . qui uero *plus* indiget *humilietur pro infirmitate*, non extollatur pro misericordia '.   The quotation from Acts and the sense are taken by St. Benedict from St. Augustine's ' Rule ' (Ep. CXI, 5 and 9), but Ferrandus seems to echo St. Benedict, and shows no likeness to St. Augustine.[1]

A few lines further on Ferrandus adds :

' Propterea sine suo consilio nec eum fratrem qui Praepositi gerebat officium sinebat aliquid agere.'

So St. Benedict c. 65 :   '' Qui tamen *praepositus illa agat* cum reuerentia *quae ab abbate* suo ei iniuncta fuerint, nihil contra abbatis uoluntatem aut ordinationem faciens.''

XXVII 53: ' Erat enim maxima ei et mirabilis gratia, *corripere inquietos* corde tranquillo . . . *Odiens enim uitia, diligens homines,*

---

[1] Ferrandus's ' nemini dans licentiam *professionis sanctae regulam praeterire* ', is not unlike St. Benedict's: ' In omnibus igitur omnes magistram sequantur Regulam, neque ab ea temere declinetur a quoquam ' (c. 3), and ' propter seruitium *sanctum*, quod *professi* sunt ' (c. 5).

tamdiu seuerus apparebat, quamdiu disciplinae spiritalis utilitas exigebat. Alias autem circa singulos ita mansuetus fuit, et communis et facilis, ut *neminem fratrum puro nomine clamitaret*, neque cum typho saecularis dominationis aliquibus quamuis paruulis imperaret '.

St. Benedict uses the proverb : '*Oderit uitia, diligat fratres*', and probably reminded Ferrandus of it, who has the more usual form (*homines*, for *fratres*) as St. Augustine uses it.[1] For what follows is like St. Benedict, c. 63 : 'In ipsa appellatione nominum, nulli liceat alium *puro appellare nomine*'; and the same chapter is again paralleled thus :

XIX, 39: ' Si quis autem nouos monachos uel in isto uel *in illo monasterio* Christus acquireret, *tempus inter se conuersionis ordinemque* seruarent '.

So St. Benedict, again in c. 63 : '*Ordines suos in monasterio* ita conseruent ut *conuers[at]ionis tempus*, ut uitae meritum, utque Abbas constituerit'. I note that for *conuersionis* we ought to read *conuersationis*, and doubtless in Ferrandus also. The following parallel is less striking :

XXIX 59: ' Aliquantos *inquietos* (clericos) uerbis, aliquantos uerberibus coercebat, quos culpa manifesta flagellari coegerat '.

So St. Benedict, c. 2 : 'id est, indisciplinatos et *inquietos* debet durius arguere . . . Et honestiores quidem atque intelligibiles animos prima uel secunda admonitione *uerbis* corripiat ; inprobos autem et duros ac superbos uel inoboedientes, *uerberum* uel corporis castigatio in ipso initio peccati coerceat '. But there is a further point, perhaps, in that St. Benedict insists that Priests and clerics

---

[1] I cite from Abbot Butler's edition of the Rule: Augustine, *Serm.* 49.5, ' *dilige hominem, oderis uitium* '; *De Civ. Dei.* 14, 6, ' oderit uitium, amet hominem '; Ep. 211. 11, *cum dilectione hominum et odio uitiorum ;* Caesarius, *Reg. ad uirg.* 22, *cum dilectione sororum et odio uitiorum.* To these I have added above (p. 48) from St. Leo to Rusticus of Narbonne: ' odio habeantur peccata, non homines '.

are as much subject to the Rule as are the other monks (c. 60), so that we are shown St. Fulgentius applying to the clerics the full severity of St. Benedict for monks.[1]

Lastly, Ferrandus tells us that his hero refused the use of baths, when the physicians urged this remedy on him in his last illness:

XXIX 63: ' Persuadentibus autem medicis ut *lauacris balnearibus* uteretur: Numquid balneae, inquit, facere poterunt ne homo mortalis expleto uitae suae tempore moriatur? Si uero proximam mortem nec aquarum calidarum possunt fomenta repellere, cur mihi, obsecro, persuadetis ut rigorem diu seruatae professionis in fine dissoluam? '

One feels that Ferrandus is proud to show that the Saint did not condescend to the indulgence allowed by St. Benedict: 'Balnearum usus infirmis quotiens expedit offeratur' (c. 36).[2]

The conclusion which this evidence suggests is that the author, writing fifteen or twenty years before St. Benedict's death, knew the Holy Rule very well, indeed almost by heart; he probably practised it, therefore, and certainly esteemed it; but he is glad to declare that an African bishop exceeded the norm laid down for monks by so high an authority.   In fact we have before us a concrete case of the clashing of the pre-Benedictine ideal with the discretion of the new law-giver.   For St. Fulgentius's ideal was the Egyptian monachism he had studied in the Institutes and

---

[1] We might also compare XXIX 62; ' et quamuis tota uita eius, ex quo monachorum professionem conuersus ex toto corde suscepit, paenitentiae fuerit tempus, in hac tamen insula ' he was yet more austere.   S. Reg. XLIX: licet omni tempore *uita monachi* Quadragesimae debet obseruationem habere tamen ' etc.

[2] Ferrandus wrote an *opusculum* ' de septem regulis innocentiae' (Epist. 7), an instruction on the duties of a Christian general.   The third rule is ' Non praeesse appetas, sed prodesse '.   So St. Benedict, c. 64: 'sciatque sibi oportere prodesse magis quam praeesse '.   But the expression is proverbial. In Dom Butler's edition we find references to St. Augustine, *Serm.* 340, 1 and *De Civ. Dei* XIX 19.

Collations of Cassian, and he had once started on a journey to Egypt to learn this observance but had turned back at Syracuse on hearing that that country was 'separated from the communion of St. Peter' by the Monophysite heresy (Vita, XII 23-4).   He is one of the last migratory monks who sought instruction from many masters.   He began in the monastery of a certain bishop Faustus.   When the bishop was driven away by persecution, Fulgentius joined an old friend, Abbot Felix, who resigned his office to the new comer, and eventually they were co-abbots.   The abbey was shifted to a new spot, to avoid more persecution.   Then Fulgentius started to visit Egypt; finding this impossible, he made a pilgrimage to Rome.   On his return to Africa, he founded a new abbey in Byzacene; but retired from it himself to become a simple monk once more in a large abbey on a rocky island.   Felix, however, induced Bishop Faustus to give Fulgentius an order under obedience to return to be his co-abbot, and Faustus insisted on ordaining him Priest, apparently to make sure of his obedience.   However, he was elected bishop of Ruspe, where he got the townspeople to make a monastery for him, of which he made Felix the Abbot.   He was soon exiled to Sardinia.   There he built a monastery at Calaris.   On the death of King Thrasimund in 523, the exiled bishops returned to Africa.   Fulgentius made himself the subject of Felix, though bishop of the see.   A year before his death, he quitted his episcopal work and his monastery, and lived with a few companions in a monastery which he had constructed on a rock in the island of Circe, and there he died on Jan. 1st, 533.

*   *   *   *   *

St. Ferreolus, bishop of Uzès, who died in 581, composed a Rule for the monastery which he founded, it is said, in

558. St. Benedict was perhaps then already dead. His Rule has clearly been used by Ferreolus.[1]

Cap. 2: ' Recte enim (Abbas) *timetur ut Dominus et amatur ut pater,* cui sanctae congregationis *grege commisso animarum* proprie *cura* mandatur: quem *sollicitudo commissa* quotidie per illud iter quod est ineuitabile morituris aut *trahit ad poenam* aut *perducit ad gloriam;* dicente Scriptura, " *Cui plus commendatur,* utique *plus ab eo exigitur* ".'

S. Reg. 2[67]: ' *dirum magistri, pium patris* ostendat affectum
 . . . . [86] scire quia *cui plus committitur,* plus ab eo exigitur
 . . . [94] ut non solum detrimenta *gregis sibi commissi* non patiatur . . . [97] ne dissimulans aut paruipendens salutem *animarum sibi commissarum,* plus gerat sollicitudinem de rebus transitoriis ' . . .

Prol. [19] 'ut nequissimos seruos *tradat ad poenam* qui eum sequi noluerint *ad gloriam.*'

Cap. 5: ' si quis ueniat religionem expetens monasterium intraturus, nisi elapso anni circulo . . . Post hoc monasterii Regula Abbatis ei iussione legatur ' . . . cp. *S. Reg.* 58[20], etc.

Cap 26. ' Ut usque ad horam diei tertiam in omni tempore lectioni monachus tam senior quam extremus uacare procuret '; cp. *S. Reg.* 48[23], and S. Caesarius, *Reg. ad mon.* 14.

Cap. 29. ' Ut loquendi temperantiam monachus in omni collocutione teneat: propter quod dicit *Scriptura: In multiloquio non effugies peccatum.* Et iterum in Euangelio: Noli multum loqui, sicut ethnici. Habetur enim in Psalmo: *Vir linguosus non dirigetur super terram.* Et ideo, quisquis ille frater, sint pauci sermones tui. Nec hoc tantum, sed etiam taciturnitatem tibi praesentia Abbatis uel etiam alterius senioris imponat: ita *ut nisi interrogatus* ab eo uel iussus silentium irrumpere non praesumas.' . . .

[1] Praef. . . . ' Regulam, quae ab eis pro lege seruetur, licentia a uobis (Lucretio) tam petita quam accepta, conscripsimus. *In qua* si quid seueritate durum, si quid remissione mollissimum, indicio scientiae adiudicaueritis. . . . cp. *S. Reg. Prol.* [117] ' *in qua* institutione nihil asperum, nihil graue ', etc.
Praef. ' et mansiones praeparent *dignis habitatoribus* praeparatas. Cp. *S. Reg. Prol.* [102] ' *de habitatore* tabernaculi eius '.
The Lucretius addressed might be the bishop of Die; but I suggest that *Licerio,* should be read, meaning the Vicar Apostolic and Primate of Arles (died 588). The request for ' permission ' suggests a superior. The immediate metropolitan of Uzès was Narbonne.

S. Reg. 6[12]: quia *scriptum* est, *In multiloquio non effugies peccatum.*
7[170] *taciturnitatem* habens, *usque ad interrogationem non loquatur,*
monstrante Scriptura, quia *in multiloquio non effugitur peccatum,*
et quia *uir linguosus non dirigitur super terram.*

Cap. 37. ' eritque [Abbas] in cunctis ita moribus dispensatus,
ut *blandimento uocet, terrore castiget ;* faciens se ab omnibus, *eo
quod uitia oderit, plus amari.* . . . totoque studio atque industria
prouidere, ne aliquis ex his *quos regendos propria cura suscepit,*
aduerso quolibet casu discedat ex numero. Et ideo *pluribus
medicamentis necesse est* illum Monach[or]um subuenire languori-
bus et aegritudinibus mentium remedium curae spiritalis
inferre . . . potionem . . . unguentum . . . antidotum,
. . . etc.

S. Reg. 2[66]: miscens temporibus tempora, *terroribus blandimenta,* dirum magistri, pium patris, etc. [100] sed semper cogitet
quia animas *suscepit regendas,* de quibus et rationem redditurus
est. 64[28]: *oderit uitia,* diligat fratres . . . studeat *plus amari*
quam timeri. 27[15]: ne aliquam de ouibus sibi creditis perdat.
28[9]: si exhibuit fomenta, si unguenta adhortationum, si
medicamina Scripturarum, etc. cp. 2[68-72].

Cap. 39: Illos igitur monachos, quos uel unius diei finis
discordes inuenerit, qui usque ad uesperum lites trahunt, et *ante
non excludunt odium quam Sol cognoscat occasum.*

S. Reg. 4[89]: Cum *discordante ante solis occasum* in pacem redire.

But the most interesting chapter is on the reception of
monks from other monasteries.

Cap. 6. ' Ut nullus monachus uel clericus alienus retinendus
recipiatur '. ' We will that no monk whatever or cleric of
another place or monastery shall be received for any cause
whatever, we forbid it, we prohibit it; taking thought for this
out of care for charity, lest they rise up and bring in some new
scandal. For the Scripture says: Do not to another, what thou
wouldst not should be done to thyself. For from hence usually
arise incurable quarrels not only between Abbots but even
between monasteries; since the one tries to keep him whom he
has lost. And in the end, unless he who is demanded back
be restored, and the injury repaired by this restoration, it
happens not that they overcome evil by good (as the Apostle

says) but that the evil are overcome by a common evil. But we have thought it right not to omit that if it should chance that a monk or cleric of another place (as I said above) should bring letters of his Abbot or Bishop, in which it is clearly proved that he is not to be avoided for his vices, but has been sent for the love of God, he only shall obtain to become a fellow of the community; if, however, it can be in any way believed that anyone will desire to be spoiled of his own good, and that another should be clothed by his own stripping '.

This clever piece of advice is obviously not independent of *S. Reg.* 61, 'De monachis peregrinis qualiter suscipiantur'. This is sufficiently shown by the quotation in both from the Old Latin text of Acts xv, 20 and 29, which was by no means an obvious proverb to cite: ' Quod tibi non uis fieri, alii ne feceris '.

St. Benedict had said that a foreign monk from distant provinces is to remain as long as he wishes if he is edifying ; and if he wishes to 'confirm his stability', he may even be urged to do so ; and if he deserves it, let the Abbot place him in a higher rank, and the same with priests or clerics. But from any 'known' monastery the Abbot should not receive a monk without his abbot's consent and commendatory letters. The bishop of Uzès to the first part of this says *nolumus, interdicimus, prohibemus!* It would be difficult to contradict more strongly. To the latter part he remarks that the commendatory letters would be given to a monk of whom his Abbot wanted to be rid.

It may seem strange that a bishop in Gaul should consider St. Benedict faulty in his idea of 'stability', for it has been a habit for centuries to regard stability as a special invention of St. Benedict, and the most striking characteristic of his Rule. This particular chapter has been supposed to apply to other monasteries only: St. Benedict will accept monks who have not vowed stability, but will not allow his own monks to go elsewhere. This does not seem tenable: he assumes that the *monachus peregrinus* belongs to a monastery (*de alio noto monasterio*), and that his Abbot has rights over him; for if he was a *gyrouagus* he would certainly not take him into his community. We have already seen St. Caesarius insisting that a monk is to persevere till death, though we have also seen St. Fulgentius changing from abbey to abbey for special reasons. Stability was the rule, and no one admired *gyrouagi*.

The ecclesiastical law in Dionysius's collections ordered monks to remain monks (St. Innocent, No 17; St. Leo, No. 26), and forbade their wandering about in cities (*Can. Chalced.* 4). So did the civil law (*Cod. Theodos.* Bk. XVI tit. 3, in 390), but allowed them in a town if they had to defend themselves in a law-court (392). Another law of Zeno and Anthemius (*Cod. Just.* I, 3, 29, of 471) again forbids them to circulate in Antioch or elsewhere. In 531, Justinian declares this law to be perpetual in intention, adding that no monk can leave his habit for any other profession or dignity; if he does so, he is to be made over to serve the curia ($\beta o \nu \lambda \acute{\eta}$) of his city, and to be punished both corporally and by fine, unless within a year he returns to religious life.[1]

From this legislation it was but a step to insist that a monk should persevere in his own monastery. In the 5th Novella, c. 4, of 535, Justinian declares that a monk who has once received the habit and leaves, in order to live a private life ($\beta \acute{\iota} o \varsigma$ $\acute{\iota} \delta \iota \acute{\omega} \tau \eta \varsigma$), must himself give an account to God; but everything he possessed when he entered remains the property of the monastery. If he enters any profession (c. 6), he becomes a servant of the governor of the province. If he leaves his own monastery (c. 7) and goes to another monastery, 'even thus his property is to remain and be

[1] *Codex Just.* I. 3, 52, No. 9. Any cleric or religious returning to a wordly life lost all his goods: ' iubemus omnes eorum res ad iura eius ecclesiae uel monasterii a quo recesserint pertinere ', *ib.* I 3, 54, No. 7, of 534.

adjudged to his former monastery'. And '*it is proper* (προσῆκον) *that the venerable Abbots shall not receive one who acts thus*; for such a life is unsettled (ἀλήτης), and very far removed from monastic fortitude, and is a sign not of a stable and firm mind, but of one which is carried about and desirous of change'.[1]

We may assume that this law, about ten years later than the Holy Rule, represents the general opinion in the East at this time, and probably much earlier. St. Benedict does not go so far in c. 58. It is assumed that a monk may possibly leave, though it is mocking God to break the vow; and his secular dress is preserved, so that he may put it on when he deserts the monastery or is expelled. And in c. 61 a strange monk may be even persuaded to stay on.

In 546 Justinian repeats his law in Nov. 123, 42. Again it is declared that the monastery of profession always keeps the property of the monk, whether he betakes himself to another monastery or to civil life. If he enters a profession, the bishop and the ruler of the province shall deprive him of his position, and send him to a monastery together with any property which he has obtained. If he leaves this monastery, he becomes an official servant of the governor.

By these laws it is made very difficult for a monk to transfer his 'stability' from one monastery to another. Before St Benedict's death they were enforced in Italy, like the rest of Justinian's legislation. It was not the Holy Rule, but imperial laws, which discouraged and prevented migration.

In St. Gregory's time the laws were well known, and the Pope puts them in force. In 591 he writes to the Rector of the papal patrimony in Campania that he hears

[1] M. Ch. Landry, in his study *La Mort civile des religieux*, 1900, points out (pp. 15 foll.) how different this Roman law is from the Frankish and mediaeval 'civil death', which prevented a religious from inheriting.

'certain monks of the monasteries in the diocese of Sorrento migrate from monastery to monastery at their own pleasure, and depart from the rule of their own Abbot out of desire for secular possessions (*rei saecularis*); and besides this, each desires to have a peculium (*peculiaritati studere*), which is known to be unlawful. Wherefore we order your Experience by this present mandate, that you are henceforth to permit no monk to migrate from monastery to monastery, nor to possess anything of his own (*peculiare quidquam habere*). But if any shall presume this, he shall be restored with the necessary coercion to the monastery where he first lived as a monk, and under the rule of the Abbot from whom he fled, lest, if we leave *such iniquity* to continue uncorrected, the souls that perish thereby should be required from their Superiors '.[1]

In the same connexion it may be worth noting that Justinian disapproves of transference to another monastery: Nov. V, c. 7 : ' Si uero reliquens monasterium, in quo con-uersationem habuit, ad aliud transeat monasterium, etiam sic quidem eius substantia maneat et uindicetur a priori mon-asterio, ubi abrenuntians hanc reliquit . . . *Erronea namque talis est uita* monachica[e] nullatenus tolerantiae proxima, neque constantis et persistentis animae sed indicium habens circumlatae (περιφερομένης) et aliunde alia requirentis'.

Erronea represents ἀλήτης, and suggests *gyrouaga* or *uaga*, as in S. Reg. c. 1 : 'genus . . . gyrouagum . . . semper uagi et numquam stabiles, et propriis uolun-tatibus et gulae illecebris seruientes'. The same law is repeated in other words in 546, Nov. 123, c. 42.

We gather from the criticisms of St. Ferreolus and from all these laws that 'stability' cannot well be regarded as the characteristic innovation of St. Benedict's legislation.

---

[1] Ep. I 40, vol. I, p. 55. From a monastery in Sicily two monks had fled; one was living with a wife, another as a secular; they are to be at once sent back to their monastery (Ep. II, 29, vol. I, p. 125.) In 597 the Pope writes very strong reprimands to a bishop and a defensor, who have allowed a nun to leave her monastery, (Ep. VIII, 8 and 9, II, pp. 10-11); she is to be instantly sent back. A similar letter is written in 599 (Ep. X, 3, II, p. 238).

CHAPTER VIII

THE DATE OF ST. BENEDICT

TRADITIONAL dates for St. Benedict based on forgeries—1. Death of St. Germanus of Capua—2. The visit of Totila—3. The visit of Sabinus in March 547—4. The episcopate of Constantine of Aquinum—5. The destruction of Montecassino by the Lombards, c. 481—The refugees did not found the monastery at the Lateran, which existed earlier—6. The first abbots of Cassinum—7. Valentinian of the Lateran—8. Honoratus of Sublacum—9. Seruandus of Alatri—10. The illustrious Aptonius. —11. The wicked priest Florentius and his grandson—12. Exhilaratus, a slave, afterwards 'secundicerius notariorum', goes to Jerusalem, and possibly becomes a bishop of undue severity—13. The rich and noble brothers, Speciosus and Gregory—14. Martin the hermit—15. The famine—List of possible dates.

IT is commonly said that St. Benedict was born about 480 and died in 542 or 543. It is often repeated that 'tradition' places his migration from Subiaco to Montecassino in 529, and the writing of the Rule in 530. There is nothing historical about these dates. They are partly conjectural, partly dependent on forgeries, such as the lives of St. Maurus and St. Placid, the donation of Tertullus and the Chronicle of Subiaco. We have to find what we can in the data provided by St. Gregory's Dialogues, forgetting Peter the deacon and Leo Marsicanus.

1. One date is certain. St. Germanus, bishop of Capua, who had been the legate of Pope Hormisdas for

the reunion of the East with the West in 519, was succeeded on February 24th 541 by Victor, the famous compiler, owner and corrector of the Codex Fuldensis, which he signed in 546 and 547. The day of his accession is known from his extant epitaph.[1] It follows that it was on February 24th, or a week or two earlier, that St. Germanus died. At that moment, we are told by St. Gregory (*Dial.* II. 35 and IV, 8), St. Benedict saw the famous bishop's soul carried up to heaven in a sphere of fire.[2] Servandus, the Abbot of the monastery founded by the patricius Liberius in Campania (probably at Alatri) was present,

---

[1] The epitaph is given by Ughelli, *Italia Sacra* (1720, 2nd ed.), vol. VI p. 306, and reproduced in Migne P. L. : ' Victor Episc. sedit ann. XIII. dies xxxviii Depositus sub die iii. Non. April. Ann. XIII. P. C. Basilii V. C. Indictione secunda.' Hence Victor died April 3rd (for *depositio episcoporum* seems to be the day of death, not of burial), 554. He became bishop, therefore, on Feb. 24th This may have been the day of his consecration; but possibly the time is calculated from the death of St. Germanus, which was therefore either Feb. 24th 541 or two or three weeks earlier. Ughelli, however, thinks that St. Germanus died on Oct. 30th, the day of his feast; this would mean 540. But more probably Oct. 30th was the day of his translation to New Capua, or even of the translation of notable relics to San Germano (unfortunately of recent years called Cassino), the principal place of his cultus. The Bollandists (Oct. 30) and Thiel with others, refused to identify this Bishop of Capua with the legate Germanus of Pope Hormisdas to Justin in 519, whose see is never mentioned in the voluminous correspondence of the Pope. In fact a misprint of *Sabinus Capuanus* as attending Pope John to Constantinople in 524 in Muratori's *Annali d'Italia* III p. 340, seemed to make it certain that Germanus became bishop later than 524. But the contemporary account by Maximian of Ravenna has *Sabinus Campanus*, and so has the *Historia Caesarea*. The editions of the *Liber Pontificalis* by Duchesne and by Mommsen have made it clear that the notice of Hormisdas was written but a few years later, and during the lifetime of St. Germanus of Capua; it identifies the latter with the legate of Hormisdas, whose interesting reports have come down to us. Paul Warnefrid (*Hist. Rom.* XVI 6) and Hincmar make the same statement, but are derived from the ' second edition ' of the Liber Pontificalis. It follows that St. Germanus was bishop before 519, so his episcopate lasted more than 22 years. His life, printed by the Bollandists from an eleventh century MS. of Montecassino, is also dependent on the Lib. Pont. and St. Gregory's Dialogues. It refuses to relate any miracles, with praiseworthy restraint, as the author says he knew of none.

[2] Such appearances at the moment of death are common enough; but the form of this particular apparition reminds one of St. Vincent de Paul's vision of the souls of St. Francis de Sales and St. J. F. de Chantal at the moment of the latter's death. He describes it very carefully in his most matter-of-fact manner in one of his letters. But it was not accompanied by a mystical vision as in St. Benedict's case, for Vincent was not by nature a mystic.

and was sent that night to Capua (about 50 miles) to inquire about Germanus.

2. One other date may be determined within a year. The visit of Totila is related by St. Gregory with some detail. He gives the names of his attendants, Riggo the spatharius, Wulteric, Ruderic and Blindinus. The visit was well attested by witnesses. Its date is placed by St. Gregory before the taking of Rome by Totila and before his expedition to Sicily. It is agreed by most writers that the visit to St. Benedict was about the time of the siege of Naples, either at the end of 542, when Totila was marching thither, or in 543 after the reduction of the city.

When St. Benedict's death is placed in 542–3 (or even 541) it is always assumed that the visit of Totila was the last event of importance in the saint's life. This may have been the case, but it was certainly not St. Gregory's idea at all. The story is related in *Dial.* II, 14, 15. Now the whole history of St. Benedict takes thirty-eight chapters, his death being described in c. 37. The visit of Totila is therefore mentioned less than half-way through the biography. It is true that St. Gregory does not preserve any strict chronological order: the visit of Totila is of 541–2, in cc. 14–15; and the death of St. Germanus, 541 also, is in c. 35. But St. Gregory is not likely to have known the exact date of St. Germanus's death; whereas the campaign of Totila in Campania was a notable event, and apparently St. Gregory does not regard it as having occurred just before the end of St Benedict's life. Nor does the prophecy related even suggest that St. Benedict died before Totila, who was to perish in the tenth year of his reign.

3. A still more important date is given by a conversation of St. Benedict with St. Sabinus, bishop of Canusium.

We are told that he was in the habit of visiting St. Benedict who loved him greatly. He was a papal envoy to Constantinople in 535, and remained there until the arrival and death of Pope Agapitus, and for the subsequent council held by the patriarch Menas, all in 536. He had been accused of magic in 528, and is said to have died in 566. Totila visited him, doubtless in 542; he was then blind (*Dial.* III. 5). St Gregory relates that when Benedict and Sabinus were conversing ' about the entrance of Totila and the destruction of the Roman city ', *de ingressu regis Totilae et Romanae urbis perditione*, the latter said : ' By this king that city will be destroyed, so that it shall not be inhabited any more '. But the man of God replied : ' Rome will not be depopulated by the nations, but by tempests, lightnings and storms and earthquake will be worn out, and decay of herself' (*Dial.* II. 15).

Obviously Bollandus was right (Acta SS. Feb. vol. II. 317, cited by Moricca) in referring this conversation to the time of the siege itself, that is to say, to the end of 545 or the beginning of 546. The city fell in December, 546, and after Totila's departure was without an inhabitant for 40 days. This was about March–April, 547. The words *de ingressu* imply that the two saints had heard that Totila was about to enter or had actually entered the city. The words of Sabinus, ' Per hunc regem ciuitas ista destruetur ut non amplius habitetur ', seem to mean that they had also heard that the inhabitants had fled. The Italians, were in terror of the new Gothic leader, and Sabinus fears the worst; the city is deserted, and Totila will destroy the buildings so that they will never return. Hence I am inclined to place the conversation in March 547, rather than in November 546.

If St. Benedict died on the 21st of March, it will hardly

be in that same year 547; so it would seem that 548 is the earliest probable year for his death.[1]

4. Another friend of the Patriarch, and a close neighbour, was Constantius, bishop of Aquinum, who sent one of his clerics to be cured by St. Benedict (*Dial.* II 16).[2]

St. Gregory, speaking of his spirit of prophecy, says ' qui *nuper* prodecessoris mei tempore beatae memoriae Johannis papae defunctus est '. John III was pope 561–573, hence *nuper* means 20 years or even 33, as St. Gregory is writing between July 593 and Oct. 594. According to Constantius's prophecy, he was succeeded by an ostler and then by a fuller; after the latter no bishop could be appointed on account of the Lombards. It seems likely that *nuper* means not more than ' 25 years ago ', so Constantius probably died about 570. If he was a bishop some time before St. Benedict's death in 541–3, he will have been over 30 years bishop. This is possible; Germanus and Sabinus had long episcopates; but we do not want to assume this of all St. Benedict's friends. Consequently it would be easier to reconcile the dates if St. Benedict died in 548, or a good deal later,—548–558.

[1] Since writing the above argument, I have received from Dr. Luigi Salvatorelli of Turin (former professor in the University of Naples) an interesting study on the date of St. Benedict, in which he argues in the same way that the visit of Bishop Sabinus to St. Benedict took place during the siege of Rome. He concludes that it was at least some days later than Dec. 17th, 546, so that the earliest date for St. Benedict's death will be 21st March, 547. Prof. Salvatorelli also points out that the episode of the Goth Galla (*Dial.* II, 31) assumes that the terrorism of Galla under Totila had lasted some time, so that it would naturally be later than 542-3. He also notes that the received date, 543, for St. Benedict's death was motived by the date of the visit of Totila: this could hardly have happened before March 21st, 542, which is the only ' traditional ' date, since it is that given by Leo of Ostia and the Acts of St. Placid. But this ' traditional ' date of 542 is impossible.

[2] According to Moricca (l. c. p. 151) the following ridiculous dates have been given for the episcopate of Constantius: Gams. 525-48; Ughelli, *floruit* c. 566; Cappelletti, c. 525. Baronius reasonably proposed 572. In discussing his date twenty years ago, I carelessly assumed that St. Benedict died in 543 (*Early Hist. of Vulg. Gospels*, 1908, p. 156). Constantine's feast was apparently celebrated at Cassinum, Aquinum having been destroyed,—so the Echternach Martyrology (*ibid.* pp. 150, 156).

5. If the destruction of Montecassino by the Lombards can be dated, it will bear upon the date of St. Benedict. St. Gregory tells us (*Dial.* II, 17) that the man of God prophesied this expulsion of the monks : ' nos autem cernimus, qui destructum *modo* a Longobardorum gente eius monasterium cernimus. Nocturno enim tempore et quiescentibus fratribus, NUPER illic Longobardi ingressi sunt ', etc. We have just seen that *nuper* was used by St. Gregory for something over 20 years. The usual date given is 589, four years before the Dialogues. Mabillon suggested 580. Lombard incursions were frequent. Paul Warnefrid gives no date, and the order of his chapters is not chronological.

St. Gregory tells us that one of his informants about the life of St. Benedict was his disciple Valentinian, ' qui multis annis Lateranensi monasterio praefuit '. This was the refuge granted by Pelagius II to the monks who fled from Montecassino, if we are to believe Leo Marsicanus. But are we to believe him? He is anxious to prove the continuity of Montecassino with St. Benedict, and he has therefore to bridge the gap between the destruction by the Lombards and the restoration under Petronax. He makes the Lateran monastery act as the bridge, by saying it was constructed by the monks who fled from Monte-cassino, and that more than a century later (his chronology is faulty) some monks from the Lateran were sent by the Pope to join Petronax, thus establishing the necessary continuity.

In 1904 I pointed out that this history is impossible.[1] Petronax went to Montecassino to be a solitary, and he

[1] *Revue Bénédictine*, 1904, vol. 21, pp. 74-80: ' *La restauration du Mont-Cassin par l'abbé Pétronax.* I followed in this article the opinion of Traube that Paul Warnefrid in *Hist. Lomb.* VI, 40, used two different sources. I remember that Dom G. Morin told me at the time that this was not in the least proved; and on looking back 24 years, I agree with him. It makes no difference to the argument of the article.

found a few solitaries there already. After a time they began to live in community; but when St. Willibald arrived there in 729, they were 'only a few monks and an abbot named Petronax'.[1] The young Anglo-Saxon drilled them in Benedictine ways, by love or fear, by word and example, so says his biographer. Clearly there had been no Benedictine tradition, nor had *aliquanti monachi* come from a flourishing monastery at the Lateran.

But it is not even proved that the Lateran monastery was the refuge of the monks of Montecassino, or was founded by them. This seems again merely an invention of Leo Marsicanus, or of previous Montecassino legend, founded upon the fact that a disciple of St. Benedict, Valentinianus, who had been a monk of Montecassino was abbot of the Lateran 'for many years', according to St. Gregory.

If we suppose that the monks who fled to Rome were settled by Pelagius II at the Lateran, when Bonitus was Abbot, we must suppose that Bonitus was succeeded by Valentinian. But the latter was dead when Gregory wrote in 593. Pelagius II was Pope from 579 to 590. Hence Mabillon dates the construction of the Lateran 580, so that Valentinian might well be Abbot from about 581 to 591–2. The year 580 goes quite well with St. Gregory's *nuper*; but ten years are not quite adequate to *multis annis*.

On the other hand, St. Gregory does not suggest that the Lateran community was identical with that of Montecassino. It is never mentioned in his letters, and when he tells us that Valentinian was for many years Abbot of it, this is the only reference to it in ancient times. We should naturally have understood, had Leo Marsicanus

---

[1] *Vita S. Willibaldi*, by a nun, his cousin, in Acta SS. 7th July, vol. 29, pp. 509-10.
' Non reperiebant ibi nisi paucos monachos et abbatem nomine Petronacem '.

never written, that Valentinus had been dead some years after being at least twenty years at the head of the Abbey. We know from *Dial.* II 13 that he had formerly been a monk under St. Benedict at Montecassino. He may have been elected Abbot by an entirely distinct community, as often happened; or perhaps he was appointed by a Pope.

If we turn to Paul Warnefrid, we find that in *Hist. Lomb.* IV 18 he simply tells us: ' Fugientes quoque ex eodem loco monachi Romam petierunt ', but he does not say that they founded a monastery there, or what happened to them; ' secum codicem sanctae Regulae quam praefatus Pater composuerat et quaedam alia scripta, necnon pondus panis et mensuram uini, et quic⁻quid ex supellectili subripere poterant, deferentes '. Evidently Paul does not know of the Lateran monastery, nor where the ' supellex ' was put. ' Ceterum post beatum Benedictum Constantinus, post hunc Simplicius, post quem Vitalis, ad extremum Bonitus congregationem ipsam rexit, sub quo haec destructio facta est '.

' Last of all Bonitus ruled the community '. This suggests that the community came to an end, and that Bonitus was its last abbot. Above, *fugientes monachi* may be rendered ' monks who fled ', so it is not clear that the community as a whole came to Rome, for some may have fled to neighbouring monasteries or stopped at monasteries on the road. Even if all came to Rome (and they were doubtless very numerous), they may have been absorbed in other monasteries. At least, Paul does not know that they continued as a community, and he distinctly suggests that they did not.

If St. Benedict's large community had been settled at the Lateran by Pelagius II, would they not have been a famous abbey? Yet we hear not a word about them.

When Petronax introduces the Benedictine ways at Monte-cassino in the first quarter of the eighth century, Pope Zacharias, who himself translated the life of St. Benedict into Greek, takes a great interest in this restoration of the abbey founded by the legislator of monks (*Hist. Longob.* VI 40), and amongst other gifts, he presents Petronax with the copy of the Holy Rule which Benedict wrote with his own hand. This autograph was at Montecassino in Paul's time, and, as is well known, he sent a very exact copy of it to Charlemagne. But if the Lateran monastery existed at that time as the legitimate continuation of St. Benedict's own community (which had carefully preserved this precious autograph, and had brought it to Rome) they would have hardly let the Greek Pope take it from them and give it to the few hermits of Montecassino.

It seems that the autograph was preserved as a relic, and belonged to the Papal treasury. Paul says ' paterna pietate concessit ', which suggests that Petronax had asked for it. Again, therefore, in *Hist. Longob.* VI 40 as in IV 18 we get the impression that the community of St. Benedict no longer existed, and had left no succession, since their prized relic belonged to the Pope.

It would seem that Leo Marsicanus and Peter of Ostia perceived that St. Gregory makes Valentinian both a monk of Montecassino (*Dial.* II 13) and Abbot of the Lateran (*ibid.* II *praef.*) ; and in order to establish the continuity they desired, they jumped at the conjecture that the refugees from Montecassino had settled at the Lateran, and that Pelagius II had given them leave to build a monastery there.[1] As Valentinian was abbot many years, Leo dated the migration in 568, although Pelagius II was not Pope until 579, and in spite of St.

---

[1] They had some justification from the life of St. Maurus, and from other forgeries, perhaps.

Gregory's *nuper*. They added the impossible, but necessary, conjecture that Pope Gregory (the second or the third ?) desired to restore the monastery, and sent Petronax with *aliquantos monachos* from the Lateran, as a return of the same community to their original seat.

If I am right in throwing overboard the whole of this characteristic invention of the two Cardinals of the eleventh century, it follows that we have no means of preferring Mabillon's date 580 for the incursion of the Lombards to the more popular one of 589. We need not suppose it to have taken place under Pelagius II. Possibly Traube's date, 581, is right. I think 589 is too near the time of St. Gregory's *Dialogues*.[1]

6. St. Gregory had known Constantine, the immediate successor of St. Benedict; a disciple of St. Benedict was still Abbot at Subiaco in 593. These two points are established by *Dial.* II *praef.* 'Huius ego omnia gesta non didici; sed pauca quae narro quattuor discipulis referentibus agnoui: *Constantino*, scilicet, reuerentissimo uiro, *qui ei in monasterii regimine successit; Valentiniano quoque*, qui multis annis Lateranensi monasterio præfuit; *Simplicio*, qui congregationem post eum tertius rexit; *Honorato* etiam, *qui nunc adhuc cellae eius*, in qua prius conuersatus erat, praeest'. We ought not to take *post eum tertius* together; Simplicius was after St. Benedict, and was the third Abbot.

---

[1] In Bethmann's posthumous *Lombardische Regesten* (*Neues. Archiv.* III, vii) he gives the date of Zotto, who was for twenty years first duke of Beneventum, as about 571 (p. 229), from Paul Warnefrid, *Hist. Long.* III, 32, no doubt because his successor, Aroges, was duke in 592 (Greg. Ep. II, 45, p. 145). Zotto may have raided Montecassino at any subsequent date. But Traube (*Textgesch. Reg. S. Bened.* 2 ed. 1910, p. 94) declares that ' the plundering of Montecassino took place unquestionably as a sequel to the siege of Naples ', and this is known to have taken place in 581 from the subscription to the St. Germain MS. 264 (239) published by Mabillon (now Paris, B.N. 11642; correct text in Knöll's *Eugippius*, CSEL ix, p. XXV). I do not see why there must be a necessary connexion between the siege of Naples and the destruction of Montecassino; anyhow the latter would be likely to precede the former. But I have no objection to 581.

Paul Warnefrid (*Hist. Langob.* IV 16) tells us that the fourth was Vitalis (of whom nothing is known) and the fifth Bonitus, under whose rule the monastery was destroyed by the Lombards. This was, we will assume, about 581.

Now St. Gregory was born not later than c. 540. He became Prefect of Rome not later than 572. He became a monk 575.[1] He was at Constantinople as Apocrisiarius of Pelagius II c. 579–586.

His informants are four abbots; he has heard nothing from any monk. But then monks were not allowed to converse with guests, even when the guest addressed them first (*S. Reg.* c. 53); whereas the abbot always dined with the guests, though he might appoint a substitute (*'cui iusserit ipse'*). There was besides the God-fearing brother who looked after their comfort.

Constantine and Simplicius both died before the expulsion, so that St. Gregory must have known them before he became a monk. For this explains why he had no information from Vitalis and Bonitus: they were abbots while Gregory was enclosed in St. Andrew's on the Caelian 574–9, or at Constantinople. It is possible, of course, that Constantine or Simplicius may have visited Rome on business, and have thus met St. Gregory. But it is inconceivable that St. Gregory should not have visited the foundation of the great wonder-worker, only 138 kilometres (86 miles) off on the Via Latina. If his father took him to visit his estates in Sicily, they would pass Cassinum, and would stay at the abbey on the mountain above as guests *qui nunquam desunt in monasterio*, even up that steep road. We gather that he stayed there under Constantine and again under Simplicius, and this not long before his

---

[1] Batiffol, S. Grégoire (1928), p. 31, points out that he was probably still prefect in 574.

own 'conversion'. Was it not because he had this vocation already in his heart, perhaps unrealised, that the young noble paid a visit and collected anecdotes of the venerable founder, and again, perhaps when Praetor, returned to examine and learn the ways which were to be introduced on the Caelian and the six Sicilian abbeys which he founded with his vast patrimony? He describes the mount as one who knows it, and the tower and the space before the door. Subiaco, with its ' cold and transparent waters ', he also knew; he may have visited it either before or after his embassy at Constantinople, more probably after; for Honoratus was still alive when he wrote, and may not have been yet abbot in 579. There is plenty of time for the visit (or for more than one visit) between 579 and 590, to a place so near.

Thus we get the dates :

> Constantine, died before 574, say 565.
> Simplicius, died after 574, say 575.
> Vitalis, (Greg. at Constantinople, 579–85), died c. 576–9.
> Bonitus, succeeded until the expulsion, c. 581 (or 589).

As Gregory seems not to have known Bonitus, the latter either died before 585 (if the expulsion was in 581), or else did not settle down in Rome. It seems that St. Gregory's visits to Montecassino were all before 574, and his notes (*see* above p. 3) of the tales told by Constantine and Simplicius were made before that date.

7. Valentinianus was a monk of Montecassino for a good many years before the death of St. Benedict. For in *Dial.* II 13 we are told that he was visited there by his brother, year by year, who arrived fasting at the abbey.

If we accepted the view that Bonitus founded the Lateran monastery, and that Valentinian succeeded him before

St. Gregory returned from Constantinople in 586, we might conjecture (as above) that Bonitus died very soon, and that Valentinian was abbot 'for many years' from 582 to 592. In this case I should argue that Valentinian must have been at least 30 when St. Benedict died, so that if this event was in the 'traditional year' 543, Valentinian was nearly 80 in 592. Hence 553 would be an easier date.

But I renounce this argument, according to which St. Gregory's acquaintance with Valentinian was only from 586 to 592. I think the foundation of the Lateran monastery by Bonitus very improbable, and I suppose that Valentinian was abbot of the Lateran before (and probably after) St. Gregory's stay at Constantinople. He was presumably Abbot at least twenty years, perhaps thirty, and we get no help from him for our chronology.

8. Honoratus, St. Gregory tells us, was still abbot of Subiaco in 593. It is not said that he was decrepit. The twelfth-century chronicle of Subiaco makes him St. Benedict's successor there. Supposing the Saint left Subiaco in 529, even so Honoratus would probably be over ninety. But I am inclined to think the date was nearer 520, and Honoratus might well be a hundred in that case. It is far more likely that he was a monk of Montecassino, sent perhaps by St. Benedict himself to govern his former monastery, or elected after St. Benedict's death. He is presumably the authority for St. Benedict's life at Subiaco. He may have been always a monk there, and have known St. Benedict by visiting Montecassino, and by seeing the founder whenever he re-visited Subiaco. All this is mere speculation. But anyhow it is easier for a disciple of St. Benedict to be alive in 593-4, if St. Benedict died in 553 and not in 543. If Honoratus was 80 in 593, he was 40 in 553,

but only 30 in 543. And we do not know that he was as much as 80.

The only point we know is that it was Honoratus who told St. Gregory about St. Benedict's prediction to St. Sabinus of Canusium that Montecassino would be destroyed, 'quamquam . . . nequaquam ex ore illius audisse se perhibebat, sed quia hoc dixerit, dictum sibi a fratribus fuisse testatur'. This is an admirable instance of St. Gregory's conscientious candour (*Dial.* II 15). I have said above that I date this event in March 547. We may assume that Honoratus was not at Montecassino at that date. But it seems to be implied that Honoratus was a Cassinese and might have been present, rather than that being a monk of Subiaco he could only know the facts from the Cassinese. Perhaps he was away for a time, or merely not present at the interview; yet possibly he was already abbot of Subiaco.

9. Servandus diaconus does not help us. He was ' Abbot of the monastery founded in Campania by the late Patricius Liberius' (*Dial.* II 35). This monastery was probably at Alatri, and is mentioned by St. Gregory again in 599 (Ep. IX 162). Its abbot was then Theodosius, whom Hartmann wrongly identified with another Theodosius, abbot of St. Martin's at Naples. Servandus had the habit (*ex more*) of visiting St. Benedict. He was present on the day in 541 when St. Germanus died.

A complete skeleton of the career of Liberius is given by Mommsen in his index to Cassiodorus's *Variae*.[1] He was still prefect of Gaul in 533 (*Variae*, XI. 1. 16), but in 534 was ambassador to Justinian from Theodahad. He was prefect of Egypt 538-541. He proved a poor general against Totila, 449-50; but he was then an ἐσχατογέρων μάλιστα, says Procopius; and his epitaph makes him nearly

[1] M. G., *Auct. Antiquiss.* XII, pp. 495-6.

ninety when he died.[1] As Servandus was abbot in 541, the abbey was probably founded while Liberius was Prefect of Italy for many years, before he went to Gaul,—say about 520.

10. We do not get much more from the case of Aptonius, whose father sent his leprous page to be cured by St. Benedict (*Dial.* II 26) : ' quod illustri uiro Aptonio narrante cognoui, qui aiebat patris sui puerum ' . . . and ' qui ad uirum Dei ab eodem patre eius missus est '. In those days (*see* pp. 164-6) *puer* meant an ' attendant ', or upper servant.

Now this distinguished personage, Aptonius, was lately dead in April, 593. For his son ' Armenius magnificus, filius quondam Aptonii illustrissimi uiri ', was reduced to extreme poverty, in spite of his high rank, and St. Gregory requested George, the Praefectus Praetorio of Italy, to grant him protection and a pension (continentiam). He had lost both parents. A man is not pitied for being an orphan (except in " H.M.S. Pinafore ") unless he is young, say, not more than 25. Evidently his father had recently died, leaving no property. If Armenius was about 22, his

---

[1] Liberius built a church at Orange, consecrated in 529. St. Caesarius of course knew him, and he was a correspondent of St. Ennodius and of St. Avitus. Cassiodorus and Liberius were among the most eminent of the aristocratic Romans who governed under the Gothic rule; and they were among the most fervent in piety. Cassiodorus will certainly have known the abbey founded by his colleague in Campania, which at that time stretched from Rome to Naples. Alatri is at an equal distance from Ferentino and Frosinone, 9 miles; both these picturesque towns are on the Latin Way, between Rome and Cassinum. Alatri stands aside, and is famous for its beautiful women. The well-known signature in the codex Amiatinus (copied from the archetype) at the end of Exodus has frequently been attributed to this abbot: ο κυρι[ο]ς Σερουανδος αιποιησε.

A letter of Cassiodorus (*Variae* VIII 6, in the name of King Athalaric) is addressed to Liberius at the end of 526, and he is mentioned in XI 1 (Cassiodorus to the senate, in 533) as prefect of Gaul, with great praise. In an earlier letter (II 16, in 507-11) his praise is in the mouth of Theoderic. He is also mentioned in III 35.

father Aptonius was born about 44 years before 593, or earlier, that is about 549. But Aptonius's father might have sent a servant to St. Benedict many years before the birth of Aptonius, who may have been born earlier, and have remembered the cure. Anyhow he may have known the servant. Thus the dates are perfectly harmonious, but tell us nothing further.

11. The Priest Florentius (*Dial.* II 8) who drove St. Benedict from Subiaco, and thus caused the foundation of Montecassino, was the grandfather of St. Gregory's subdeacon Florentius, 'huius nostri subdiaconi Florentii auus'. The subdeacon distressed the Pope by refusing to become bishop of Naples in 592, hiding himself to escape consecration (Ep. III 15). Though the priest Florentius was no lover of chastity, we need not suppose the subdeacon's father was illegitimate, so he will have been born before Florentius was in major orders, and therefore several years before the foundation of Montecassino. If Florentius the younger was 52 in 592, he was born in 540. His father may have been born, therefore, in 520 or earlier, even before 500 perhaps. Hence the foundation might be in 530, the traditional date, or much earlier. It is easy to place it about 520 :

Son of Florentius born	505
Florentius ordained Priest	510
Florentius jealous of St. Benedict	515–20
St. Benedict goes to Montecassino	520
Florentius the grandson born	540

But I am not arguing from this. I am only showing that the two Florentii cause no difficulty with regard to a date much earlier than 530 for the foundation of Montecassino.

12. Exhilaratus is a more promising subject. He must have been young when he was sent by his master to carry

two wooden barrels of wine to St. Benedict (*Dial.* II 18) : 'Quodam quoque tempore Exhilaratus noster,[1] quem ipse conuersum nosti, transmissus a domino suo fuerat . . . praedictus Exhilaratus *puer*'. Doubtless the wine was carried on a mule. *Puer*, as we shall see, means an upper servant of any age, let us say of 17, at youngest.[2] But *quodam tempore* shows that St. Gregory did not calculate from the age of Exhilaratus that his dishonesty and its discovery took place at the very end of St. Benedict's life. Let us suppose that Exhilaratus was only 20 when the saint died, though St. Gregory may have thought he was more ; for we need not press *quodam tempore*, nor imagine that St. Gregory knew exactly the date of Exhilaratus's birth. But he knew him to be still in 593 a vigorous man.

He says to Peter : ' you knew him when he was a monk '. Peter had been a monk of St. Andrew's on the Caelian. But Exhilaratus would have been middle-aged when that Abbey was founded in 573-4. Probably he became a monk at Rome after the miraculous discovery of his greediness, and Peter would have known him then. But Exhilaratus was no longer a monk : *conuersum nosti.* Was he dead? No. Like Gregory and Peter, he had become an important Papal official, after years in the cloister. That is why he is *Exhilaratus noster.*

---

[1] The word *noster* is often used by St. Gregory to mean simply a friend, e.g. ' ut uestros nos credamus reputare qui nostri sunt ', and ' quia noster est ' (Ep. IX 92, vol. II p. 104), cp. VI 14, I p. 394, etc. But there is also a special sense in which *noster* means one of St. Gregory's officials at Rome, who lived with him. We have already seen ' Florentius, huius *nostri* subdiaconi auus ' (*Dial* II 8), and we find that Exhilaratus is called *noster* here and in Ep. V 6 because he was *secundicerius notariorum* (Ep. VII 29). Similarly Vitus is made a member of the *schola* of defensors in Jan. 599 (Ep. IX 97), and later carries a letter to the defensor Romanus (Ep. IX 118): ' experientia tua *olim nostrum fuisse* cognoscat '. Similarly in a letter to John, bishop of Syracuse (Ep. VII 36) we hear of ' Caesarius, uenerabilis abbas, *qui olim noster fuit* . . . in saecularibus causis omnino inexpertus est '.

[2] Exhilaratus would probably be manumitted on his entrance into monastic life. But a slave who entered the monastery with permission only, was obliged to go back to his master, by the laws of Justinian, if he left the monastery.

A year after the Dialogues were concluded, St. Gregory wrote to Sabinianus, his *apocrisiarius* at the Byzantine Court, about an important piece of business (Sept. or Oct. 594) : *Exhilaratum* autem *nostrum* pro ea re dirigere uolui ', ' I had intended to send our Exhilaratus to the Emperor on this question '. Nearly three years later, St. Gregory writes to Jerusalem to a certain Abbot Anastasius (June 597), and thanks him for relics sent from Jerusalem to Rome by the hands of Exhilaratus and afterwards of Sabinianus : ' Benedictionem uero, quam et prius per *Exhilaratum secundicerium* et postmodum per Sabinianum diaconum transmisistis '. So that Exhilaratus has been to Jerusalem, and returned before June 597. In January 599 the *secundicerius* is St. Paterius, whose extracts from St. Gregory's works are found in Migne P.L. 79. Consequently Exhilaratus either died in 598, or was promoted to be *primicerius.*[1]

---

[1] The *primicerius notariorum* in July 593 was Gaudiosus (St. Greg. Ep. III. 54, p. 213). The will of a certain ' Gaudiosus presbyter ' is mentioned in Sept. 595 (Ep. VI. 12, p. 341), but he is not called *primicerius.* Did Gaudiosus become a bishop? Gregory writes to Gaudiosus, bp. of Nola, in 595, and to Gaudiosus, bp of Eugubium in 599.

As for Paterius, he was merely a notary in Feb. 595 (Ep. V. 26, p. 307) and Sept. 595 (Ep. VI. 12), but he has become *secundicerius* in Jan. 599 (Ep. IX. 97) and is again mentioned with this title on Oct. 5th, 600 (Ep. XI. 15.) Johannes diaconus says of him two hundred years later: ' Paterium, aeque notarium, qui ab eo secundicerius factus, ex libris ipsius aliqua utillima deflorauit ' (*Vita S. Greg.* II. 11). It is possible that Gaudiosus became bishop of Gubbio in 598, and was succeeded as primicerius by Exhilaratus, the latter being succeeded as secundicerius by Paterius. But Exhilaratus may have died in that year.

It seems to me more probable, however, that he neither died nor became primicerius, but was promoted by St. Gregory to a bishopric, as one of his most trusted intimates. For in Sept. 603 we find an Exhilaratus, bishop of an unknown see in Sicily, of whom St. Gregory says (Ep. XIV. 4) that he ought to have been severely punished; but as his case had been tried by Leo, bishop of Catania (a frequent correspondent of St. Gregory) and he had been let off lightly, he is to be restored to his see. He had been kept for some time at Rome by St. Gregory and had done penance there, and this must suffice: 'iudicantes sufficere illi hoc quod eum diutius hic retinentes affliximus '. The papal defensor at Palermo is to watch Exhilaratus's morals and actions, and to see that he is kind to his clergy, and that the clergy are obedient. I am inclined to think that the fault of Exhilaratus had been a cruel severity to his clergy, who had rebelled and complained. That St.

If he was twenty or more in 543 (the 'traditional' date of St. Benedict's death), he was born in 523, and was at least 74 in 597. Would St. Gregory have sent him to Jerusalem at such an age, or to Constantinople at 71? Possibly, if he was very vigorous. But it is surely more probable that St. Benedict died later, 547-556, and that Exhilaratus, born about 527-536, was only 58-67 in 594 and still only 61-70 in 597, and very strong for his age.[1]

Thus the weaker arguments from Valentinian, who lived till nearly 593, and Honoratus, who was still alive in that year, are singularly reinforced by the case of *Exhilaratus noster*, and confirm the proof that St. Sabinus visited St. Benedict in 547 some years before the death of the latter.

13. In *Dial.* IV 9 we hear of two brothers, Speciosus and Gregory, rich men and learned, who gave themselves to the Rule of St. Benedict in the holy life of monks. He sent them to Terracina, to the monastery whose building is spoken of in II 22.[2] St. Gregory only knows of these two by the report of St. Benedict's disciples. Speciosus was sent on business of the monastery to Capua, and died there, appearing to his brother at the moment of his death. We may with some probability identify this *uir nobilis*

Gregory, though not acting as his judge, had taken him into his house and 'afflicted' him there, would be natural if he was a former inmate of the quasi-monastic Papal headquarters; and the words used to the defensor Fantinus are curiously reminiscent of St. Benedict's style and ways,—perhaps because Exhilaratus had been a monk.

[1] If the former note was right in suggesting that he was made a bishop in 598, and was tried for over severity in 603, the later dates for St. Benedict become more probable still. Suppose Exhilaratus was 65 at most when he was sent to Sicily as bishop in 598, he was born in 533, and would be only ten years old at the 'traditional' date of St. Benedict's death. Hence I should place that event about 553 at the earliest.

[2] *Dial.* IV. 9: 'Eisdem quoque discipulis illius narrantibus, didici quia duo nobiles uiri atque exterioribus studiis eruditi, germani fratres, quorum unus Speciosus alter uero Gregorius dicebatur, eius se regulae in sancta conuersatione tradiderunt ; quod idem uenerabilis pater in monasterio quod iuxta Terracinensem urbem construxerat, fecit habitare. Qui multas quidem pecunias in hoc mundo possiderant, sed cuncta pauperibus pro animarum suarum redemptione largiti sunt, et in eodem monasterio permanserunt.

Speciosus, who had possessed much riches, and was learned in secular studies, with the Speciosus who was an important official of King Theodoric.   In 509 a letter to Speciosus in the King's name orders him to see that no less a person than the consul Inportunus, and the patricius Theodorus (who had been consul in 505) shall send proxies to stand trial for violent behaviour before two other patricii.   Not more than two years later another letter of Theodoric to him addresses him as a *deuotus comitiacus*, and commits to him the execution of some business connected with Agapita (presumably a relative of the patricius Agapitus and of the deacon who was later to become Pope).   It was the office of a *comitiacus* to see to the carrying into effect of important commands of the government.[1]   Such a position for a youngish man of noble birth might be the stepping stone to higher offices.   If Speciosus was really a comitiacus in 509-11, it will be surprising if his conversion is later than 528-9, the ' traditional ' date of the foundation of Monte-cassino.   But I have argued above that St. Benedict probably migrated to that spot soon after 520.   Now St. Gregory speaks as if the brothers were at least approaching middle age, and Speciosus was the elder.   He may have been 30 in 510, and 45 when he entered the monastery about 525.   These considerations are slightly in favour of the earlier date for St. Benedict's migration.

14.   Martinus, a famous hermit on Mount Marsicus, was told by St. Benedict to do away with the chain with which he had bound his foot to a rock (*Dial.* III 16).   St. Gregory says he lived *nuper*, and that the information about him was derived from Pelagius II and others.   This does not prove that he lived until Pelagius became pope in 579, for Pelagius is more likely to have visited him before he was

---

[1] See the elaborate discussion of the duties of a *comitiacus* (and of an *agens in rebus*) in Mommsen's *Ostgothische Studien*, in *Neues Archiv.* XIV. pp. 468-74.

Pope. All we can infer is that a man who was grown up some time before St. Benedict died, had lived until *nuper*. This is a shade easier if St. Benedict died as late as 553, than if we took 542-3.

15. The famine in Campania, mentioned in *Dial.* II 21 and 28, is usually identified with the great famine of 537-8, spoken of by Procopius. He tells us it was at Urbino and Orvieto, in Aemilia, in Tuscany, and Picenum, where fifty thousand farmers died ; it was worse north of the Ionian Gulf, and it caused a frightful plague, which he describes (*Bell. Goth.* II 20). He tells how two women near Ariminum ate seventeen men, whom they successively took in as lodgers : the eighteenth lodger killed them both! The Liber Pontificalis relates that in Liguria, women ate their children. But Campania is not mentioned by these authorities, while Gregory does not speak of the plague. The identification is therefore doubtful, as St. Gregory seems rather to refer to a local famine.

The conclusion I draw from all this rather vague evidence is that the ' traditional ' dates for St. Benedict—founded Montecassino in 529, wrote the Rule in 530, and died in 542-3—are not tenable.

The Rule was written before 530, as it is quoted by Justinian in that year. St. Benedict was still alive when he conversed with bishop Sabinus in 547. The facts as to Valentinian, Honoratus, Constantius of Aquinum, and especially Exhilaratus, impel us to suppose that St. Benedict lived until 550 or later.

The usual date given for his birth, 480, seems a good one. The ' traditional date ' of his death puts it at the early age of 63. Hermits and ascetics are in general tough and hardy, and 75 seems a much more likely age.

St. Gregory does not suggest that he lived to a great age, but he certainly does not suggest that he was a middle-aged man during his years of fame as a thaumaturgus at Monte-cassino. It seems more reasonable to suppose that he lived to 70-77 than to insist that Honoratus and Exhilaratus were all octogenarians or nonagenarians, though St. Gregory does not say they were.

The dates I suggest as moderate are:

Birth	±480	
Leaves Rome	±496	
Founds Montecassino	±520	
Rule commissioned	c. 523	
Rule published	c. 526	
Justinian	530	quotes
Caesarius	534	quotes
Ferrandus	534	quotes
Cassiodorus	c. 542	puts in practice
Death of St. Germanus	541	
Visit of Totila	542	
Visit of Sabinus	547	
Death	±553-5	

St. Gregory never saw St. Benedict. As St. Gregory was born somewhere about 540, it would be rash to put St. Benedict's death later than 560.

CHAPTER IX

LANDS, SERFS AND SLAVES

MONASTERIES were founded by the rich on their estates.—
Examples of monastic lands and gardens—The endowments
to convents—The cultivation of lands in the Roman Empire
by coloni, ascripticii and mancipia—The laws as to originarii—
The serfs on monastic farms made into a 'Third Order' by
Cassiodorus—Pagan rustics at Nola, in the village near Montecassino, and in Sardinia—Distinction between 'pueri' and
other 'mancipia'—Slaves belonging to monasteries—The
work of the monks not agricultural, but by St. Benedict's Rule
always within the clausura, the fields being worked by the
rustici.

CASSIODORUS'S idea of a monastery is clear enough: it is
a community of contemplatives nestling on the property
of some noble lord who protects them. He explains of
monks the words of Psalm ciii. 17, *Illic passeres nidificabunt:*

' *There* (that is, *in the cedars that Thou hast planted*) *the sparrows
shall make their nests.* For a sparrow is a tiny and a very timid
bird, and signifies the littleness of the monks, who *in the cedars
of Libanus,* that is to say, in the patrimony of powerful Christians
as if in branches, are shown to make their nests; by whose
power they are sustained and sing forth the praises of the Lord
with continual voice. A celestial life upon earth, an imitation
of the faithful angels, to live spiritually in the flesh, and not to
love the vices of the world. . . . But great is the glory of that
tree wherein this nest is built: let him understand that he was
planted by the Lord, since he bears in his branches such an institute '. (P.L. LXX. col. 734-5).

Cassiodorus himself became such a tree, when he founded on his patrimony of Squillace a monastery of monks and solitaries; but he did more, he renounced his dignities and became a monk there himself, *feliciter conuersus*.[1]

Such had been the example given at the end of the fourth century by St. Paulinus, who expended a part of his vast wealth on the foundation of a monastery and hospice at Nola, and there embraced the religious state. And in the century of Cassiodorus a yet greater man, Gregory, prefect of Rome, founded in his father's house on the Caelian hill an abbey whence proceeded the conversion of this island; and he became there a humble monk. Out of the rest of his patrimony, says St. Gregory of Tours, he founded six monasteries in Sicily.

Liberius, who like Cassiodorus was made a 'patricius' for his services to the Gothic kings, founded a monastery in Campania, of which more has been said in another chapter (pp. 138–9). Bishops founded monasteries; so did Popes, with their greater riches and influence. In the fourth century St. Sixtus III founded one at S. Sebastiano. St. Leo the Great another by St. Peter's, St. Hilarus one by S. Lorenzo and another *ad Lunam* in the city. Later, Pope Vigilius founded the monastery of St. Juvenal, which he endowed with many possessions and gifts.[2]

Monasteries possessed a garden and had income from lands.

---

[1] So he describes himself at the head of his Tripartite History, and elsewhere in MSS.

[2] *Liber Pontificalis, Xystus III:* 'Fecit autem monasterium in Catacymbas.' *Leo I:* 'Hic constituit monasterium apud beatum Petrum apostolum' (so most MSS.), some MSS. add 'quae nuncupatur sanctorum Johannis et Pauli'. *Hilarus:* 'Hic fecit monasterio ad sanctum Laurentium et balneum et alium sub aere . . . fecit autem et bibliothecas II. (viz. Old and New Testaments) in eodem loco. Item monasterium intra urbe Roma ad Luna'. (The spelling is Mommsen's). These and other interesting references to monasteries of the fourth and fifth centuries will be found in E. Spreizenhofer, O.S.B. *Die Entwicklung des alten Mönchthums in Italian von seinen ersten Anfängen bis zum . . . h. Benedict,* Kirsch, Vienna, 1894.

Pope St. Gelasius (492–6) tells us how Marcus, priest (and abbot) of the monastery on the *fundus Lucianus*, complained of the depredation of his monastery by two priests assisted by a *conductor regius* (that is, of the imperial patrimony).[1] On the other hand the holy hermit, Isaac of Spoletum, would not accept any land; many disciples settled around him, but he built himself a humble house (*humile habitaculum*) in a desert spot. ' Alii ad construendum monasterium praedia, alii pecunias . . . offerre uolebant ', yet he refused to accept ' pro usu monasterii possessiones quae offerebantur ', ' sollicitus suae paupertatis custos ' (*Dial.* III 14). But he was a Syrian, and was not a cenobite.

One of the greatest contemporaries of St. Benedict affords an example : in the life of St. Fulgentius we read :

' There is offered to him by a certain man, Sylvester by name, a good Christian and a noble (*primario*) of the province of Byzacene, a place suited for the construction of a monastery, whose soil (*gleba*), rich and fertile, was adapted by its desirable fecundity for being laid out as gardens '. (P.L. LXV, 131).

As for St. Benedict himself, when he founded his twelve small monasteries at Subiaco, the valley was rough, and possibly he could occupy uncultivated spots with merely a permission from the authorities, without receiving any grant of land from the owner.[2] We hear in one case of a Goth cutting away thorns at the edge of the lake to make a garden (*Dial.* II, 6). But at Montecassino it is clear (see p. 163 and note there) that a private property must have been given to the Saint.

[1] Ep. 3, p. 2 of Löwenfeld's *Epistolae Pontificum Romanorum* ineditae (Leipsic, 1885); from the collection in Brit. Mus. MS. addit. 8873, discovered by Edmund Bishop.
[2] Three of these cells, of 12 monks each, were high up on the rocks (*Dial.* II, 5). The sites of most of them are unknown. Moricca (*S. Gregorii Dial.* pp. 84-5) quotes the three very different lists made up by mediæval tradition. Probably the twelve were near together.

In the case of the only other foundation made by St. Benedict, we fortunately have a statement by St. Gregory :

'Also at another time he (St. Benedict) was asked by a certain faithful man to send disciples and construct a monastery in his property (*praedium*) near the town of Terracina' (*Dial.* II 22).[1]

This monastery is mentioned again, IV 9. These disciples, among whom were included two holy brothers, Speciosus and Gregorius, who had been very rich men, were the 'sparrows nesting in the estate' of the donor.

A letter of Pelagius I (555-61) to John, bishop of Larinum speaks of the monasteries in Lucania and Samnium, and of their *possessiones* or estates. No layman must interfere with them, nor must the bishop himself, in their private matters ; but he must see to the regularity of the communities and the cultivation of the lands which belong to them.[2]

From St. Gregory the Great we get a good deal of information about the lands of the Roman Church and the properties of bishops ; and we have some corresponding mention of lands belonging to monasteries, though the details are sparse and accidental. He tells us of the estates and gardens (*possessiones*[3] *uel hortos,—uel* means 'and' at

---

[1] According to Novella V., cl., of 535, ' if anyone shall wish to build a holy monastery, at every time and in the whole of our empire, he has no permission to do so, until he has invited the right reverend bishop of the place, and the bishop shall have stretched forth his hands to heaven, and *shall have consecrated the spot to God* by prayer, *planting in it the symbol of our salvation*, we mean the truly adorable and honoured Cross,—and thus shall he commence the building '. This consecration and the foundation cross were ancient customs, no doubt.

[2] This letter is] to be found, I think, only in Baluze, *Miscell.* V. p. 465. The important words are: ' ea tantum quae ipsis monasteriis utilitatisque eorum, tam in dispositione congregationum, quam in cultura possessionum ad ea pertinentium, necessaria esse perspexeris, competenter exerceas et diligenti studio peragere non praetermittas, omni[bus] quibuslibet laicis, siue in praefatis monasteriis, siue in possessionibus eorum, quicquam gerendi uel disponendi interdicta licentia '. This bishop John is mentioned in 592 by St. Gregory (Ep. II. 38. p. 139) as already dead.

[3] *Possessiones* are lands, and *possessores* are landlords. For the technical use of the latter word examples are in Cassiod. *Variae* VIII, Ep. 29 and 31.

this date) of the monastery of St. Martin at Naples (Ep. III 23, p. 181). He gave over the well-known church of St. Pancras outside the walls to monks from the Caelian, with all its *terrae and reditus*, lands and rents (IV 18, pp. 252-3). A house near the Thermae of Agrippa is given to an abbot whose monastery was in a ruinous condition, together with a garden and rents, including the *Massa Maguliensis*,[1] an estate about eleven miles off on the *via Nomentana*, together with a tavern in the city, and a fruit store opposite the monastery. Owing to the difficulty of the times this transfer was not carried out, and the house and property were later made over to a convent of nuns (VI 42, p. 417, and IX 137, vol. II, p. 135).

The land is therefore not to be tilled by the nuns, nor was it to be worked by the monks. It is an endowment, just like the lands owned by mediaeval abbeys. Such property was often at a distance.

For example, Stephen, Abbot of St. Mark's, in the orchards just outside Spoleto, claims that Pope Benedict I (574-8) had adjudged to him the *Massa Veneris* in Campania.[2] An outlying portion (appendix), called *Agellus*, of the *Massa Gratiliana* near Viterbo, and a *terrula* of xxx *modii* from the same *Massa* is given to the monks of Bieda, who were very poor. Bieda must be more than a dozen miles from Viterbo (IX. 96, II pp. 106-7).[3] The Abbey of SS. Erasmus, Maximus and Juliana, founded at Naples by Alexandria, *clarissima femina*, has a right to divide the *Massa Papyriensis* in Sicily with the xenodochium of St. Theodore (IX 170, vol. II, p. 167). A deed by which

---

[1] A *massa* was an estate comprising a number of *fundi* or farms.

[2] IX. 87, p. 101. A former Abbot of this monastery Eleutherius, is frequently mentioned in the Dialogues (III. 14, 31, 33, IV. 36).

[3] With still greater generosity the Pope sent a ship to relieve the Abbess Adeodata in Africa. In another case, a monastery which is poor or nearly deserted is joined to a flourishing one (X. 18, II. p. 253 and XIII. 4, II. p. 369).

St. Gregory, when still a deacon, makes over property to his former monastery of St. Andrew on the Caelian, is apparently genuine (Ewald-Hartmann's ed., Appendix I, vol. II, p. 437). The gift (to which the Abbey had a right— *uestra uobis reddimus*) is of one-third of three *fundi* (*Laueriani, Speiani* and *Ancessani*) and their *castellum* with its appendages, ' together with the *mancipia* and *coloni* thereof, with full right and property of the same, with cottages[1] and party-walls, and all that is joined or adjacent, with woods, plains, fields, meadows, osier-beds, standing crops, vineyards, olive-yards, fruit-bearing or not fruit-bearing trees, wells, springs ', etc. This is merely a legal formula.

But a formula for the foundation of a monastery of nuns is particularly interesting. It occurs twice among the surviving letters of St. Gregory, and was taken over into (or from) the *Liber Diurnus*, No. 11 (*Ed.* Rozière or Sickel).[2] But it is not the formula itself, but the detail filled in which interests us here.

A. VIII. 5, vol. II, p. 8, Oct. 597 : To the bishop of Luna, who wishes to found a convent in his own house. Permission granted by the Pope, on condition that no corpse has been buried there, that the necessary gifts have been made over, the municipal forms complied with. Consecration is to be without public Mass, ' and the rest according to custom ', which implies probably what we find added in the *Liber Diurnus*, that there shall be no baptistery, no ' cardinal ' priest, but for masses a priest shall be appointed by the bishop, no other being allowed

---

[1] The word *casale* is taken to mean a cottage of rustics or *casarii* by the new Thesaurus. But from the examples there I gather that *casa* is a cottage, and *casalia* are ' cottagings ', if one may coin a word: the cottages with the gardens or yards and appurtenances, belonging to the *coloni* and *adscripticii*.

[2] The early formulæ (1-63) of the Lib. Diurnus are generally ascribed to the seventh century, but embody older formula. That used by St. Gregory is evidently well known, and the editor has not completed his copy in either case. It is probably very much older than St. Gregory.

to officiate; and the relics (*sanctuaria*) are to be reverently received and placed.[1] The donations are as follows:

A silver chalice of 6 oz.
A silver paten of 2 lb.
2 Sindones (altar-cloths)
1 Altar covering
6 beds with bedding
20 pieces in brass (kitchen utensils?)
30 pieces in iron (tools?)
The farm Faborianum and Lumbricata, about two miles from Luna, by the river Macra.
With 2 slaves (*serui*), Maurus and John,
And only 2 pairs of oxen.

The other endowment is larger:

B. IX. 233, vol. II, p. 228, Aug., 599: Adeodata, *gloriosissima femina*, founds a monastery of handmaids of God in the city of Lilybaeum. In this case the *donatio legitima* consists of:

x shillings (*solidi*), free from tax.
3 *pueri* (slaves of better training)
3 pair of oxen
5 other slaves (mancipia) to serve within the monastery (presumably women).
10 mares
10 cows
4 segments[2] (hastulae) of vineyard
40 sheep, ' et caetera secundum morem '.

The land given is not specified, but is implied by the number of oxen for ploughing and of mares, cows and sheep

---

[1] Requests for and grants of *sanctuaria* occur many times in St. Gregory's letters. They were never at this date in Italy portions of flesh or bones, but ' secondary relics '.

[2] MSS. have also *iostulas* and *iastulas*. The word *hasta* or *asta* was a measure of land in the 13th century. But I suppose *astula* or *assula* (probably a little *as*) is meant: a fragment. I do not know whether the word occurs elsewhere as a measure for vineyards. ' Four vine-poles ' would not be worth mentioning between cows and sheep.

for pasture or roots.   The convent at Luna has only six beds
as a beginning ; that of Lilybaeum, was perhaps larger.[1]

How were these farm-lands cultivated?   Obviously in
the usual manner.   In earlier centuries the *latifundia* of
great nobles may have been cultivated by vast troops of
slaves ; but in the fifth and sixth century the whole country
appears to have been worked by dwellers on the land, all
of them irremovable.   Some of these were slaves (*mancipia*
or *serui*) ;   a larger number were nominally freemen,—
coloni or *originarii* and *ascripticii*.

The code of Justinian has a collection of laws *de agricolis
censitis* (Bk. XI, 48, al. 47), which makes the position of
these 'rustics' quite clear.   They are *ascripti glebae* like
villeins in the Middle Ages.   In law they are free, not
slaves ; but they are bound to work on the land and cannot
leave the estate.   A law of Constantius (357) insists that
they must be bought and sold with the land.[2]

Another law of 366 provides that they shall pay in kind,
not in money, unless there be a custom of the estate to
the latter effect.[3]   Presidents of provinces in Gaul (366)
are ordered to compel fugitive *coloni* or *inquilini* to return to

[1] We hear also of a house and garden in Rome, known as 'The White
Hens ', being given to the Abbess Flora (III. 17), and of the garden of a
deceased priest, Felicissimus, being granted to nuns (III. 10).   Rustica, a
' patricia ' (perhaps wife of a ' patricius ') bequeaths a third of her fortune
to found a nunnery at Naples (the formula here is that of *Lib. Diurnus* 16).
A convent is founded in a house at Caralis (IV. 8; also IV. 10 and V. 2;
cp. XI. 13).

[2] So a law of 369 in the code of Theodosius, IX. 42, 7, where among the
questions set to discover the value of landed property, we find ' quot *mancipia*
in praediis occupatis, *uel urbana uel rustica*, uel quarum artium generibus
imbuta teneantur;   quot sint *casarii* (" cottagers ") uel *coloni* ', etc.

[3] This is to be compared with the later law of Justinian, of 529, Codex XI.
48, 20.   A *massa*, or many *massae*, might be leased to a *conductor*, who would
receive the payment in kind from the rustics, and pay the owner in money,
making a profit on the transaction.   This would save the owner from the
trouble of looking after the estate himself or by a paid agent.   Cp. Greg.
Ep. I 42, p. 65, against the exactions of *conductores*.   A *conductor* might be a
slave, like Ampliatus in the 28th fragment of Gelasius's letters, (Thiel, p. 499),
who in old age was so impious as to make an invalid will, knowing that his
peculium belonged to the Roman Church.

the place where they are registered (*censiti*), and were brought up, and born.[1] A law of Valentinian, Valens and Gratian declares that just as *originarii* (that is, *coloni* born on the property) cannot be sold without the land, so *rustici et censiti serui* cannot. If a farm or a part of it is sold, it must be sold with as many *serui* and *originarii* as it has had under the seller. Laws of Arcadius and Honorius (of 400 or just before) order all absent *originarii* and *serui* and *tributarii* and *inquilini* to be returned to their owner and farm. An owner may transfer *inquilini* and *coloni* from a part of his property which is overstocked with them to another part which is in want of more workers. But if he sells the latter portion, he must transfer the families of the transferred *coloni* to the part sold (400). The same law declares that there is no difference in practice between *inquilini* and *coloni*; it is merely a matter of name.

These severe laws have the evident object of insuring the cultivation of the land, by forbidding any movement of labourers into towns, or transference to other occupations. This was so important, that these labourers could not enter the army, nor even any *humilior militia*[2] (426), and can even be recovered from the camp (like the sons of municipal functionaries, who had severe *onera* to fulfil, —decurions, later called curiales) by a law before 386 (Bk. XI, 64, 1) and an earlier law of Constantine (Bk. XI, 68, 3), even if they have taken the military oath.

Hence by the time of Justinian, these rustics are no longer regarded as 'free', though they are not slaves. Returning to Bk. XI, 48, we find Justinian in 530 declaring that there is no real difference between an *ascripticius* and a *seruus*; a marriage between them is lawful, and the

---

[1] No one must wittingly take a *colonus* for his property from the farm of another. If he did so in good faith, he must restore the man with all his *peculium* and his family.

[2] *Militia* means any 'profession'.

children (as always) follow the condition of the mother. And if a woman goes off with a free man, her children can be brought back to the land (419). If the son of a *colonus* goes to another condition in a town, because the work of the fields is done sufficiently by his father or by some other of his kindred, he cannot benefit by prescription, but if he is needed for the land, he can be brought back after thirty years, or even forty (531). Hired men after thirty years are bound to remain and go on cultivating, though remaining free (before 519) ; hence the class of *ascripticii*.[1] We see that ' back to the land ' was not a mere proverb in the fifth and sixth centuries.[2]

On the other hand, these rustics have their rights. If they are obliged to remain on the land, they have also a right to be undisturbed : as far back as 383 (or there-abouts) the law declared that *coloni* could not be turned out of their holdings, and other *coloni* or slaves substituted (Bk. XI, 63, 3) ; they had also their own savings, *peculium*, which might be large. But this they could not sell or give away, except with the permission of the *dominus*, for it was a surety for the rent. Justinian (531-4) assures them the right of appealing against injury or violence or over-exaction ; they are to dwell tranquilly on the lands their fathers cultivated. But in no other cases can they bring any action against the *dominus*, any more than could a slave or a freedman, since ' it is nearly as if they were subject to a kind of slavery ' (XI, 50, 2).

We find a curious example in a fragment of a letter of Pelagius I (555-61). Dulcitia, a serf or slave (*famula*) of

---

[1] This law of Anastasius left it doubtful whether the children would be free to leave. Justinian (c. 23, in 531-4) declares that the children cannot leave the land, though they are free.

[2] After the conquest of Africa, Justinian justly insists that no man who obtained his freedom under the rule of the Vandals can now be recalled to the condition of *colonus* (*ad colonatus condicionem*). A law of 555 (Appendix to Novellae, no. 6) is reinforced in 558 (no. 9).

the Roman Church, after her husband's death lived with a certain Celerinus, whose mother was a slave (*ancilla*) of the Church, (he would be of the same condition as his mother[1]). He deserted Dulcitia, and is said to have retained a field which formed part of the *peculium* of his first wife, and to have other things as his *peculium ;* for he pretends now to be a free man and a *curialis*. Now his first wife was a *colona* of the Church ; therefore this *peculium* of hers must be restored to the Church, and Celerius himself as well, if all the facts are found to be true.[2] This case shows that a *peculium* might be in land, as well as in furniture, tools, produce or money.

An interesting case of a ' rich ' rustic is the story of St. Honoratus (*Dial.* I, 1), whose father was a *colonus* on a property in Samnium belonging to Venantius, the *patricius*, who had been consul in 507, and was made *comes domesticorum* by King Theodoric.[3] This rustic made a

---

[1] If an *ascripticius* marries a free woman, the *dominus* may punish him *moderata castigatione*, but the children are free. But of course, if a free man marries an *ascripticia*, the children are bound to the soil. This is in a law of 531-4 (XI, 48, 24). But earlier such a mixed marriage was invalid. An example from Gaul is among the letters of St. Sidonius Apollinaris (Bk. V, Ep. 19). The daughter of the Saint's nurse has been run away with by the son of the nurse of a certain Pudens. In order to put this right, as the woman is already a free woman, the man must ' become a *cliens* not a *tributarius*, and change his colonarian condition for the plebeian state ', in other words, ' si laxat libertas maritum '; and this was to be done. The importancé of the nurse of a great noble (Sidonius's father was Prefect of Gaul, he himself had been praetor of Rome, and had even been made a *patricius ;* and his father-in-law Avitus became emperor, until deposed and made a bishop) is an interesting commentary on the history of St. Benedict and his nurse not many years later. St. Benedict, however, was only ' of good family ', see p. 184. St. Gregory's nurse was living when he was pope, in August, 594. Apparently she was at Constantinople with St. Gregory's friend and cousin Rusticiana patricia (a great lady at court), Ep. IV, 44 (p. 279): ' Domnam uero illam nutricem meam, quam mihi per litteras commendatis, *omnino diligo*, et grauari in nullo uolo '.

[2] In Migne, P.L. 69, col. 418. Dulcitia lived at the *Tarpeiana Massa*. Celerinus is ' ex ancilla, ut perhibetur, ecclesiae procreatus '. His first wife ' in ecclesiae possessione genitam ex colonis ecclesiae . . . ex cuius peculio quemdam agellum dicitur hactenus detinere '.

[3] His father Decius was consul in 484, his son Paulinus in 534, and probably another son Decius in 529. This eminent family claimed a glorious descent from the Decii of Republican times.

feast for his neighbours; and when they wanted water (to put into wine, I presume), a *mancipium* is sent to draw it from the well in a wooden bucket. A *colonus* might thus quite naturally possess a field or a slave.[1]

The state of things which we have described, whatever its origin, tended to become universal throughout the Empire,[2] from Constantine onwards. The fact that hired labourers and slaves with families became attached to the soil by thirty years' prescription, must have caused exceptions to be extremely rare. Free ownership of an acre or two, worked by sons or an occasional slave, would not be exceptions; but it would seem that any property from a hundred acres upwards, must have had its own *casarii* (whether *mancipia, coloni* or *adscripticii*), working by hereditary right and obligation, at least by the time of St. Benedict's beginnings as an Abbot, c. 500. In St. Gregory's letters, the laws of Justinian are copiously exemplified some forty years after St. Benedict's death.

We saw above (pp. 150 ff) that monasteries in St. Gregory's time possessed farms (*fundi*), or groups of farms (*massae*) and rents (*reditus*). We also saw that these farms were at a distance from the monastery,—as far as Spoleto from Campania, or Naples from Sicily, or merely some miles away. These were not cultivated by monks, but by the *rustici* who were given of necessity with the lands to the monastery, and could not be dispossessed.

On a larger scale, bishops, Patriarchs, and the Pope especially, possessed lands with *coloni*, who are often

---

[1] So a law of Valentinian and Valens (*Cod. Theod.* Bk. V. tit. 4) speaks of *arua* as possibly a part of *peculium* : similar references to land as possessed by *coloni* in Justinian; see p. 495 of Jacobus Gothofridus's essay on *coloni* in his edition of the Code of Theodosius II. (vol. I, pp. 492-6 ; Lipsiae, 1736).

[2] We find in the laws references to *coloni* etc. at Constantinople, in Thrace, in Palestine, in Illyria, in Gaul, in Africa as well as the general laws for all the Empire. It should be remembered that under the Ostrogothic domination, Italy was governed by the Imperial laws, including new laws, so far as the Italians were concerned.

referred to as *familia*, just as though they were slaves.
St. Gregory's letter, Bk. I, 42, is well known, in which
he protects the *coloni* and *rustici* on the patrimony of the
Church against unjust exactions. One point is interesting.
Too large a fee for permission to marry has been charged:
for the future only one *solidus* is to be charged, even to
rustici diuites, and *rustici pauperes* may be let off with less.
We thus learn that *rustici* might become relatively rich.

We saw above (p. 152) in St. Gregory's donation to
his own monastery of St. Andrew's that the land is given
cum mancipiis, colonis, etc. Forty years earlier, probably
before the death of St. Benedict we find Cassiodorus
speaking of the rustics belonging to his monastery, and of
the duties of the monks towards them:

'The very rustics who belong to your monastery you must
instruct in good behaviour, and not increase the load of their
legal obligations, for it is written: " My yoke is sweet and My
burden is light ". Let them be innocent of thefts, which are
known to be the common fault of rustics; let them be guiltless
of worshipping groves; let them live a sinless career and in
happy simplicity. Let a SECOND ORDER of monasticity (CONUER-
SATIONIS) of the present character be imposed upon them;
let them frequently assemble at the holy monasteries; and
let them blush to be yours, if they are not recognised to be
of your own institute. Let them know that God graciously
grants fertility to their lands, if they are in the habit of invoking
Him with faith' (*Instit. div. litt.* 32).[1]

[1] The text, from a photograph of the Bamberg MS. is as follows: ' Ipsos
autem rusticos qui ad uestrum monasterium pertinent, bonis moribus erudite,
quos adiectarum pensionum pondere non grauetis; scriptum est enim:
Iugum meum suaue est et onus meum leue est. Illud uero quod familiare
rusticis conprobatur, furta nesciant, lucos colere [MS. locos colore] prorsus
ignorent: uiuant innoxio proposito et simplicitate felici. Secundus illis
[MS. illi] ordo CONUERSATIONIS purissimus imponatur: frequenter ad monasteria sancta conueniant, et erubescant uestros se dici, et non de uestra institutione cognosci.
Sciant etiam Deum ubertatem agris eorum dignanter infundere, si eum
fideliter consueuerint inuocare. Data est itaque uobis quaedam urbs propria,
ciues religiosi ', etc. Dom Garet's inferior MSS. read *leue* (om. *est.*), *secundo
ut erubescant, Facta est itaque.*

This passage is extremely interesting. This chapter is
addressed to the two Abbots, Chalcedonius and Geruntius,
whose two new monasteries evidently possess the lands
immediately adjoining, as we should expect; since Cassiodorus founded them upon his property. The right
reading appears paradoxically to be the earliest example
of a ' third Order', in the words *Secundus illis ordo
conuersationis purissimus inponatur.* The *coloni* are to be
treated as *confratres ;* they are to frequent the monastery
and they are to be subjected to a very simple rule of
quasi-monastic life, by the observance of which they will
be recognised by others to belong as much to the religious
Institute by their life, as they belong to its estates by their
condition.

These *coloni* were probably families, living as *casarii*
in their ancestral cottages or farmsteads, *casalia*, father
and married sons and their children. There were no
village schools for them; they were wholly uninstructed,
and Christianity had not always reached them. Even
when baptized, as they must have been for the most part
by the middle of the sixth century, they had not lost their
' pagan ' habits and traditions and superstitions.

For it is significant enough that before the end of the
fourth century the name *paganus* had lost its sense of
' *villager* ' and had come to mean an idolater of the old
religion. The enormous privileges given by Constantine
at the beginning of that century to the clergy and the
bishops, and the progressive disabilities inflicted upon
heathens, fashion, and also the manifest superiority of
Christianity, had converted the towns, which were full
of churches, but had left the country to itself. The
shutting of the pagan temples and the gradual intensifica-
tion of the laws against ' pagans ' in the course of the fifth
century made the latter outlaws in cities, yet the rustics

were untouched by most of the laws, such as those which forbade a heathen to have a Christian slave, which prevented his inheriting even from his father, and so forth. The *coloni* continued to inherit their obligations. They were not exempted, as slaves were, from a heathen *dominus ;* for the land at all costs must be tilled. In the sixth century the fierce persecutions of pagans and heretics by Justinian had not been extended to Italy when Cassiodorus wrote. But even after them, many 'villagers' remained 'pagani' in both senses of the word.

How a monastery might convert its rustics, according to the desire of the pious Cassiodorus, is illustrated much earlier in the case of Nola. St. Paulinus describes in one of his poems the fresco paintings of his church in honour of St. Felix. After relating the series of old Testament pictures in the portico (XXVII, vv. 511–541), he explains that of the multitudes who come to honour St. Felix, the vast number are rustics, who till lately have offered profane sacrifices, but now are converted by the miracles at the Saint's shrine. They travel far, and then spend the night in revels, and get drunk in their simplicity and ignorance, when it would have been better to sing hymns and fast. The pictures will strike their imagination, and make them forget to over-eat themselves 'dum fallit pictura famem ', and they will learn by the moral examples and miracles represented. (Carmen 27, lines 542–595.)

When St. Benedict migrated from Sublacum to the mountain above Cassinum, he found there ' a most ancient temple, *uetustissimum fanum*, in which Apollo was worshipped by the stupid population of rustics after the manner of the heathen of old ' (St. Greg. *Dial.* II, 8). This *stultus rusticorum populus* apparently means those who lived around. The hill was far above the town of Cassinum, and evidently the magistrates did not interfere with effect. ' Besides all around groves had grown up in honour of the devils, in which at that time the insane multitude of heathen was busied with sacrilegious sacrifices. Thither came the man of God, broke up the idol, over-turned the altar, cut down the groves, and built in the very temple of Apollo the chapel, *oraculum*, of St. Martin, and where the altar of Apollo was, the chapel of St. John ; and with continual preaching he called the multitude who dwelt all around to the faith '.

The *insana multitudo* is the same as the *commorantem circumquaque multitudinem*, and must be the *originarii* of the fields within a radius of a few miles round Montecassino. Consequently the site was inhabited and cultivated when St. Benedict arrived.   St. Gregory tells us elsewhere :

' Not far from the monastery there was a village in which no small multitude of men had been converted to the faith of God from the worship of idols by the exhortation of Benedict. Certain nuns lived there also; and Benedict the servant of God took care frequently to send brethren thither to give spiritual exhortation '.[1]

How far the land of the monastery extended we do not know.   We find St. Benedict going out with brethren *ad agri opera* (*see* p. 171), evidently to help his *coloni* with the harvest (*Dial.* II, 32).   He used every year to meet his sister St. Scholastica at a spot ' not far off, outside the gate, on the estate of the monastery '.[2]   Whether there is any probability of the chapel now pointed out being the true site it is impossible to say.   It is conceivable that some traditions might survive the destruction of the Abbey by the Lombards, but it is not likely.

---

[1] *Dial.* II, 19: ' Non longe autem a monasterio uicus erat, in quo non minima multitudo hominum ad fidem Dei ab idolorum cultu Benedicti fuerat exhortatione conuersa ', etc.

[2] *Dial.* II, 33: ' ad quam uir Dei non longe extra ianuam *in possessione monasterii* descendebat '.

The lands on the mountain were as a rule safer against troops than the valley below;[1] hence the Italian cities are generally on hills. When St. Benedict left Subiaco in haste with a few monks, he must have had in view this estate, a superb site for a new monastery, already offered to him by some noble client,[2] just as in the case of his later foundation at Terracina (*Dial.* II, 22). During the many years (about 520 until 555) that the patriarch lived on the mountain, he will have received many farms or *massae* as dowers or gifts or legacies, but probably at a distance.

Consequently it is very likely that the nearest of the ' rustics ' of whom St. Gregory speaks, were serfs of the new monastery. We may even imagine that a pious owner of the property had wished St. Benedict to settle upon it, with a view to the removal of the scandal caused by their idolatrous habits. They are probably assumed to have been baptized Christians, but wholly uninstructed.[3]

The parallel between Cassiodorus and St. Benedict is here so close, that it suggests that the former, knowing, as he must have known, the apostolic work of the latter at Montecassino, wishes his Abbots to imitate it at Squillace.

In St. Gregory's time the rustics in Sardinia were often actually pagans.[4] He writes with grief to the metropolitan

[1] I foolishly ventured to say in 1919 (Downside Review, vol. 38, p. 92): ' St. Benedict himself had, indeed, " squatted " in an uncultivated valley, and on a barren mountain top '. My short stay at Montecassino induced me to write (p. 96): " There was no farm at Montecassino and no room for one ". The latter statement was refuted by Abbot Butler in the second edition of his *Benedictine Monachism*, p. 390.

[2] A donation of Montecassino to St. Benedict by the ' patricius ' Tertullus, and a bull of Pope Zacharias confirming this, were forged there at a later date. It is unlikely that there was any tradition on the subject.

[3] These heathenish rustics at Montecassino are also mentioned by the monk Marcus, in his poem on St. Benedict. He evidently uses St. Gregory's account, together with later legends. See additional note, p. 173.

[4] But not all rustics were inclined to idolatry. St. Gregory (*Dial.* III, 27) tells us of 40 rustics in 578 (' fifteen years ago ') who were slain by the Lombards because they would not eat meat offered to idols. The place of this martyrdom is not given.

at Calaris that he hears this to be the case even with the
serfs of the Church. The bishop is reproved for negligence,
and is ordered to see to their conversion. ' If I find a
pagan rustic belonging to any bishop in Sardinia, I shall
punish that bishop severely, *in eodem episcopo fortiter
uindicabo* ', says the Pope. But if any rustic should be
found of such infidelity (*perfidiae*) and obstinacy, that he
will not consent to come to God, he is to be weighed down
with so great a burden of payment, that by this penalty
of exaction he may be compelled to hasten to the straight
path '[1] (Ep. IV, 26, p. 261).

Besides the *rustici*, who were sometimes slaves but mostly
serfs, the monasteries possessed household slaves : *mancipia*
and *pueri*. The general words, *serui* and *mancipia* cover
the *pueri* ; but *pueri* are a higher grade within the general
class.

We saw above that the small beginning of a convent
at Luna is given two *serui*, Maurus and John ; another
convent received three *pueri* and five other *mancipia*,
' quae seruiant in ipso monasterio '. These quotations
established both the fact that nuns possessed household slaves, and the distinction between *pueri* and other
slaves.

The distinction was pointed out in a letter of Pope
Pelagius I, some forty years earlier (555–60). He writes
to a bishop : ' For as to the slaves (*mancipia*) remember
that our order was this, that you should grant them men
who might perhaps be useful in the cloth-mill (*gynaecaeum*),
but on condition that the churches should be compensated
in farm-workers (*agricolae*) for the merit of their industry

---

[1] St. Gregory's method of compelling those in the high ways and hedges
to come in, reminds one of St. Francis Xavier's recommendations to the
Governor of Goa as to the treatment of the heathen who would not be converted. St. Gregory orders (Ep. II, 38, p. 134) that the Jews who dwell
on the *massae* of the Church in Sicily shall have their rent (*pensum*) lowered,
if they wish to become Christians, as an encouragement!

(*artificii*). For an artisan (*artifex*) or a household slave (*ministerialis puer*) has a very different value from that of a *colonus* or a *rustic*. Grant therefore what will be useful for their house, in such wise that you do not let them off compensation to be given in farm labourers. Take care therefore not to give men who can keep up houses or cultivate and get back men who are useless. . . . For as to rustics and those who can be *conductores* or *coloni*, if you let a hair of them go, no excuse you can make will content me. . . . Whatever you neglect you will be obliged to make up.'[1]

Here it is clear that *pueri* are artisans, not mere labourers ; *pueri ministeriales* I have translated ' household slaves '. We find the same in St. Gregory : in Ep. IX, 200, of 599, Petrus *puer* is a *mancipium* and a baker, who has to be sent back to his owner ; in Ep. IX, 74, of 598, Consentius *puer* is the guardian of the goods left by Primogenius the notary in his will, an office of trust. In Ep. III, 1, of 592, about a riot in the castellum Lucullanum at Naples (the Castello dell' Uovo, where was the monastery of St. Severinus, founded by Eugippius), the slaves of the ' glorious ' Clementina are said to have committed excesses merely from pride, as being the *pueri* of a noble lady, ' utpote nobilis feminae pueri, ex sola superbia deliquerunt '. In 593 (III, 18), St. Gregory[2] makes a present of a *puer* called

[1] This fragment (printed only in Baluze, Miscell. V, p. 466) is not easy to explain. A *gynaecaeum* was a public factory where hired women or slaves worked at weaving: men were condemned to it as a punishment; and evidently in the sixth century men regularly worked there. I presume this energetic Pope is anxious to get the land of the Church better stocked with *coloni* in the March of Ancona (the letter is to the bishop of Cinguli, near Osimo). To ' keep up houses ', *continere casas*, seems to mean ' to support a family in a cottage '. *Continere* in St. Gregory means ' give means of subsistence ', and ' continentia ' means an allowance for support. The bishop is to get more men, by exchanging some artisans for strong young slaves, who can become farm-labourers, *casarii*.

[2] In Ep. VI, 10, of 595, Candidus is told to buy in Gaul clothing for the poor, and *pueros Anglos* of 17 or 18 years of age. Here *puer* may mean ' servant ', as they are bought, or ' boy ', as they are young.

Acosimus, a Sicilian, to a counsellor, Theodorus, who is in want of slaves.[1]

A *puer* and *puella* are not necessarily young; they may be of any age. In Ep. IX, 235, a blind man possesses a *puer*, Maurus, whose wife is called *puella*, though they have children and grandchildren.[2]

Julian, a Defensor, afterwards a bishop in the Sabines, was sent by a former Pope to bring the Abbot Aequitius very honourably to Rome, to be examined as to his unlicensed preaching. Julian reached the monastery in Valeria, accompanied by a *puer* very proud and stubborn, so that he himself could scarcely keep him in order. This pampered menial was sent by his master into the valley to find the humble Abbot, who was cutting hay. The *puer* in an overbearing manner (*proteruo spiritu*) bounced into the field, but when he saw the holy Abbot a great way off, he was suddenly terrified, and approaching him with trembling, embraced his knees.[3]

In the Rule of Serapion, Paphnutius and the two Macarii, more than a century before St. Benedict, there is a curious passage (c. 7) :

' If (the aspirant) be rich, and having great wealth in the world wishes to be converted, he must first fulfil the will of God . . . " sell all thy goods and give to the poor " . . .

[1] Similarly he makes a donation, with more formality, to Felix, bishop of Porto, of John, ' iuris ecclesiastici famulum, natione Sabinorum, ex Massa Flauiana, annorum plus minus decem et octo ', IX, 98, p. 107. In 594 the Pope sends a notary to buy *mancipia* for the use of the *Barbaricina parochia*. (Ep. IX, 123). The *Barbaricini* were a Sardinian tribe, whom St. Gregory had been converting by means of their Christian duke (Ep. I, 46, IV. 26, 27).

[2] The use of *puer* as a household attendant is abundantly illustrated in St. Gregory's dialogues: e.g. Bk. IV, 27: ' in domo praedicti Valeriani puer Armentarius '; 32: ' citius ad ecclesiam B. Laurentii . . . puerum mittite '; 27: the advocate Cumquodeus is ill in bed, ' uocauit puerum, parare sibi uestimenta ad procedendum iussit ', ' ordered him to get his clothes ready for going out '.

[3] The rest of this vivid story may be read in St. Gregory, *Dial*, I, 4 (Morica, p. 34)

But if he should wish to confer a part on the monastery . . . and *if he should wish to bring of his slaves with him to the monastery*, let him know that he has him no longer as a slave but as a brother, that in all things that man may be perfect '.

There is apparently no suggestion that the slave will become a monk; he will belong to the monastery, but his former master is to reach perfection by treating him as a brother (as St. Paul recommended to Philemon, v. 16).

In St. Benedict's own day St. Caesarius writes thus in his Rule for nuns, c. 4 *fin*. ' ANCILLAM PROPRIAM nulli, nec etiam abbatissae, liceat in seruitio suo habere; sed si opus habuerit, de iunioribus in solatium accipiat '. This seems to imply that female slaves were to be in common, the emphasis being on *propriam*.

In the rule of St. Ferreolus, written about 558, perhaps a few years after St. Benedict's death we find the following law :

Cap. 36. ' That the Abbot shall not presume to free a slave (*manumittere mancipium*) of the monastery.'

' The Abbot shall not have permission without the consent of all the monks to make free (*liberum facere*) a slave of the monastery; except on condition that he make over at the time to all the brethren from his own possession a substitute of the same merit and age. For the slave of many cannot pass over to freedom by the permission of one, nor become a freedman unless he is released by all unanimously; since it is manifest that he has as many masters as there are monks '.[1]

Some further examples may be given of slaves belonging to monasteries. In 595 (Ep. V 33, p. 314) Theodosius, Abbot of St. Martin's in Campania, and a successor

---

[1] 'Mancipium monasterii liberum facere Abbas absque consensu omnium monachorum licentiam non habebit; nisi ut tradat cunctis fratribus in praesenti eius meriti uel aetatis de propria facultate uicarium; quia non potest multorum seruus unius ad ingenuitatem remissione transire; nec libertus fieri, quem omnes unanimiter non absoluunt, cum manifestum sit illum tot dominos habere quot monachos '.

of St. Benedict's friend Servandus, had three monks in
Sicily on business, and wishes them sent back; he further
complains that officials of the Roman Church have
unjustly detained slaves belonging to his monastery,
mancipia eiusdem monasterii; St. Gregory says they must
be restored to him, if his statement is found to be correct.
In 598 (Ep. IX, 10, vol. II, p. 47) Romanus, of the rank
of *spectabilis*, left his house at Naples for a monastery;
messengers have been sent to Sicily to collect his *mancipia*,
who had fled there (I suppose); the papal Defensor is
to hire land (*possessiones*) for them to work. All that they
gain over and above their own keep, they are to send
yearly to the monastery.[1]

Similarly, in 599 (IX, 191) vol. II, p. 180), the Abbot
of St. Demetrius at Rome, called also 'the Bath of
Cicero' (*Dial.* I, 4), Fortunatus by name, a close
friend of St. Aequitius, sends two monks to some
place unknown, where the papal Defensor was a certain
Boninus, to find and bring back some slaves of his
monastery who had run away. Boninus is instructed
by the Pope to help in this good work, with the Divine
assistance.

Trajan, an Abbot at Syracuse, is made bishop of Malta
in succession to Lucillus, deposed towards the end of
598 (Ep. IX, 25), and finds that Lucillus has made away
with all the property he can lay hands on. St. Gregory
permits him (599, X, 1, vol. II, pp. 237-8) to take to
Malta four or five monks from the monastery at Syracuse
of which he was Abbot, lest he shall be too unhappy without
friends in a new place; but John, bishop of Syracuse
must be asked to consent to this. Trajan also asked the

---

[1] 'Et quicquid eorum labore accesserit, reseruato unde possint subsistere,
reliquum ad praedictum monasterium Experientiae tuae cura annis singulis,
auxiliante Domino, transmittere '. This monastery, St. Sebastian's, is again
mentioned in X, 18; cp. IX, 165.

Pope's permission to take with him the slaves he had bought with his own money, '*pueros quos de propria pecunia comparauit*', and the books (*codices*) which were his own or his father's, and other possessions which were in his monastery. St. Gregory says this is reasonable; and he may take with him freely whatever he bought or in any way acquired after he ceased to be Abbot, and also whatever he brought with him to Syracuse from the monastery in the province of Valeria where he first became a monk (*in quo conuersus est,*—one MS. has *conuersatus*, wrongly), which his father built, and whence he was driven out by the enemy. But anything which he acquired while he was Abbot at Syracuse, belongs, he must know, to the monastery, and not to himself, and he cannot remove it. Capitulina, the foundress of the monastery, had left him by will a legacy to be received every year from the monastery, and this is to be paid to him. It would seem therefore that she had died after his appointment to his bishopric.

*   *   *   *   *

There are so many things which St. Benedict does not mention in his Rule, because they are a matter of course, that we need not be surprised that he says nothing of the *pueri* or *mancipia*, the *rustici* and *coloni*. But we shall not rightly understand his teaching, if we do not realise the regular conditions of monasteries in his day.

It is natural to us to think of farms let out to farmers as constituting monastic estates. We think of the work of the Abbey done by lay-brothers for the choir-monks; but there were no lay-brothers, though almost all the monks were lay. It would be useless to conjecture how much in the monastery was done by *pueri* or how much in the garden by *mancipia*, for this must have varied in different monasteries.

It is quite clear that the monks actually did the cooking, for later practice as well as earlier rules prove that this was meant by *coquinae officium* (*S. Reg.* 35) ; but the *hebdomadarii coquinae* seem to have served the monks in the refectory ; so that in spite of the severe exclusion of all lay persons from the kitchen by later saints (*see* Martène's commentary) it is possible that in many monasteries under St. Benedict's Rule *pueri* assisted with some professional knowledge. St. Gregory speaks occasionally of some monk as ' the gardener ', as though the other monks did not work in the garden. It is clear from c. 48 that the monks did no agricultural work, except under stress of necessity.

' Si autem *necessitas loci* aut *paupertas* EXEGERIT ut ad fruges recolligendas PER SE occupentur, non contristentur; quia tunc uere monachi sunt, si labore manuum suarum uiuunt, sicut et Patres nostri et Apostoli '.

St. Benedict however assumes that this might easily happen. *Necessitas loci* implies the want of sufficient *rustici* to gather in the crops in haste while good weather lasts. *Paupertas* implies the need to economise in hiring extra men on such occasions. So we find in c. 40 the two suppositions for harvest time, after Pentecost : ' si labores agrorum non habent monachi ', and for other monasteries : ' si opera in agris habuerint '. There is also a chapter for the case which might arise if this summer work was far off (or perhaps some building or other labour) as well as for those who are on a journey : c. 50 : ' De fratribus qui longe ab Oratorio laborant, aut in uia sunt '. We know that on one occasion at least St. Benedict went out working in the fields with his monks (*Dial.* II,

32) : ' Quodam die cum fratribus ad agri opera fuerat egressus '[1] We hear of the humility of Abbot Aequitius who made hay (*Dial.* I, 4) ; but hay has often to be made in a hurry, and the field was near.

These exceptions are definitely permitted by St. Benedict : they happened for a month or so in the year, but only in some monasteries. They are exceptions allowed for. The *officina* of work, as of the virtues is within (c. 4, *fin.*) : *claustra sunt monasterii.*

The enclosure for monks is not so strict as for nuns in St. Caesarius, and St. Benedict's sister was not shut up *usque ad mortem,* like the sister of Caesarius. But monks are to have everything necessary within their enclosure (c. 66), ' water, mill, garden, bakery and diverse arts, so that there may be no necessity for the monks to wander abroad, *uagandi foras,* for it is altogether bad for their souls '.

It is clear that the idea that monks were agriculturalists would have horrified St. Benedict, as much, perhaps, as the opposite error of the African monks, for whose instructions St. Augustine wrote his *De opere monachorum,* who wished for a contemplative life with no work at all.

We do not learn from St. Benedict what all the work was, for *artes diuersae* is vague. These arts varied according to the ability and training of particular monks, and we learn from c. 57 : ' Artifices si sunt in monasterio ', that there might be no artificers. The best list (which resembles c. 66, just quoted,) of work is in c. 46 : ' Si quis in labore quouis, in *coquina,* in *cellario,* in *ministerio,* in *pistrino,* in *horto,* in *arte aliqua* dum laborat . . .' The ' arts ' will be perhaps illuminating, cabinet making, carving in wood or stone, polishing marble, working in iron or

---

[1] At Montecassino the monks were at first few in number, and apparently poor, for the monastery was not built for them by a donor, but they did the masons' work themselves, *Dial.* II, 9 and 11.

brass or precious metals; some monks might be archi-
tects or masons.

Every monk could probably copy a book for his own
use; some would copy books for the use of others; a
few would be expert calligraphers to write in fine uncials
for the Church.

A good many would be teaching the younger monks
and the boys who were offered as monks by their parents.
Some might teach Christian doctrine to the *rustici* or
their children.

To ' study ' or to write books would be rare. Apart
from the Venerable Bede,[1] it is seldom that we hear
in history of a monk being an author.   The vast literature
of ' Benedictines ' was composed by Abbots and Bishops.
Here and there a St. Anselm may have begun to write
before he was a bishop.   The congregation of St. Maur
is an exception : they had not the Benedictine government : no Abbots and no Bishops ; and the monks,
drafted from one monastery to another, could be combined
for ascetical, scriptural, patristic, historical study, so that
they produced very large and useful tomes.   But St.
Benedict contemplated nothing of the sort, nor did
Cassiodorus or Gregory the Great.

The sixth-century monk was not a scholar and author
like some of the Maurists, nor a farm-labourer like the
Trappists.   But he worked hard, and he read enormously.

---

[1] St. Bede is also apparently the only Benedictine monk, or well-known
monk (if we except martyrs), who is venerated as a saint.

ADDITIONAL NOTE

ON THE POEM OF MARCUS

I do not agree with Traube that these verses were written by a monk of Montecassino, who came there ' after the death of Benedict and before the destruction of the Abbey, that is between c. 542 and 581 ', nor do I think ' he does not know the written Dialogues of Gregory ', (Traube, *Textgesch. der Reg. S. Bened.* 2d ed. p. 95).

Paul Warnefrid quotes the poem as to those points which are not mentioned by St. Gregory (*Hist. Langob.* I, 26, *fin.*) The points are a great contrast to the Pope's traditions, and they are obviously legendary: Benedict was ordered by God to come from Subiaco to Montecassino,—no other reason is given,—' iussus ', and ' Ad quam tu ex alio *monitus* cum monte uenires, Per deserta tibi dux, uia Christus erat '; two angels at every turning, *biuium*, showed the way. A ' just man ' lived there (a hermit, evidently,—he was later identified with Martin), but Christ warned him to leave and give place to Benedict. Three crows followed the Saint all the way. The rocks made way for him, the thorns let him pass, the water in the way dried up!

Are we to believe these inventions were current at Montecassino after the Saint's death, c. 553 and before 581? Yet they were unknown to St. Gregory in 593!

Marcus is correct in one point: he speaks of the Altar of Jove: it was discovered in modern times, and was probably visible when Marcus was at the place.

But, though it is not his intention to relate the miracles told by St. Gregory, he appears to know the Dialogues just in the one point where he agrees: that is, as to the pagan rustics and their cult:

'Hunc *plebs stulta* locum quondam uocitauerat arcem,
Marmoreisque sacrum fecerat esse diis'.

Dial, II. 8: 'ubi uetustissimum fanum fuit, in quo ex antiquorum more gentilium *a stulto rusticorum populo* Apollo colebatur'.
With *marmoreis diis* cp. *contriuit idolum.*

The only mention of a monastery is in the words:

'De qua stelligeri pulsatur ianua caeli,
Dum canit angelicis turba beata modis'.

There is also a reference to the cultivation of gardens and
fruits on the summit of the mountain. All this refers back
to the time when the Saint was alive.

The poem is simply a glorification of Montecassino as a
shrine of St. Benedict and a place of pilgrimage. The life
and miracles of the saint do not interest the writer; only the
miraculous guiding to the place, the destruction of the temple
and altar, and all that sanctifies the place itself to the pilgrim:

'Huc properet caelos optat qui cernere apertos,
Nec remoret uotum semita dura pium.'

The date of the poem cannot conceivably be near that of
St. Benedict. It was written by a pilgrim to Montecassino
after the days of Petronax (died 747), when it was a flourishing
abbey. So I understand Paul the deacon, (6. c.):

'Haec omnia ex Marci poetae carmine sumpsi, qui *ad eumdem
Patrem huc ueniens*, aliquot uersus in eius laudem composuit.'
It would be wrong to translate this 'coming to be a monk under
St. Benedict's rule as Father'. We have but to look at the life
of St. Willibald by his cousin, written in the same age, on that
saint's visit to Montecassino in 729:

'Cumque . . .uenissent *ad sanctum Benedictum*, non reperiebant ibi nisi paucos monachos', etc.

When Paul says Marcus 'came to St. Benedict', he simply
means that he made a pilgrimage to Montecassino. His excellent verses belong to the Carolingian revival. Marcus may
have been a monk: he was probably not a monk of Montecassino. He seems to have been a visitor at the abbey in the
last years of the eighth century. By that time a legendary origin
for the abbey had been invented, the angels and the crows which
led St. Benedict.

In St. Gregory's days the pilgrimage in honour of St. Benedict
was to Subiaco (*Dial.* II 38), where many miracles took place;

we gather that there was no pilgrimage and no miracles at the place where his body rested, else St. Gregory's discourse to Peter has no meaning. But in the 8th century, Willibald was succeeded by visitors of fame like Carloman and Sturmius, and the new abbey was already beginning to adorn its history with legends.

CHAPTER X

THE SOCIAL CONDITION OF MONKS

THE imperial laws forbidding censiti to become clerics or monks to the neglect of their hereditary obligations—The wicked curiales—The other conditionarii or obnoxii : the coloni, whether originarii or ascripticii—Relaxations granted by Justinian—Examples from Gelasius and Gregory—The upper classes and the mediocres—A list of the monks at Subiaco who are known to us by name—The small numbers of the Arian Goths—The monks mentioned at Montecassino—These were probably more aristocratic than elsewhere.

THE imperial laws were numerous on the subject of would-be clerics or monks who belonged to the classes of *obligati*. The most difficult point was the *decuriones*, later called *curiales*, whose expensive and necessary duties in the towns of which they were hereditary town-councillors tied them to their burdensome position. Originally they had an honourable status, wearing a ring and possessing privileges. St. Augustine's father was a *decurio* at Tagaste ; so was St. Patrick's at Bannaventa, in Britain. This was still in the fourth century. Not much later Salvian, no doubt with his usual exaggeration, regards *curiales* as hateful persons. They had to collect the taxes, and make up themselves what was lacking, and even when they were not in default ; they were answerable for the public works. ' What cities are there, or even towns and villages where there are not as many tyrants as there are *curiales*? ' says this Christian pessimist, and again : ' Quid aliud est curialium quam iniquitas? '[1]

But the unfortunate *curiales* became as pitiable as they were reported to be wicked. A monk who left his monastery was condemned to serve the *curia* as a punishment ; and other free men were punished in the same way. To escape from these hereditary bonds was very difficult. The army and the Church were forbidden, except under severe restrictions. Constantine in 320 ordered curiales who had been ordained to return to their *curia*.[2] Later on *curiales* might get ordained by relinquishing the whole of their patrimony (law of 383) ; in 386 they may provide a substitute ; again in 390 they are ordered to surrender all their property ; but in 399 both alternatives are permitted. This severity was tempered, however, by the admission that the agreement of the whole *curia*, especially when supported by the voice of all the people, would free a *curialis* for ordination (361).[3]

Consequently we are not surprised at an angry edict of Valens that Egyptian solitaries who had been *curiales* are at once to return, or to relinquish their property (about 373).

If we jump to the sixth century, we find that *curiales* (βουλευταί) are now a proverb for badness. A law in Justinian's code (of 531) declares that no *curialis* or *cohortalis* can henceforward become bishop or priest. For it is unjust that one who has exercised violent exactions and committed many sins, unless he was received among monks before he was grown up, should be ordained. If this be

---

[1] Salvian, *De Gub. Dei.* V, 18, and III, 50.
[2] *Cod. Theodos.* XVII, 2.
[3] These laws will be found in *Cod. Theod.* Bk. VI. No wonder Pope St. Innocent in 404 bitterly complained of them, for they claimed that not only lower clerics, but even those *in sacerdotio constituti* should be restored to their municipal duties, which included the giving of diabolical games and spectacles. The Pope had besought the Emperor in person, without result (Ep. 2, *Ad Vitricium Rotomag.* c. 14).

the case, he must give up a quarter of his patrimony to the curia or the fisc.[1]   In 546 Justinian permits ordination even to a bishopric, if a *curialis* has spent 15 years in a monastery.[2]   In order to enter a monastery with due permission from the *curia*, a *curialis* has to surrender the usual portion of his property, not the whole.

We now turn to the humbler ranks of the *conditionarii* or *obnoxii*, as they were called, that is to say, the *coloni*, *adscripticii* (or ' *censibus adnotati* ') and the *mancipia*.   These had originally no right to leave the land, which had to be cultivated, except by the express permission of their *dominus*.   And in any case the work must be done by a substitute.[3]   A law of 484 forbids *adscripticii* to become monks without permission, whereas slaves cannot become clerics even with permission, for if their master wishes it, he can free them.[4]   If, however, they have become solitaries with permission, they return to slavery if they should leave religion.

But the pious Justinian altered this legislation, in favour of monastic life.[5]   In 535 slaves are allowed to become monks if they have good vocations, and do not merely wish to escape from servitude.   After three years in a monastery they are free men.   A slave who is ordained without his master's permission can, however, be recalled. His master's permission and the ordination make him

---

[1] *Code* I. 3, c. 52; repeated Nov. 6, I, 1.
[2] Nov. 123, I, 1 and 15.
[3] *Cod. Justin.* I, 3, 16, in 409.
[4] St. Leo writes to the bishops of Italy in October, 443, that persons are being everywhere ordained who have neither morals nor free condition, and even to the priesthood.   This is a double crime, because not only is the clerical state disgraced, but the rights of the *dominus* are violated when his slaves are ordained without permission.   For the future, not only slaves, but any who are *originali aut alicui conditioni* obligati, (that is, coloni, adscripticii, etc.) cannot be ordained (Ep. 4, 1).   Compare the canon 4 of Chalcedon (451): ' nullum uero recipere in monasteriis seruum obtentu monachi praeter sui domini conscientiam '.
[5] Nov. V, 2.

free (546). *Ascripticii* are allowed to become clerics, but must remain on the spot and till the land (Nov. 123, 17). Bishops are altogether freed from the servile or colonarian condition (*ibid.* c. 4).[1] A postulant whose condition (τύχη) is unknown cannot receive the monastic habit until three years have passed. If during this time he turns out to be a *seruus, colonus* or *ascripticius*, he is to be sent home together with any property he brought with him. If unclaimed for three years, he is free; but if he leaves the monastery at any time, he must revert to his original condition (*ibid.* 35).

This legislation of 546 is towards the end of St. Benedict's life; that of 531 is just after his Rule was published. Until then the laws of Zeno were in force. We find examples of their application in the letters of Pope St. Gelasius, about the time when St. Benedict was in his cave at Subiaco. In 494 he writes to the bishops of South Italy and Sicily that it is a general complaint that *serui* and *originarii*, to escape the rights of their masters and estates under the excuse of religious life, betake themselves to monasteries, or are carelessly admitted by the connivance of bishops to the service of the Church. This invasion of the rights of others is un-Christian: and bishops, priests, deacons and superiors of monasteries who harbour such persons are threatened with deposition and excommunication.[2]

Of about the same date is a formula *Probabilibus desideriis* for informing the clergy and people of any town

---

[1] A law of Valentinian III of 452 says: 'Originarii and slaves, who have transferred themselves to the ecclesiastical order, avoiding the yoke to which they were born (bishops being excepted, and priests, as has been said), unless they have filled the same office for 30 years, return to the possession of their *dominus*. A deacon, however, of this condition shall provide a substitute, and relinquish his whole peculium'. If he cannot provide this *uicarius*, he falls back under the general law.

[2] Gelasius, Ep. 14, 14, Thiel, p. 370.

within the archiepiscopal jurisdiction of Rome, that the Pope has consecrated a bishop for them :[1] the bishop has been warned what classes of person are not to be ordained, including *curiae aut cuilibet conditioni obnoxium notatumque.* The importance of this document lies in the fact that the same form is used by St. Gregory just a century later and remained the style of the Roman chancery until the Middle Ages.[2]

St. Gregory tells us how a deacon manumitted two slaves that they might be monks. One quitted the monastery, so he is to be sent back to religious life (Ep. IX, 107, vol. II, p. 113. On another occasion the *domina* (the ladies are harsh) refuses to let her maid become a nun, and the good Pope himself proposes to buy her, in order that she may follow her vocation (III, 39, p. 197). This case suggests that the permission given by Justinian with regard to slaves (*Nov.* V, 2) had not been carried out in practice, or had been modified by a

[1] This formula, *Probabilibus desideriis*, is first found among Gelasius's letters (Ep. 15, Thiel, p. 379). It is found a hundred years later among those of St. Gregory twice, Epp. III, 11, and IX, 210, but was so well known that the excerptor of his register is content to copy a couple of lines, adding ' et caetera secundum morem '. It is given in full in the *Liber diurnus*, no. 6. Hartmann says it was still used by Nicholas II in the XIth century. References to intermediate traces of it will be found in the note of Rozière's edition of the *Lib. Diurn.* (Paris, 1869, pp. 22-4).

[2] Some other letters of St. Gelasius are concerned with the ordination of *conditionarii*, and they interest us here only on account of the parallel between ordination and ' conversion ' to religious life. Men belonging to the *uir illustris* Amandianus have been ordained against his will. If they are proved to be *obnoxii*, they are to be restored to him, unless they are priests, in which case they retain their position, but forfeit the whole of their *peculium* (Ep. 20, in Thiel's ed.). Two slaves of Placidia have been ordained. They are to be restored to her. But one is a priest: if she claims him, he will be chaplain in the place,—' pro mysteriorum celebratione susceptum ' (Ep. 21). Two *originarii* of the magnificent lady Maxima have been ordained deacons, against imperial laws, against the rules of the Fathers, against recent admonitions: they lose their dignity (Ep. 22). On the other hand, two clerics, who had been granted their liberty, and had served in the clerical office since almost their cradle, are being prosecuted unjustly by the heir of their former master, so as to lose their right of serving at the altar (Ep. 23 and 24). Again it is a lady who is claiming her rights, Theodora, after the manner of Maxima and Placidia. These females had hard hearts.

subsequent Emperor. Presumably it was included in the law of Maurice of 592, of which we learn only from St. Gregory (Ep. III, 61, p. 220, etc.), which renewed the old law as to *curiales* and such like, that ' quisquis publicis administrationibus fuerit implicatus ' should not receive an ecclesiastical office,—so far St. Gregory agrees,—nor be ' converted ' in a monastery, to which latter point St. Gregory objects; for he says the accounts the man has to render can be attended to by the monastery, which could make itself answerable for his debts; for any one who with devout mind wished for ' conversion ' would certainly be careful to restore whatever he had wrongly taken. The same law forbade any soldier, *manu signatus*, to become a monk, unless his term is finished, or he is dismissed for bad health. On reading this, the Pope writes to the Emperor, ' I was sore afraid ': some can indeed, he explains, live a religious life in the world; but many there are who can by no means be saved, unless they renounce all.

What is specially interesting is the appeal which follows : ' But perhaps it is believed that none of them becomes a monk with a pure intention. I myself, your unworthy servant, know how many converted soldiers in my monastery in my own days have done miracles, have worked signs and wonders !¹ Yet by this law it is prohibited for any of such to be converted '. This shows that at St. Andrew's on the Caelian, which Gregory had entered as a monk about 574, having founded it not long before, a good many soldiers had entered within about twenty years. We need not ask any further about converted soldiers, however; for it is of St. Benedict's time that we are making an inquiry, and there were no Roman soldiers in Italy

¹ St. Gregory relates miraculous events at St. Andrew's monastery in Ep. XI, 26, p. 288-9 and in his Homilies, and many more in the Dialogues. But we do not hear of any particular monk there that he had been a soldier.

until the later days of his life, after the invasion by Justinian. It is most unlikely that soldiers from the small
army with which Belisarius accomplished so much, until
Totila temporarily reconquered all the Goths had lost,
would be allowed to enter a monastery during war time.
Hence for the whole of St. Benedict's life there would
be no question of soldiers being 'converted' in Italy.

An example of a *colonus* is St. Honoratus of Fundi.
On account of his piety as a boy he was given his liberty
by Venantius the patricius, and became the father of
200 monks.

An example of a slave is Exhilaratus, a *puer* who was
sent by his master with wine to St. Benedict. He later
became a monk (being evidently freed by his pious
master) probably at Rome. For his subsequent career
see pp. 141, 142.

As to rich persons becoming monks we have the obvious
examples of Cassiodorus, of St. Benedict, of St. Gregory.
St. Fulgentius was of a good African family. In the
Dialogues we hear of Maximus, a monk, son of the noble-
man Chrysaorius of Valeria (*Hom. in Evang.* XII 7), a very
rich man (*Dial.* IV 40). Of the 'middle class', known
as *mediocres*, we have an instance in *Hom. in Evang.* XXXIV
18: 'In our times lately there was a certain Victorinus,
who was also called Aemilianus, not a poor man for the
middle class to which he belonged', 'non inops sub-
stantiae *iuxta mediocritatem uitae*'. He lived a life of great
humility and severity in a monastery.

From these data, how are we to tell what classes were
most frequent in a monastery? It is obvious that no
answer can be given. It must depend on the monastery.
1. On account of the necessity of cultivating the land,
it must have been difficult for *coloni* to get their freedom;
they were wholly uneducated; they were inclined to

pagan superstitions. Yet they were numerous, and doubtless their children might be accepted in monasteries, educated and professed. 2. Domestic slaves, *pueri* and *puellae*, were not so rough. Some of them were well educated, and might exhibit ' good vocations '. 3. At the opposite extreme of the social order were the great families, proud of honours and antiquity. Few in number, some of their members were ambitious, worldly, or wicked, and those who became monks were many, considering the exclusiveness of this high rank. Beneath the great consular families, there were provincial nobles, ' country gentlemen ', of all varieties of wealth and influence, *defensores* or magistrates of importance. A number of these had vocations. So had even the ' publicans ' of the times, *curiales*, officials with power and some wealth, which they could not legally part with. 4. Then there are the *mediocres*, of whom we know so little,—undistinguished as to family, of mixed race and blood, largely commercial; of such there must have been great numbers in the principal cities, and some in every town. 5. From these we may distinguish the small tradesmen, the ' butchers and bakers and candlestick-makers ', the tailors, livery-stable owners, inn-keepers, and so forth. In many cases slaves managed shops, giving a *pensio* to their masters, or freedmen did so, or descendants of freedmen, who still remained clients and dependents of the nobles who had owned their fathers.

The upper middle class (4), and the lower middle class (5), presumably made the largest contingent in most monasteries, together with a few *pueri*, an occasional rustic, caught young, and a noble or two. Some country monasteries may have had a good many of the poorer classes. Some monasteries of renown had a good many *nobiles*, and an occasional *illustris* or a ' splendid ' and

' most magnificent' scion of a consular family which traced its dignities back to Republican days.

Two centuries after St. Benedict, Paul Warnefrid describes the restoration of Montecassino under Petronax (*De gestis Langob*. VI, 40) : ' multorum ibi monachorum *nobilium* et *mediocrium* Pater effectus ',—it would not have been to the point to add *et pauperum*, for such monks could more easily be had, as it would be a rise in life for them.[1]

It so happens that the only sixth century monasteries for which any details are extant are St. Benedict's own principal foundations, Subiaco and Montecassino.

St. Gregory tells us nothing about the origin (except as to the soldiers) and parentage of any of the monks he mentions in his own monastery at Rome, but he happens to speak of the condition of many religious sons of St. Benedict.

Of St. Benedict himself he says that he was ' liberiori genere ex provincia Nursia exortus' (*Dial*. II *praef*.). By *liberior* is clearly meant that he was not of servile or colonarian or libertine or (especially) curial condition. The comparative is equal to a superlative, and implies not merely the upper middle class, but that he was 'of

---

[1] St. Augustine wrote, about 400, in his *De opere monachorum*, c. 22 (25): ' But now it is quite usual that to this profession of the service of God should come men even from the condition of *slaves* (or even freedmen, freed or promised freedom for this purpose by their masters) and from *rustic life* (*uita rusticana*), and from the exercise of artizans and plebeian labour (*ex opificum exercitatione et plebeio labore*), who have been brought up in a hardy manner,—and so much the better for them.   It is a grave crime to refuse admittance to such; for many out of these classes have been truly great and examples of virtue (*uere magni et imitandi*) '.   But the wise Doctor goes on to explain how many of these come only to escape poverty and hard work, in order to be fed and clothed and to be honoured by those by whom they have been accustomed to be despised and trodden down.   St. Augustine clearly describes here the lower classes of his age, 1; slaves, 2; *coloni* 3; artisans and other free workmen.   His first words are noticeable: ' *Nunc* autem ueniunt *plerumque* . . . et ex conditione seruili '; ' nowadays ', ' almost everywhere ', ' even of the lower classes '.   We understand that religious life is now more common, and has spread *even* to the lower classes, who are received in the greater number of monasteries after due trial.

good family'. But it is quite clearly implied that he was not *nobilis uir*, and still more that he did not belong to one of the great families.[1] His parents were of good position and of good fortune, and sent him to Rome to do the best studies possible when Odoacer ruled and Gelasius was Pope.

1. St. Benedict having been unsuccessful in his attempt to reform a community near Subiaco, was surrounded by disciples in his solitude, on account of his miracles. 'Cum sanctus uir in eadem solitudine uirtutibus signisque succresceret, *multi* ab eo in loco eodem ad omnipotentis Dei sunt seruitium congregati', so that he settled them by twelves in twelve monasteries. '*Even at that time, etiam tunc*, the nobles and religious men of the city of Rome began to hasten to him : ' ad eum Romanae urbis NOBILES ET RELIGIOSI concurrere '. These words are of some importance, as they imply that later on—evidently at Montecassino—the nobles and religious men ran together to St. Benedict, though this had already begun at Subiaco.

2. Two examples are given, Eutychius (MSS. EUTHI-CIUS, Euitius, Equitius) brought his son Maurus. It is implied that Eutychius was a Roman noble, apparently a person of consequence. Perhaps he is of the same family as the Eutychus (MSS. EUTHICIUS, Eutichus) mentioned by St. Gregory as *uir magnificus*, ' qui se inlustrem praefecturium esse memorat ',—asserted that he had been a prefect, or had that dignity (Ep. IX, 115, vol. II, p. 120).

3. ' And Tertullus, *uir patricius*, brought his son Placidus ' (*ibid.*). The patriciate was an honour granted for life to a distinguished public servant. It ranked next after the consulship, and most of those who received it had been

---

[1] Later forged documents insisted that St. Benedict (and St. Gregory as well) belonged to the Anician gens, so much extolled by St. Jerome, whose consul-ships and inscriptions are so frequent in the fifth century.

consul, and if not, then prefect of Rome, praefectus praetorii or magister militum. A uir consularis et praefectorius would rank above others who had held the same office, if he was also a patricius[1]. Sidonius Apollinaris, who himself was made a patricius by Anthemius in 469, congratulates his wife on his brother-in-law Ecdicius's reception of the same honour in 475;[2] both their families had been praefectorial: now both have become patrician; may their children make both consular! This is remarkable, for the father of his wife and of Ecdicius was Avitus who was Emperor of the West (by the grace of Ricimer) 455-7, until he was made bishop of Placentia, in order that he might not claim the throne again. Ricimer himself was proud to become a patricius in 461, and so was Odoacer after him. It is obvious that St. Placid was of one of the great families of the time. On this point an additional note will be found at the end of this chapter, p. 190.

4. The Goth in *Dial.* II, 6 is interesting: 'At another time a certain Goth, poor in spirit, came to religious life (*ad conuersationem*), whom the man of God Benedict received most willingly'. This was at Subiaco. When this Goth cut away the thorns by the lake with such zeal that the iron of his reaping-hook came off the handle and fell into the lake, 'he came trembling to the monk Maurus'. A humble Goth, who trembled before a young Roman was an unusual sight. St. Gregory tells many stories about the insolence and cruelty of these

---

[1] A law of Gratian, Valentinian and Theodosius, 382, in the Theodosian code (Lib. VI, lit. 6) says: ' Consulatus praeponendus est omnibus fastigiis ', but one who has also had *praefectura* or *culmen militare*, ranks higher. If to these is added the *patriciatus splendor*, ' oportet huiusmodi uirum inter ceteros eminere '. The order of rank was consules, patricii, praefecti praetorio, praefecti urbi, magistri militum, praepositus cubiculi, quaestores et magistri officiorum, the various ranks of counts, primicerius notariorum, magistri scriniorum.

[2] Sidonius, ed. Lvetjohann in M.G., V 16, p. 89.

barbarians, and he would regard Zalla (cap. 31) as almost typical. The *libentissime suscepit* is noticeable : St. Benedict was extremely willing, even pleased, to receive a Goth among Romans.

It must have been very rare about 505-15 to find a Catholic Goth. Their Arianism was in power, and the Emperors were obliged to tolerate Arianism even in the East to some extent, to placate the Gothic rulers of Italy.[1] It was only when Italy had been subjugated by Narses, —say, from 555 onwards—that a serious effort could be made, according to the method of the time, to convert the Arians by applying to them the regular laws against heretics, by which they could neither buy nor sell property, nor bequeath nor inherit it, could have no Churches or religious rites. From that time the Arians quickly disappear from history.[2]

But in St. Benedict's time they were dominant. The army consisted of Goths with Gothic leaders. The Civil Service consisted of Romans, administering Roman law. But the Goths were not numerous, possibly 300,000 about 535,[3] and fewer in the early years of the century

[1] We learn much on this subject from the embassy and death of Pope St. John I.

[2] In 535 the first conquest of North Africa was followed by a severe law (*Novella* 37) forbidding Arians or Donatists in Africa to baptize or ordain, or to have churches.

[3] Belisarius, after conquering half Roman Africa with 15,000 men (Procopius, *Bell. Vand.* I, 12) proceeded to conquer Sicily, South Italy and Rome with a tiny army of 8,500, consisting of 4,000 regulars and auxiliaries, 3,000 Isaurians, 200 Huns and 300 Moors, and his own body guard, perhaps another 1,000. For the battles round Rome he received 1,600 more (I, 27); 500 Campanians were collected by Procopius, and 4,800 arrived from Byzantium (II, 5). Eventually Narses brought 5,000 more and 2,000 Heruli, in all 13,300 men to reinforce what remained of the victorious 8,500. The Goths had enormously outnumbered the original army; we hear of a camp of 7,000 of them outside Rome, between the aqueducts (II, 3), and we hear of 4,000 being killed (I, 27). But it is unlikely that the total number of Goths capable of bearing arms was much more than 30,000—say a nation of 300,000, who had never settled down on the land or taken to city life. For when Narses came to Italy in 551 to reconquer it from Totila, the 15,000 men he brought were sufficient for his purpose (IV, 26 and 31).

after the wars between Odoacer and Theoderic. We may assume that up to the Gothic war in 535 conversions were very few and Gothic monks practically unknown. From that year until after St. Benedict's death the wars continued, and there will have been no Gothic converts or monks at all. That even one should have been found at Subiaco is a tribute to St. Benedict's fame at that date.

5. We now turn to Montecassino. 'A certain noble-man, Theoprobus, (*uir quidam nobilis*) was 'converted' by the advice of Father Benedict' (*Dial.* II, 17), and he was in St. Benedict's confidence. The Saint sent him to Capua to inquire whether St. Germanus was dead (II, 35).

6. 'From the same disciples of St. Benedict I have learnt that two men, noble and learned in worldly studies, (*duo nobiles uiri* adque exterioribus studiis eruditi), brothers, of whom one was called Speciosus,[1] the other Gregory, gave themselves to his rule in holy monasticity (*con-uersatione*), whom the same venerable father caused to dwell in the monastery which he had constructed near the city of Terracina' (IV, 9). Of this monastery we hear in *Dial.* II, 22. 'They had possessed much money (*multas pecunias*) in this world, but they gave it all to the poor, for the redemption of their souls, and remained in that monastery (IV, 9).

7. We hear in *Dial.* II, 20 of a young monk, son of a *defensor*, who thought himself too grand to carry a candle-stick while St. Benedict dined. A defensor was often a powerful noble of a district, chosen by a town as its pro-tector. A papal *defensor* was also an important official.

---

[1] There is no reason for connecting this monk Speciosus with the priest of that name who was St. Gregory's authority for the story of Redempta (*Dial*, IV, 16 and *Hom. in Evang.* II, 40, 11); he was of the title of St. Damasus or of St. Clement (Council, Ep. V, 57ᵃ, p. 367). St. Gregory evidently did not know the brothers Speciosus and Gregory personally. But perhaps we may find the same Speciosus in *Variae* I, 27 and II, 10. On this point see p. 143.

8. The boy-monk (*Dial.* II, 11) who was crushed by the falling of a wall was ' the son of a certain curialis '. We may remember the law of Justinian (*see* p. 177) that a *curialis* may become a priest or a bishop if he has lived among monks since he was a child. Here is an instance of a curialis offering his son as a monk, according to the Holy Rule c. 59, so as to keep him from the contamination of his disgraceful though wealthy condition.

9. Valentinianus, a monk of Montecassino, afterwards abbot of the Lateran, had a brother who used to visit him every year, and always came fasting. He is called ' a layman, but religious ', ' uir erat laicus, sed religiosus '. He came on foot, out of devotion, perhaps, rather than poverty. He probably lived at no great distance. Apparently he was a free man, perhaps from Cassinum or Aquinum; he is probably not *nobilis*.

This is the whole of our information. To sum up: there is no slave, or colonus or rusticus mentioned. All are nobles,—Maurus, Placid, Theoprobus, Speciosus, Gregorius and the defensor's son,—except the upper middle class *curialis* and the lower middle class (?) Valentinus.

We gather that St. Benedict's fame for miracles and his nearness to Rome obtained for him a particularly aristocratic clientèle,[1] far above the average of monasteries at a distance from the capital, which would have only a few of the local *nobiles*, and would consist mainly of the middle class, with some converted *pueri* and an occasional rustic boy offered by his parents.

---

[1] Abbot Butler wrote (*Benedictine Monachism*, pp. 291-2): 'A simple life it was, made up of a round of simple duties [very true]; and the monks were quite simple men [I hope so]; though no doubt some were of the same station of life as St. Benedict himself, the great majority of them were recruited from the Italian peasantry, or from the semi-barbarous Gothic invaders '. But the peasants were *censiti*, and St. Benedict could not receive them; the Goths were heretics, and he would not receive them.

ADDITIONAL NOTE

ON THE FAMILY OF ST. PLACID

It was rare that anyone who had not held an ordinary consulship, the highest of all offices, should be made a *patricius*. It is probable that the *Variae* of Cassiodorus mentioned all the patricii of the West during the thirty years they cover, 507-37. Not counting two previously dead (Aetius, Basilius) we find nineteen:

		Consul		
1.	Agapitus,	517	last heard of	525
2.	Agnellus		dead before	527
3.	Albinus	493	last heard of	507–11
4.	Avienus	501 or 502	,,	528
5.	Boethius	510	killed	525
6.	Cassiodorus, elder,		patricius c.	507–11
7.	,, (author)	514		
8.	Cyprianus		patricius c.	527
9.	Decius	486	alive	510–11
10.	Festus	472	,,	507–11
11.	Inportunus	509	(patr. c. 508)	523
12.	Liberius		died after	554
13.	Maximus	523		
14.	Paulinus	534		
15.	Probinus	489	alive 507, dead	511
16.	Symmachus	485	killed	525
17.	Theodorus	505	alive	525
18.	Venantius	507 or 508		
19.	Volusianus	503	,,	510–11

It is seen that only four out of the nineteen were probably never *consules ordinarii*. In nearly all cases we know something of the families. The Symmachi are sufficiently celebrated. The two sons of Boethius were consuls in 522. The Cassiodori were related to the Petronii, or to the Anician family (a lady called Proba being a relative) to which Maximus belonged. The brother of Cyprianus was consul in 524. Decius, Inportunus and Venantius traced their descent to Decius Mus. The genealogy of the Volusiani has been traced by Seeck.

These nineteen patricii were not all alive at once. The number at any time will not have exceeded a dozen. Who then was *Tertullus patricius*, father of Placidus? There is no consul of the name; but then for seven years, 473-9, there were no Western consuls. No Tertullus is known to have been distinguished at this time, except a Tertullus, deacon of the Roman Church, who twice signed his name in Pope Symmachus's council of 499. He may have been of noble birth.

From the name Tertullus[1] we can infer no particular family. But the name Placidus gives us a lead. Rufius Placidus was consul in 481, and Mommsen remarks of him: ' The Placidi belong anyhow to the noble families of the West (C. I. L. VI 1757, X 1700) '. The first of these references gives us a Placidus Severus who erects a memorial of his father (name lost), who had been proconsul of Africa, praefectus urbi, and consul ordinarius,—very likely the Placidus who was consul in 543 and praef. urbi in 346-7. Apparently this consul is meant in C.I.L. X 1700, where his full name is given: *M. Maecius Memmius Furius Babuinus Caecilianus Placidus.*

Of Rufius Placidus,[2] consul 481, nothing is known except from Ennodius (ed. Vogel in *Mon. Germ.*, opusc. CDLII, p. 314), who makes him the father of Probinus patricius, and grandfather of Cethegus patricius. Now an inscription (C.I.L. VI 32200) gives us a *Rufius Achilius Maecius Placidus, vir cl.,* and Cethegus's full name is known from a papyrus, Flavius Rufius Petronius Nicomachus Cethegus. This Cethegus was consul in 504, but patricius later than 537, and was at Constantinople with

[1] For a consul of this name we have to go back to Attius Insteius Tertullus, consul 307. The bases of two statues of him are extant, C. I. L., VI, 1696 and 1697. Junius Tertullus acted as vicar for the prefect of the city in 340. Both these are given by the Chronographer of 354.
[2] An inscription *fius Placidus*, suggested to de Rossi the name Rufius (*Inscr. Christ.* I. p. 387,) and later he discovered an inscription confirming this (p. 606).

Pope Vigilius in 552.[1] His father Probinus must have had this name from relationship with the Petronii, who had regularly used the names Probus, Probinus, Probianus, ever since a Petronius married a Proba Anicia[2] at the end of the fourth century. *Achilius* is for Acilius. The consul for 488 was Sifidius, or rather Siuidius (Sibidius). His full name is known from a diptych (C.I.L. XII 133) to be *Rufius Acilius Sifidius*. He is presumably closely related to Cethegus. ' Rufius ' is a name of the Volusiani and Albini (alternate names, see genealogy in O. Seeck's ed. of Symmachus, 1883, p. CLXXV); but it is found with Acilius again in C.I.L. VI 32200, ' Rufi Achil ex quaestore ', and 32017, ' Mellita mat Rufi Acili '. Hence the family names of the father, son and grandson, Placidus, Probinus and Cethegus, imply the junction of three ancient families, Maecius Placidus, Petronius Probinus,[3] and Rufius Acilius. This last race carries us back to an Acilius Glabrio Sividius at the beginning of the fourth century; and it doubtless claimed descent from the Glabrios, one of the most noble families among the *optimates* in Cicero's time and earlier, though plebeian in origin.

In two letters of Pope Pelagius I we hear of another *Placidus patricius* in Gaul, the father of the metropolitan of Arles,

[1] This Cethegus was elderly in 545 when Procopius (*Bell. Goth.* III, 13) describes him as head of the Roman senate. Pope Pelagius I writes to him, 559-60 (*Epp. Pontt. Rom. ined.*, Löwenfeld, 1885, p. 14). This is 56 years after his consulship. But the sons of Boethius were mere boys when they were consuls in 522, Boethius being only forty, and Cethegus was consul only 23 years after his grandfather, and 15 years after his father. Probinus, with Festus and Faustus, was a leader of the Senate against Pope Symmachus at the time of the Laurentian schism, 501-14. Let us hope that Tertullus was on the side of the lawful Pope, against the Senators and the Arian King.

[2] See De Rossi. *Insc. Christ.* pp 68 and 238. The son of this distinguished lady, cons. 405, was Anicius Petronius Probus, whose sons bore the Anician names of Anicius Olybrius, An. Probinus, An. Probus; and similarly, Petronius Probianus had a son Petr. Probinus, whose son was Petr. Probus; and so forth. For it was a great thing to have Anician blood.

[3] As the great Roman families sometimes became Roman priests or deacons, I will note that a priest Probinus acts as messenger between St. Gregory and Spain (St. Leander, bishop of Seville, and King Reccared whom he converted) in 595 and in 599 (Ep. V. 53 and 53ᵃ, IX, 227ᵃ, 228), He may have been a Spaniard, or he may be the same Probinus who in 605 signs a local Roman council as priest of the title of St. Cyriacus (XI, 15, vol. II, p. 275, 14). As the priest of that title in 595 was Aventinus (V, 57ᵃ, p. 367, 17), it is possible that Probinus received this Church on his return from Spain. He may be a Petronius, and therefore of the Placidus family; or more directly an Anicius, or of a freedman's family, or merely christened with a fancy name.

Sapaudus.[1] This is in 556. Names commonly went from grand-father to grandson; so this Placidus is very likely a grandson of Rufius Placidus, and perhaps brother to Cethegus. For the same reason it is probable that the Cethegus mentioned by St. Gregory the Great in 598 (' Gloriosi filii nostri Cethegus et Flora, iugales', and ' praedictorum filiorum nostrorum Cethegi atque Florae gloriosarum personarum ', Ep. IX, 72, vol. II p .91) is a grandson of the other. The epithet *gloriosus* suggests the son of a patricius, as no office is mentioned for Cethegus himself. Another Placidus (' filius noster, uir magnificus ', Ep. XI, 32, vol. II, p. 302), mentioned as claiming justice against the bishop of Messina, probably owning property there, is clearly of the same family. He may be a brother or cousin of Cethegus the younger.

To sum up, this family supplied four consuls in a few years; Placidus 481; Sifidius 488; Probinus, son of Placidus, 489; Cethegus, son of Probinus, 504, and had four patricii in the sixth century; Probinus, Tertullus, Cethegus, Placidus. Now Tertullus probably brought his son to St. Benedict about 504. He may have been a son of Rufius Placidus, brother of Probinus, and his son St. Placidus would be named after his grandfather.

But Tertullus is never mentioned in the *Variae* of Cassiodorus, so that we may suppose he retired from all public functions through illness, old age, or (most probably) death either before 507 or not much later. We presume that it was a younger son whom he offered. Hence he might well be elderly, brother to Rufius Placidus and uncle to Probinus. We can hardly say that he retired from the world to become a Roman deacon, as Tertullus the deacon is a deacon in 499, which seems too early for the entrance of St. Placid to Subiaco, unless St. Benedict was born somewhat earlier than 480.

At all events the fact that Tertullus was patricius though not consul agrees well with the fact that his family had three consulships in the sixteen years, 589-604, which certainly cover the years of his patriciate. Even so great a family could not get consulships for all its members in so short a time; and Tertullus was out of the running, or dead, soon after this.

---

[1] Filius noster uir magnificentissimus patricius Platidus, is collecting the rents of the Roman Church in Gaul. The Gothic King Gontramnus conferred the title *patricius* on Celsus (St. Gregory of Tours, *Hist. Franc.* IV, 24) about 562; but he did not take Arles till about 568; so Placidus (as we should guess from his name) is a Roman patricius, appointed by Justinian.

CHAPTER XI

ST. BENEDICT did not found an order but wrote a rule—St. Gregory's witness that in his time the Holy Rule was of obligation in Italy and Sicily, and that he himself had observed it as a monk—A summary of the evidence accumulated in the last ten chapters—The Rule was quoted immediately after its publication by an Emperor at Byzantium, a metropolitan in Gaul, a canonist in Africa, and the learned Prime Minister of the Gothic kings of Italy—The writing of the Rule was preceded by an intensive study of all previous monastic literature and of the canons and the decretals—It was written to be the general monastic law—Perhaps under the influence of Dionysius, the Rule may have been commissioned by Pope Hormisdas before 523 and published about 526.

IT is time to summarise the conclusions reached in the preceding chapters. It is a great surprise to me, as the author of this book, that it is possible to summarise them, as if they formed a whole. For they embody observations and conclusions arrived at by me at different dates, disconnectedly, and written down as chapters in a book of unattached essays on the sixth century. I never expected them to make a logical whole; but they have grouped themselves, and have forced me to group them.

Long ago I felt sure that Ferrandus knew the Rule, that Caesarius was not a source but an excerptor of it, and that Cassiodorus quoted it here and there. But when six months ago I found that Justinian knew it also, the other witnesses became much more important: the emperor set himself at their head, and they became a potent and disciplined army. The Holy Rule was famous at Constantinople in 530, in Gaul in 534, in Africa at the same date, as well as in Italy. Much more, it was an Emperor who used it at Constantinople in laws for the world. It was the most influential ecclesiastic in Gaul who dipped into it, the metropolitan of Arles and papal Vicar. In Africa it was a legist, a canonist, of no little fame in the Western Church.

And in Italy it was the Prime Minister of the Gothic Kings, the leader in literary conservatism, and the cousin of half the patricii and prefects and consuls of the day, who retired to his lands in the South to observe the Rule of St. Benedict.

There is something curiously official in all this. We might expect a new Rule to be borrowed by a monastery or two or by an Abbot who was a friend of the writer, but not by a Justinian, a Caesarius, a Cassiodorus, a Ferrandus; —rulers and administrators, writers of laws or collectors of laws.

I was beginning to feel this, when I sat down to write the second chapter to the effect that the Holy Rule is not an account of the life at Montecassino, but an instrument for the reform of Italian monasteries, composed at the request of neighbouring abbots, admirers of the Thaumaturgus. If the reader has read that chapter (pp. 25-9 above) he may remember that it did not turn out as I expected! I found that I was forced by the Rule itself to show it clearly as it is: a Rule for many monasteries, many climates, many provinces,—a Rule which calls itself Mistress, Holy, to be observed by ' whosoever ' becomes a monk, to be obeyed by Abbots, with no discretion of their own, save where itself gives explicit permission: a Rule written with great humility and modesty by a Saint—who calls himself ' Magister ' and broadcasts his precepts with confidence that they will be respected.

In the third chapter the manner in which the Rule was created was elucidated further than was known before. St. Benedict prepared himself for its composition by an intensive study of all previous monastic literature, from St. Antony to his own day: this was known, for Abbot Butler had exposed the armoury whence the legislator drew his *fortissima et praeclara arma*, choosing and altering, rejecting or rewriting what Jerome and Augustine and Cassian and Pachomius and Rufinus and so many more had laid down. But he also studied the laws of the Church, the Greek councils translated by the venerable Dionysius, and his edition of the papal constitutions which made up the canon law of the West; and he must have read also the imperial laws concerning monasteries.

In order to write so short a Rule, so much careful labour preceded. Scarcely a chapter where we cannot trace this study, and observe the practical genius which seized upon what was necessary and phrased it shortly *luculento sermone*, so that none could mistake the meaning.

Thus I found myself driven along to a conclusion as unexpected as it was both obvious and traditional:

1. *Unexpected:* I had never supposed that the Holy Rule was anything but a private venture, accidentally so successful by its sheer practical common sense that it became the universal law of Latin monks, though intended for a few friendly Abbots.

2. *Obvious:* since the Rule so admirably met the situation, summing up all that was practical and durable in the monastic experience of two hundred years, how paradoxical it was to suppose its suitability to be a mere chance: it was adaptable because it was intended to be

adaptable, it was masterful because it was meant to have authority and to receive obedience, it has endured because it was meant to be a permanent code of religious law.

3. *Traditional:* why, the idea that the Rule was anything less than this was unheard of in ancient times. To St. Gregory it was already 'the rule of monks'.

A. In a well-known passage of St. Gregory's letters (IX 20, vol. II, pp. 54-5) he says: 'Your Affection had wished the monk Catellus to be made prior in the monastery of Lucuscum. After we had ordered this to be done, we found out that he was no monk. For he was not afraid to cause a contention on the journey, by begging for a portion of a small *eulogia* ('present', like *benedictio* or *xenia*) which the monk Bonus had received. Your Affection could recognise how great a bitterness of heart was the source of this, if you had chosen to be acquainted with the Rule of Monks', *si regulam monachorum nosse uoluisset*, 'for we have learnt by your disciple that you who are called an Abbot, do not yet know how to be a monk'.

The reference is to

S. Reg. 54: 'Nullatenus liceat monacho neque a parentibus suis neque a quoquam hominum, *nec sibi inuicem*, litteras, *eulogias*, uel quaelibet munuscula accipere aut dare sine praecepto Abbatis . . . Qui autem aliter praesumpserit, disciplinae regulari subiaceat'.

St. Gregory takes for granted in 598 that there is but one Rule for monks, and that is St. Benedict's *Regula monachorum*, as he calls it in *Dial.* II, 36, and as most MSS. entitle it. The *monasterium Lucuscanum* (SS. Maximus and Agatha) was one of the Pope's own foundations in Sicily, for he says 'in congregatione monasterii *nostri* confusionem'.

He is writing to Urbicus, Abbot of Palermo, apparently another of his foundations.[1]

B.   In another letter (in 593, to the bishop of Syracuse (*Ep.* IV, 11, pp. 243-4) the Pope declares that a clergyman cannot become an abbot, unless he renounces his clerical profession (*militia*).   ' For it is sufficiently incongruous, if one of these offices is so great that with diligence it cannot be fully performed, that a man should be judged fit to hold both, and thus the ecclesiastical duty (*ordo*) should impede the monastic life, and the *Rule of monkship* should impede the work for the Church '.   *Regula monachatus*—this would be true to some extent of any monastic life.   But it is especially verified of St Benedict's *Regula monachatus* :

S. Reg. 60: ' Si quis *de ordine sacerdotum* in monasterio se suscipi rogauerit, non quidem citius ei adsentiatur;   tamen si omnino perstiterit in hac supplicatione, *sciat se omnem* REGULAE disciplinae seruaturum, *nec aliquid ei relaxabitur* ' . . . and so of lesser clerics.

C.   The Pope writes on the same subject to John, bishop of Ravenna in 594 (Ep. V, 1, pp. 281-2) :

' Nemo putet et ecclesiasticis obsequiis deseruire, et *in mona-chica* REGULA *ordinate persistere*, ut ipse *districtionem monasterii* teneat, qui cotidie in obsequio ecclesiastico cogitur permanere '.

The reason for thinking that the *S. Reg.* 60 is again in St. Gregory's mind is that it was presumably a not un-known practice in towns that a monk should act as a priest attached to a public church, an abuse to which moderns are more accustomed ; (though we do not hear of any monasteries going so far as to have their own churches open to the public).   St. Gregory appeals against

---

[1] In the same letter (p. 55[13]) we have ' aspicio quomodo dissoluta sit *regula monasterii*, where we should translate ' the regular observance of the monas-tery ';   for the monks would not be obedient to the papal visitor, Urbicus,

this to the *Regula monachatus*, or *Regula monachica*, c. 60. The expression *districtio Regulae* was familiar to him from c 37[5].

D. To the monks in the little island of Montechristo, which Dumas afterwards made famous, the Pope writes (I, 49, p. 75) :

' Peruenit ad nos, nulla uos *monachicae* REGULAE praecepta custodire '.

St. Gregory is sending Orosius, an abbot, to hold a visitation, to enquire into their behaviour and report. A definite Rule is clearly intended, ' THE Rule of monks ', though no definite article exists to be employed.[1]

E. Again we have a reference to the Rule in the past, when it was merely a custom at Montecassino, *mos cellae Dial.* II, 12 :

' Mos enim cellae fuit, ut quoties *ad responsum* aliquod egrederentur fratres, cibum potumque extra cellam minime sumerent. Quumque hoc *de usu Regulae* sollicite seruaretur ', etc.

This is the Rule, perhaps before it was written ; for in *S. Reg.* 51 we find :

' Frater qui *pro quouis responso* dirigitur, et ea die speratur reuerti ad monasterium, non praesumat foris manducare, etiamsi omnino rogetur a quouis: nisi forte ei ab abbate suo praecipiatur. Quod si aliter fecerit, excommunicetur '.

The brothers in the Dialogues invited themselves to a certain woman, who fed them well. They had no permission from the abbot. They returned back rather late, and St. Benedict without second sight might have

---

[1] As opposed to the general *Regula monachorum*, we have the rule (abstract) of the abbot, *Ep.* I, 40, p. 55: ' a propria abbatis regula . . . abscedere ', and ' sub abbatis sui regulam . . . reddatur ', i.e. his government, authority. So Gregory writes to his former Prior, St. Augustine: ' tua fraternitas, *monasterii regulis* erudita, seorsum uiuere non debet a clericis suis ' (*Ep.* XI, 56, vol. II, p. 333).

guessed the reason, if he knew of their kind hostess.   And he refrained from excommunicating them, thinking their fright was sufficient.   Thus every point in the short chapter of the Rule is accounted for.

If these five mentions of the Rule occurred in the ninth century, no one would trouble to deny that the Rule of St. Benedict is referred to in each case.   But it may be said that in 590–600 we have conversely to prove that this is so.   I prefer, therefore, a *reductio ad absurdum* : if we say that in all these cases, A, B, C, D, E, the Rule of St. Benedict is not meant, then we have to assume the existence of *a general custom having the force of the Law* which contained all the points raised by St. Gregory :

1. Eulogiae not to be given by one monk to another.
2. Monks not to exercise clerical Orders outside.
3. Definite ' praecepta Regulae ', which could be inquired into at a visitation.
4. The points raised in Ep. I, 40 (quoted in the note), that monks went as they pleased *de monasterio ad monasterium,* and also had property of their own, *peculiaritati studere,* of which St. Gregory says ' quod non licere *notum est* '.

It would surely be parodoxical to take such customary law for granted :   and in fact there seem to have been no such customs !

But the Rule of St. Benedict exactly applies in each case, so that this Rule is meant, and it was already the *Regula monachorum.*

F.   I do not doubt that the commentary on the first book of Kings is by St. Gregory. It differs greatly from the *Moralia,* because it was spoken not written, and we possess therefore an uncorrected shorthand copy ; it differs also in that it is spoken to monks in particular, and it therefore quotes the Holy Rule more often than the *Moralia* do. But it would be pure ignorance that could attribute its doctrines of contemplation to anyone but St. Gregory; and I quote without any hesitation the reference to the Holy Rule by St. Gregory, and written down by Claudius,[1] on 1 *Reg.* VIII 18, Bk. IV 17, P.L. 79, col. 215 (199):

' Facile quidem uobis regem petistis: sed quia dignitas regia grauis est, eorum potestatem effugere facile non potestis. Hoc quia ad historiam dicimus, notandum esse censemus, quia omnipotens Deus, dum ius regis praedicit, *religiosis praepositis formam institutionis* impendit. Quare? Ut qui arctissimam conuersationis uiam imperant, *nouiter accedentibus facile aditum* non impendant. Quare et eiusdem arctissimae uitae MAGISTER optimus, summae ueritatis discipulus eruditus, praecipit dicens: " Probate Spiritus, si ex Deo sint ", et item: " Nuntietur ei dura et aspera, per quae itur ad Deum, ut sciat ad quod intrat " '.

The citations are not exact; St. Gregory quoted from memory, and his dear son Claudius wrote down his words inexactly. But c. 58 is quoted without doubt, and the Magister optimus of the very strait way is St. Benedict.

G. Let us now examine the passage of *Dial.* II, 36:

' Hoc autem nolo te lateat, quod uir Dei inter tot miracula quibus in mundo claruit, doctrinae quoque uerbo non mediocriter fulsit. Nam scripsit MONACHORUM REGULAM, discretione praecipuam, sermone luculentam. Cuius si quis uelit subtilius mores uitamque cognoscere, potest in *eadem institutione Regulae* omnes *magisterii* illius actus inuenire, quia sanctus uir nullo modo potuit aliter docere quam uixit '.

---

[1] Claudius wrote down, or rather ' composed ' (*dictauit*), the lectures which St. Gregory had been too ill to write himself. Claudius wrote *suo sensu*, and St. Gregory says ' quae cum mihi legisset, inueni dictorum meorum sensum ualde in utilius fuisse permutatum ' (*Ep.* XII, 6, in Migne XII, 24). The Benedictine editors and Hartmann agree in reading *ualde inutilius*, so that Claudius is accused of altering ' very uselessly ', or rather ' much more uselessly than I expected '. But Père de la Taille has most ingeniously proposed to read *in utilius*, which seems much better. If he is right, we can use the commentaries on Kings and Canticles with all the more confidence.

'The man of God, amid the many miracles which made him famous, had no little glory by the word of his doctrine. For he wrote *the Rule for monks*, remarkable for its discretion, and clear in its diction '.

Here ' non mediocriter fulsit ' means that the Rule made him almost as famous (though mainly among monks) as the miracles (which impressed the uneducated as well as the educated). This was naturally no news to Peter; but St. Gregory uses his usual literary artifice; just as he presumed at the beginning of the book that nobody knew of St. Benedict, so now he assumes that it was not known to Peter that he wrote the Rule under which Peter had lived. Yet he had said that Benedict was a lamp on a lamp-stand to give light to all, and that his Rule had no little fame!

The invention of the Chronicle of Subiaco that St. Gregory approved the Rule and propagated it has evidently no truth in it.[1] The Rule was *the* Rule in Italy before St. Gregory became Pope.

[1] There are other instances of citation of the Rule by St. Gregory. I give two in particular, as possibly not noticed:

A: Ep. V, 47, p. 347: ' ut in defuncti abbatis locum, alium quem dignum communis consensus congregationis elegerit debeat ordinare. His autem ita perfectis, *in Dei opere estote solliciti*, et adsiduae orationi operam date '.

The first sentence may be from *S. Reg.* 64: we find the same in the accompanying letter (V, 49, II, p. 349):

' Abbatem uero eidem monasterio non alium, sed quem dignum moribus atque aptum disciplinae monasticae communi consensu congregatio tota poposcerit, ordinare te uolumus '.

But this procedure was equally according to imperial law (above, pp. 62–3). I wish rather to call attention to the clear quotation from *S. Reg.* 58¹⁵, *si sollicitus est ad Opus Dei*, the first quality necessary in a novice.

B. In VII 10 (II, p. 453) we hear of an abbot, Agnellus of Rimini, who is overworked because he has no prior: ' quod dilectio tua, praepositum non habens, omnino in regendis fratribus elaboret '. St. Benedict in fact thought it best to do without a praepositus, if possible. But the Pope orders: ' Si qui uos ex ordine sequitur talis est, ut circa cellae ordinationem fratrumque custodiam, nec non in lucrandis animabus sollers ualeat inueniri, is debet ad hunc locum incunctanter accedere. Si uero talis non est qualem locus exposcit, de quolibet etiam ultimo gradu, si talis inter fratres Domino fuerit protegente reppertus, qui uitae meritis dignum conuersationis suae praebeat documentum ', etc.

qui uos ex ordine sequitur, (cp. *laws of Justinian* pp. 59ff.).

Notice *magister* in E, and *magisterii* in G ; they remind us of the solemn opening of the Rule : ' Obsculta, o fili, uerba Magistri '.

* * * * *

St. Benedict would hardly have made so elaborate a study of monastic, ecclesiastical and civil law merely in order to govern his own Abbey. He did so to compose a law for Italy for all monasteries,[1] and he was confident that it would be obeyed.

It is scarcely possible that Justinian, who was not emperor till 527, and had no power in the West, should have commissioned the famous wonder-worker to write a Rule. It must, therefore,[2] have been the Pope who did so.

I suggest that Dionysius is behind the scenes. St. Benedict quotes his books and must have known him. A ' code ' for religious would appeal to this Scythian Abbot, who had collected councils and decretals. Was not the idea due to Dionysius?

And would not Dionysius, who had a copy of his translation of the councils prepared for the use of the Pope, suggest to St. Hormisdas the advisability of adding to his new canon law a new Rule for all monks?—not a collection of rules, but a selection,—*a minimum standard of cenobitic*

---

cellae ordinationem   S. Reg. 66, De praepositio monasterii . . . uidimus expedire . . . in abbatis pendere arbitrio *ordinationem monasterii sui.*
in *lucrandis animabus* sollers, 58[12] aptus sit ad *lucrandas animas,*
qualem *locus exposcit,*   66[31] Quod si *aut locus expetit,*
de quolibet *ultimo gradu*   64[7] etiam si *ultimus fuerit in ordine* congregationis.
Si uero *talis non est*   61[19] quod *si* non fuerit *talis qui*

It is obvious that St. Gregory knows c. 66, and remembers two words from c. 58.

[1] The necessity for such a Rule is illustrated by a letter of St. Gregory (*Ep.* VII 32, p. 481) to an Abbot, Cumquodeus, who complained that his monks *would* run away, when he tried to keep them in order!

[2] See above, p. 30–2.

life, not too hard to be enforced by ecclesiastical penalties and papal visitations, nor too easy-going to be a means of perfection.

The very idea of such a Rule would seem to be paradoxical and preposterous ! Yet this is what Benedict set out to write,—I believe, at the bidding of the Pope, and by the persuasion of the venerable Dionysius, to whom (if this conjecture is right) we owe not only the Christian era but the *Regula monasteriorum.*

At all events the Abbot of Montecassino accomplished the impossible. He produced a Rule which was so practical and moderate that it could be enforced as a minimum, and so wise and holy that it could lead saints to perfection.

St. Hormisdas died August 7th, 523. It is hardly possible that St. Benedict should have started on his preliminary studies later than this ; so no other Pope is probable as the Rule's originator. Suppose the idea was started in 522, the work might be completed in 526. I cannot believe it was done quickly.

I leave this hypothesis about Hormisdas and Dionysius, (not as a wild one, but as the only one I can think of, which at all fits the facts or probabilities of the case,) to the judgment of others. It is wholly impossible to prove, and will cease even to be reasonable if a more probable theory can be invented.

ADDITIONAL NOTE

THE VERSES ABOUT SIMPLICIUS

A difficulty may be raised on the score of Simplicius. Peter the deacon says of him: ' Simplicius SS. Benedicti discipulus, ac post eum tertius in Cassino abbas effectus, Regulam quam suus Magister condiderat, publice legendam omnibus monachis tradidit '. (*De uiris ill. Cas.* V). Peter did not invent this: he made it up out of the verses found in a few copies of the Rule. Traube edited them carefully from 11 MSS. (*Textgesch. der Reg. S. Ben.* 2d ed. 1910, pp. 86-7). I quote the last 5 of the 9 lines:

hocque Benedictus pater	constituit sacrum uolumen,
haec mandauitque	suis seruare alumnis.
Simplicius Christi	quod famulusque minister
magistri latens	opus propagauit in omnes.
una tamen mercis	utroque manet in aeternum.

They are meant for hexameters. A Turin MS., 10th c., has *late* for *latens*, and Mabillon knew another witness.

Closely connected with these verses is the letter of the abbot of Fondi to Simplicius, which I cite from Mabillon, *Annales*, vol. I, p. 17:

Reuerentissimo monachorum Patri Simplicio, B. Abbas Monasterii apud Fundanam urbem, *obedientiae subiectionem.*

Experientia compertum est, multorum Rectorum mores uarias uiuendi normas in monasteriis peperisse. Hinc factum est ut iam omnia monasteria Campaniae, Samniae, Valeriae, Tusciae, Liguriae, et aliarum prouinciarum Italiae, certam et rectam regulam uiuendi, quam sanctissimus et Deo acceptus Benedictus Magister tuus instituit, seruare decreuerint, ut iuxta illam uiuentes, nec ad dexteram nec ad sinistram declinare praesumant. Hanc ergo proposui seruandam huic congregationi, cum nuper me in suum Abbatem elegit indignum.

Quam cupientes in hoc monasterio *sicut in Cassinenensi* obseruare inuiolabiliter, decrevimus *ad Sanctitatem uestram* destinare religiosos ex eadem congregatione uiros Hugonem et Paulum fratres nostros, *iuxta praedictam sanctam Regulam et obseruantiam plenius instruendos in Cassinensi sacra congregatione :* quos commendatos apud *Paternitatem tuam humili obsequio* rogamus. Datum in monasterio prope urbem Fundanam 7 Kal April.

I have underlined the passages which seem to indicate that the forger of this letter was engaged in proving that Fondi had great reverence for Montecassino and particular obligations to it. The date is obviously later than St. Willibald's residence 729-39 when regular observance began; the letter is not quoted by Paul the deacon 780-90. The name *Hugo* and *paternitas tua* will pass in the 8th or 9th century, I think.

The letter does not suppose that Simplicius propagated the Rule; *therefore it is not founded on the verses.* It supposes the Rule to be already universally followed in Italy, except at Fondi, which is 11 miles from Terracina, within easy reach of Capua or of Cassino. Yet it is unlikely that the verses and the letter are wholly independent. On the other hand, the writer of the verses may easily have understood the letter as if Simplicius himself had sent the Rule to Campania, Samnium, Valeria, etc., and so have composed his poem. Traube was obviously wrong in supposing that Simplicius wrote the lines himself; for he would not have put himself by the side of St. Benedict: ' una tamen mercis utroque manet in aeternum '. But some of the MSS. are of the ninth century, so the verses are probably of the eighth.

But if anyone wishes to read *latens,* and to believe in the tradition enshrined in the poem, it might easily be said that during the wars of Justinian in Italy from 354 onwards, and during the ten years that Pope Vigilius was at Constantinople (during which no bishops were consecrated for Italy) there was no monastic reform, and that the propagation of the Holy Rule had ceased; so that Simplicius had to begin anew to publish and advertise it. But it is much more likely that the verses are of no historical value whatever.

CHAPTER XII

CONUERSATIO MORUM

THE reading *conuersatio morum* is certain—In St. Gregory's Dialogues 'conuersatio' means 'monastic observance' and also in his letters—It corresponds to 'conuersari', which is ' to live as a monk '—In the official translation of the Novellae we have irrefragable proof of this meaning—Other examples from the sixth century: Gallican councils, Ferrandus, Cassiodorus—St. Benedict's use is undoubtedly the same.—' Conuersatio morum ' means ' monasticity of behaviour '—This cant meaning is parallel to many such uses—The new Thesaurus has explained the word wrongly—Approximations to this meaning from the fifth century in Cassian, Jerome, Paulinus and others.

IT has long been admitted as certain that the best MSS. of the Holy Rule are to be followed in the reading *conuersatio morum* for the usual *conuersio morum*. I propose to show that in St. Benedict's time *conuersatio*, though still retaining its old significations, had come to be used absolutely for *monastica conuersatio*, *monachica conuersatio*, *sancta conuersatio;* so that the mere word *conuersatio* alone meant ' monastic observance ', ' monastic life '.

It will be interesting to trace the origin of this usage, if possible. But it will be best to work backwards, by first giving proof of the usage itself, after St. Benedict's time, by St. Gregory the Great and others, and only afterwards outlining the earlier evidence which anticipates or approximates to the developed meaning.

I take St. Gregory's Dialogues, which I have examined myself for this purpose, and his Letters, where I have used Hartmann's admirable index. The amount of matter is more than sufficient, without his other writings.

Dialogues.

I 1, cumque tam magna CONUERSATIONE polluerit ('extreme asceticism' in a boy at home).

ibid. exempla eximiae CONUERSATIONIS dedit

ibid. usus quidem rectae *conuersationis* est ut praeesse non audeat qui subesse non didicerit.

II *Praef.,* sanctae CONUERSATIONIS habitum quaesiuit

1, quanta Benedictus puer CONUERSATIONIS gratia in perfectione coepisset.

ibid. sanctae CONUERSATIONIS habitum

3, praeconio itaque eximiae CONUERSATIONIS celebre nomen eius habebatur.

ibid. deflectere a CONUERSATIONIS itinere

ibid. suaeque conuersationis longe dissimiles

6, Gothus ad CONUERSATIONEM uenit[1]

8, sancti uiri studiis coepit aemulari, eiusque CONUERSATIONI derogare

ibid. CONUERSATIONIS illius opinionem crescere

ibid. CONUERSATIONIS illius appetebat habere laudem

III 14, sanctaemonialis uitae CONUERSATIONEM quaereret

15, multis annis monasterium rexit, discipulorumque animos in studio sanctae CONUERSATIONIS exercuit

18, et in sanctae CONUERSATIONIS regula se fortiter stringens

21, contempto patre CONUERSATIONIS habitum suscepit

22, ibi enim quidam uenerabilis sacerdos erat, qui cum clericis suis, Dei laudibus bonisque operibus intentus, sanctae CONUERSATIONIS uitam ducebat.

IV 9 (*al.* 8), eius [*scil.* S. Benedicti] se regulae in sancta CONUERSATIONE tradiderunt

---

[1] The ordinary editions (usually after the Benedictine Ste Marthe) read *conuersionem ;* but the edition of Dom Rupert Mittermüller (1880) had *conuersationem.* Of Moricca's MSS. only one has *conuersionem* (V1); V 2 has *conuersationis ordinem ;* the rest (including all the best) have *conuersationem.* So Abbot Butler was justified in his view, before Moricca's edition, that *conuersationem* must be right (*Reg. Mon.* p. 149).

37 (*al.* 36), ut inferni eum [Petrum monachum] uidisse et pertimuisse tormenta, etiam si taceret lingua, *conuersatio* quippe loqueretur

40 (*al.* 38), numquam se ad sanctae CONUERSATIONIS habitum uenire . . . iurando testabatur

Twice in the above passages I have italicised *conuersatio* as being used in its ordinary and classical sense. But in the other places it is in small capitals, as it has the particular meaning of 'monastic observance'.

It may be urged that in some places it takes on this meaning by the force of the sentence, or else by the limiting adjectives *magna, recta, eximia* (twice) and *sancta* (seven times). It is more natural to take *eximia conuersatio* to mean 'remarkable observance' than merely 'remarkable way of life'. As to *sancta*, it is an *epitheton ornans;* for we have *sanctae conuersationis habitus* three times, but once merely *conuersationis habitus* (III 21). Other passages are equally convincing: II 1, *quanta conuersationis gratia*; II 3, *conuersationis itinere*; II 6, *Gothus . . . ad conuersationem uenit.*

We find all this confirmed in St. Gregory's letters. The *habitus* CONUERSATIONIS, without epithet, reappears (III Ep. 39, Ewald-Hartmann, vol. I, p. 197, 9). *Sancta* CONUERSATIO of Priests (V 58, Vol. I, p. 370, 7)[1]. Often

---

[1] So *pia conuersatio* of a priest VI, 60, p. 436, 15. The general use of *conuersatio* is fairly common in St. Gregory's letters, besides the special employment illustrated above. In V, 18 (p. 300, 2) 'si CONUERSATIO forte meruerit', as a penitent Abbot is in question, we should probably understand 'monastic behaviour'. Similarly in Ep. XIII, 49, p. 413, 4, of bad monks 'ad uiam rectae CONUERSATIONIS reducere, evidently means 'the way of true monastic life'. Again III, 17 (p. 175, 13-5): 'Religiosam uitam eligentibus, congrua nos oportet consideratione prospicere, ne cuiusdam necessitatis occasio aut desides faciat, aut robur (quod absit) CONUERSATIONIS infringat'. II, 35 (p. 131, 17): 'antiqua eius CONUERSATIO', of an Abbot. The monastic sense of *conuersatio* is particularly common in the commentary on I Kings, delivered orally by St. Gregory, and taken down in shorthand by Claudius. These lectures were obviously given to monks; and their testimony to this usage is just as valuable for the period as if we had St. Gregory's own words. But I do not quote the instances, as I am told I have already given too much evidence.

we have *monachica* CONUERSATIO (VI 12, p. 391, 5);
gratiam monachicae CONUERSATIONIS *appetit* (IX 157, vol.
II, p. 159, 1); so I 40 (p. 55, 19) in one MS.; whereas
all the MSS. read *monachica conuersio* in XI 15 (vol. II p.
277, 21) and *religiosa conuersio* in VII 33 (p. 482, 10); but
in XI 216 (vol. II p. 203, 18) one MS. has *religiosa* CON-
UERSATIO rightly.

That *monachica* is not wanted for the sense is shown
by V 28 (p. 309, 1) 'postquam *a monachica* CONUERSA-
TIONE culpae lapsus abripuit, iugum dominii, quod
euadere *in* CONUERSATIONE permanens poterat, recog-
noscat', since *in* CONUERSATIONE alone has the same
sense. (The reference is to a slave who became a
monk, and had to revert to servitude on quitting
the monastery.) The same use in X 9 (vol. II p. 244,
12), 'praeterea monasteriis omnibus fraternitas uestra
districtius interdicat, ut eos quos *ad conuertendum*
susceperint, priusquam biennium *in* CONUERSATIONE compleant, nullo modo audeant tonsorare'. Compare also
II 42 (p. 142, 5) 'inculpabiliter in qua sunt CON-
UERSATIONE *uel habitu* perseuerent', of deacons and
religious persons.

In another passage *conuersatio* seems to mean a
particular religious discipline: when an Abbot dies,
his successor is to be elected out of the monastery
itself, or from some Abbey 'of the same observance',
VIII, 17 (vol. II, p. 19, 24): 'non extraneus, nisi *de
eadem* CONUERSATIONE'.

Of a *praepositus* to be appointed 'qui uitae meritis
dignum CONUERSATIONIS suae praebeat documentum'.
(Ep. VII, 10, p. 453, 13) and 'arto CONUERSATIONIS
(*apto* MSS.) itinere' (*ibid.* as in *Dial.* II 3).

Conuersio, on the other hand, is used to mean not
only conversion to the faith (as II 4, p. 103, 19;

VI 45, p. 420, 21)[1], but also 'entrance into the religious state':

I 40 (p. 55, 19): 'a clericatu in monachicam *conuersionem* uenire' (one MS. *conuersatione*).

III 64 (p. 226, 5): 'non poterant ea ipsa monasteria quae milites suscepissent, alienas res reddere, atque ad *conuersionem* homines tantummodo habere?'

VI 47 (p. 422, 24): 'tibi eius *conuersio* proficiat ad mercedem'.

VIII 9 (vol. II, p. 13): 'in monasteriis *conuerti* festinant . . . iuxta normam regularem debent in suo habito per triennium probari, et tunc monachicum habitum Deo auctore suscipere . . . non est eorum *conuersio* renuenda; . . . Imperator . . . libenter eorum *conuersionem* suscipit (of soldiers).

XI 30 (pp. 300, 27; 301, 1) illius *conuersio* . . . *conuersionis* gratia.

I 14 *a* (p. 14, 31): '*conuersionis* meae primordia reducens in animum'.

On the other hand we ought probably to read *conuersatio* in VII 33 (p. 482, 10): 'dilectionem uestram religiosam *conuersionem* non solum nomine sed etiam tenere uita monstrauit', since it is not entrance but perseverance which is in question.

It is thus beginning to appear that as *conuersio*, 'entrance into the religious state', is the noun connected with the verb '*conuerti*', 'to enter into the religious state', so, on the other hand, *conuersatio* is 'living as a religious', while *conuersari* is the verb 'to be a religious'.

Instances of these two verbs are therefore needed:

A. *Conuerti festinant* has just been seen.

Also 'quos ad *conuertendum* susceperint, priusquam biennium in *conuersatione* compleant . . .' just above.

[1] Other instances (XI, 36, vol. II, p. 308: *Dial.* II, 19 multitudo . . . conuersa; II, 31 ab arrianae hereseos prauitate conuersus est) of the verb suggest that we should read *conuersio* in IV. 46 (*al.* 44) 'ad fructuosam paenitentiam eorum corda conuertere (conuerti, 2 MSS.) atque ipsa conuersione (conuersatione, 4 MSS.) saluare'.

Dial. I 2 in discipulatu illius *conuersus*[1] atque eruditus est.

II 17 eiusdem Benedicti Patris fuerat admonitione *conuersus*.
18 quem ipse *conuersum* nosti (i.e. ' after he became a monk ').
IV 40 (*al* 38) *conuerti* paratus sum (' to become a monk).
IX 197 (II, p. 185, 34), intransitive: ingredientibus monasterium *conuertendi* gratia.

These examples will suffice for *conuerti*, as the usage is not strange, and it continued into the Middle Ages, so that ' lay-brothers ' were known as *conuersi*.

B.   For *conuersari* the evidence is more limited as to date, so St. Gregory's use[2] is important :

Dial. II 23, sanctimoniales feminae . . . in loco proprio CONUERSABANTUR.

III 18, frater quidam mecum EST in monasterio CONUERSATUS. 33 in hac urbe in meo monasterio CONUERSATUS.

Epp. IX 114, vol. II p. 119, 29: ut CONUERSANTES ibidem (nuns) magnum in uobis subsidium, sicut decet, inueniant.

I 14 *a*, p. 15, 1 : propter quod in eo (monasterio S. Andreae) monachicum habitum et CONUERSANDI sumpsi (diuinae potentiae gratia protegente) principium.

I 40, p. 55, 15: in monasterio quo ab initio CONUERSATUS EST (one MS. *conuersus*).

---

[1] For *conuersus*, the second hand of one MS. has the correction *conuersatus*, wrongly.   So *Ep.* X, 1, (II, p. 237, 17), one MS. has *conuersatus* wrongly, and also in X, 9, (II, p. 244, 4).

[2] I add *ex abundantia* a few extra examples from St. Gregory: *Hom. in Evang.* XXXVIII, 15, uno omnes ardore *conuersae*, . . . cumque diutius essent in eadem CONUERSATIONE. . . .

ibid. 16. Ante biennium frater quidam in monasterium meum, quod iuxta beatorum martyrum Joannis et Pauli ecclesiam situm est, gratia CONUERSATIONIS uenit, . . . quem frater suus ad monasterium, non CONUERSATIONIS studio, sed carnali amore secutus est. Is autem qui ad CONUERSATIONEM uenerat ualde fratribus placebat. . . .
ferre non poterat si quisquam illi de sancti habitus CONUERSATIONE loqueretur . . . Nunquam se ad sanctae CONUERSATIONIS habitum uenire . . . *conuerti* paratus sum (as in *Dial.* IV, 40).
longis et continuis in CONUERSATIONE eadem flagellis eruditus.
Hom. XIX, 7 : Praesenti anno in monasterio mea quod iuxta . . . frater quidam ad *conuersionem* uenit, deuote susceptus est, sed ipse deuotius est CONUERSATUS.   Hunc ad monasterium frater suus corpore, non corde secutus est. Nam ualde *conuersionis* (?) uitam et habitum detestans, . . . quis illum umquam seruari ad *conuersionem* crederet?

V 51, p. 351, 9: quem diu mecum didicere in monasterio CONUERSATUM.

V 57 a, p. 365, 13-4: in monasteriis CONUERSARI.

VIII 17 (p. 19, 13): quatenus CONUERSANTES illic in Dei seruitio.

VIII 32 (p. 34, 13): si quemquem illic praue CONUERSARI (at Cassiodorus's monastery).

Let us now turn to earlier evidence in the same century. We have seen St. Gregory's usage 593-600; I take next the testimony of the ' Vulgate ' translation of Justinian's *Novellae.* It seems to be an official rendering: its Latin is redolent of the sixth century; it is earlier than the more accurate translation given at the foot of the page by Schoell and Kroell (Berlin, 1895), which is itself early. I think we may date the ' Vulgate ' rendering as a whole soon after Justinian's death in 565; but the translations of the various laws may well be contemporary with the laws themselves, which range from 533 to 565 (not counting the five of Justin II of 566-575).

The crucial importance of these translations is obvious, for the sense in which CONUERSATIO is employed is not merely to be gathered from the context, but can be determined by the Greek original.

Novella V. de Monachis, A.D. 535.

1. *Praef.* ὁ ἐν ἀσκήσει μοναστικὸς βίος, CONUERSATIONIS monachilis uita.

2. *Ibid.* εἰ τοίνυν μέλλοι τις ἔσεσθαι μοναχὸς ἀκριβής, δεῖ καὶ τῆς τῶν θείων αὐτῷ λογίων παιδείας καὶ ἀσκήσεως ἀκρίβους, si quis igitur futurus est monachus perfectus, indiget et diuinorum eloquiorum eruditione et CONUERSA-TIONIS integritate.

3. c. 2. τοὺς εἰς μονήρη βίον παραγγέλλοντας, eos qui singularem CONUERSATIONEM profitentur.

4. *ibid.* καί τινα τῶν εἰς ἄσκησιν παραγγελλόντων, et aliquem horum qui CONUERSATIONEM professi sunt.

5. *ibid.* Ζώσιμος ὁ θεοφιλέστατος, ἀνὴρ περιβόητος ἐν ἀσκήσει, Zosimus Deo amabilis, uir famosissimus in CONUERSATIONE.

6. *ibid.* μοναχικὴν ὑποδυόμενος ἄσκησιν, monachicam simulans CONUERSATIONEM.

7. *ibid.* φαίνοιτο δὲ ὁ τὰ τοιαῦτα ἐγκαλούμενος καὶ ἐξ αὐτῆς τῆς ἀσκήσεως σεμνός τε καὶ ἐπιεικής, appareat is qui in talibus accusatur ex ipsa CONUERSATIONE honestus ac mitis.

8. *ibid.* μένειν αὐτὸν ἐπὶ τῆς ἀσκήσεως βουλόμεθα, manere eum in CONUERSATIONE uolumus.

9. c.3. ἐπείτοιγε τοὺς ἀλλοὺς ὅσοις εἰς πλῆθος ἡ ἄσκησις ἐστίν, alioquin alios, quibuscumque inter multitudinem CONUERSATIO est.

10. *ibid.* γενήσεται γὰρ ἡ τῶν παλαιοτέρων πολιτεία τῆς νεότητος ἀκριβὴς παιδαγωγία, fiet enim seniorum CONUERSATIO iuuentutis educatio perfecta.

11. *ibid.* καὶ τὴν παραδεδομένην αὐτοῖς ἄσκησιν ἀμέμπτως τηροῦντες, et traditam sibi CONUERSATIONEM inculpabiliter obseruantes.

12. c. 7. εἰ δὲ ἀπολιπὼν τὸ μοναστήριον καθ᾽ ὅπερ τὴν ἄσκησιν εἶχεν, si uero relinquens monasterium in quo CONUERSATIONEM habuit.

13. c. 8. εἰ δέ τις τῶν μοναχικὴν ἐπαγγειλαμένων ἄσκησιν, si quis autem monachicam profitentium CONUERSATIONEM.

14. *ibid.* καθαρὰν φυλάττων τὴν ἄσκησιν, puram seruans CONUERSATIONEM.

15. *ibid.* οἷα τὴν προτέραν ἄσκησιν, καὶ τὸν μονήρη

καταισχύνων βίον, tanquam priorem CONUERSATIONEM et solitariam confundens uitam.

Nouella 76, A.D. 538.

16. χωρίσαι μὲν ἑαυτὴν τῆς κοινῆς ταύτης, διαίτης, ἐν δέ τινι γυναικῶν ἀσκητηρίῳ καταμεῖναι, segregare se a communi ista *conuersatione*, et in quodam mulierum monasterio commanere.

Nouella 123, A.D. 546.

17. c. 1. ἴσασιν αὐτὸν ἐν μοναστηρίῳ οὐχ ἧττον δεκαπέντε ἐνιαυτῶν μοναχικὸν βίον ἐκτελέσαντα, sciunt eum in monasterio non minus quindecim annis monachicam CONUERSATIONEM implesse.

18. c. 35, ἀποπειράσθω τῆς τούτου ἀναστροφῆς ὁ τοῦ μοναστηρίου ἡγούμενος, experiatur huius CONUERSATIONEM monasterii praesul.

19. c. 36. ὥστε ἀμοιβαδὸν ἀλλήλοις μαρτυρίαν τῆς σώφρονος διαγωγῆς παρέχειν αὐτούς, ut mutuum alterutris testimonium castae CONUERSATIONIS praebeant.

20. *ibid.* διὰ τὴν χρονίαν ἐν μοναστηρίῳ ἄσκησιν, propter longaeuam in monasterio CONUERSATIONEM.

21. c. 37 ἐπὶ γὰρ τοῖς προσώποις ἅτινα εἰς μοναστήριον ἢ ἀσκητήριον εἰσέλθωσι, καὶ καταλείψωσι τὴν τοιαύτην σώφρονα ἀναστροφήν, in personis enim quae in monasterium uel asceterium ingrediuntur, et relinquunt huiusmodi castam CONUERSATIONEM.

Nouella 133, A.D. 539:

22. c. 1, μίαν εἶναι τὴν αὐτῶν συνέλευσιν, una sit eorum [*sc.* monachorum] CONUERSATIO.

23. c. 4. τὸν . . . μοναστηρίου προεστῶτα συνεχῶς
ἐποπτεύειν καὶ περιεργάζεσθαι τὴν ἑκάστου πολίτειαν τε καὶ
κατάστασιν, monasterii praesulem frequenter inspicere
et perscrutari uniuscuiusque CONUERSATIONEM et disciplinam.

24. ibid. μηδὲ ἀπολέσθαι ψυχὴν πρὸς τὴν ἐκ τῆς
ἀσκήσεως σωτηρίαν καταφεύγουσαν, et perire animam ad
salutem CONUERSATIONIS confugientem.

25. c. 6 οἷα τὸν ἐν αἰσχύνῃ βίον τῆς ἀγγελικῆς ταύτης
καταστάσεως ἀλλαξάμενον, utpote in confusionem uitae
angelicam hanc CONUERSATIONEM mutantem.

If we take the Latin by itself, we see that in every case
but one (No. 16) the meaning of *conuersatio* is ' monastic
discipline '. In most cases this meaning is induced by
an adjective; but the word is sometimes absolute: 4.
qui conuersationem professi sunt; 5. *famosissimus in conuer-*
satione; 8. *manere in conuersatione,* etc.

When subsequently we turn to the Greek, we find that
the translator means nothing less than ' monastic discipline '
in the great majority of cases. This confirms the previous
conclusions with regard to St. Gregory the Great, that
he intends this sense even when he adds *monachica, sancta,*
eximia, etc., as epithets.

As for our translator, he takes *conuersatio* to be the
natural rendering of ἄσκησις, the life of a monk or
ascetic, monastic discipline. FIFTEEN TIMES ἄσκησις is the
word translated; once it is κατάστασις (which he has
elsewhere alternatvely rendered by *disciplina*). But the
meaning of the word is so definitely monastic that he
uses it also to translate βίος (twice), πολιτεία (twice),
ἀναστροφή, (twice), διαγωγή, when they have a monastic

epithet. Once it is for συνέλευσις (living in community); only once for 'worldly conversation' (No. 16), κοινή δίαιτη.

This equivalence of ἄσκησις and *conuersatio* in laws of 535–546, exactly in St. Benedict's time, is of great interest. Ἄσκησις had long been the technical word for monastic observance. In the fourth century it is already the ordinary word in St. Basil (ἄσκησις, ἀσκήτης, ἀσκητήριον ἀσκητικὸς βίος), Palladius, Evagrius, etc. The word had never meant merely 'mode of life', but always implied a life of training, usually severe training. So Galen is quoted for ἄσκησις τῆς ὁσιότητος, an inscription for ἄσκησις ἱππική, Lucian for ἀσκούμενος τὴν κυνικὴν ἄσκησιν. Josephus has this last expression. But when Cynics were forgotten, and monks were counted by tens of thousands, 'ascetic' and 'asceticism' gained their modern meaning. Just in the same way, CONUERSATIO from meaning 'way of life' came to mean that particular way of life which the Greek world called ἄσκησις, and for which the moderns have invented the expressions 'monachism' or 'monasticism'.

The verbs *conuerti* and *conuersari* are less common in the translation of the *Novellae* :

Nov. 5, c. 5, καὶ μετὰ τὸ παραγγεῖλαι τὸν ἀποτατόμενον εἰς μοναχούς, et postquam abrenuntians CONUERSATUS FUERIT inter monachus.

Nov. 123, c. 1. ἐπί δεκαπέντε ἐνιαυτοὺς ἐν μοναστηρίῳ διαγαγόντα, qui . . . quindecim annis in monasterio CONUERSATUS EST

Elsewhere it is in a bad sense: *Nov.* 123, c. 29, 'cum muliere conuersari'; 133, c. 6, 'in aliquam tabernarum conuersari'. We find *conuerti* for entrance into religious life or 'renunciation', *Nov.* 76, c.1, τοῖς μετ' αὐτὴν (sc. διάταξιν) ἀποτατομένοις ἀνδράσιν ἢ

γυναιξί, et his qui postea *conuertentur* uiris et mulieribus
posita sit.[1]

We have seen the technical use of *conuersatio* in the
official letters of a great Pope, and in the probably official
translation of a great Emperor's laws. We can find it
also in ecclesiastical councils in Gaul of the same date.
The excellent edition by Friedrich Maassen in M.G.
makes investigation easy. In the first place I take a series
of canons which deal with a period of one year's strictness
of life before the ordination of laymen to the diaconate,
priesthood, or even episcopate. The first council is given
from Mansi (VII, 883), as it is before Maassen's period
(date uncertain) ; consequently no MSS. can be quoted.

1.   *Conc. Arausicanum*, can. (p. 43): nisi qui prius *con-
            uersionis* proposito professi fuerint castitatem.

2. 524.   *Conc. Arelatense*, can. I (p. 36): episcopatus uero
            uel presbyterii honorem nullus laicus ante
            praemissam CONUERSATIONEM uel ante triginta
            aetatis annos accipiat.

3.   *ibid.*   can. II (p. 37): nisi anno integro
            fuerit ab eis praemissa *conuersio*.

4. 538.   *Conc. Aurelianense*, can. VI (p. 75): De clericorum
            praemittenda CONUERSATIONE id omnimodis
5.   obseruetur, ne ullus ex laicis ante annualem
            CONUERSATIONEM uel aetatem legitimam . . .

6.   *ibid.*   can. XI (p. 76): pro nouitate
            CONUERSATIONIS ac fidei (of newly baptized
            persons).

7. 549.   *Conc. Aurelianense*, can. IX (p. 103): ut nullus ex
            laicis absque annua CONUERSATIONE prae-
            missa. . . .

---

[1] A Latin law in the code, I, 3, 54, in 534, supplies the following examples:
No. 2: ' se diuino deputare seruitio, et a saeculari conuersatione recedere
ac sanctimonialium uitam uiuere '.

ib. 3: ' saeculi istius uitam contemnens, in sanctimonialium *conuersatione*
uiuere.

ib. 6: nullo eis impedimento ex sanctimoniali *conuersatione* generando.

ib. 7: in monasterio uel clericatu . . . sanctimonialem uitam elegerint,
ad saecularem autem conuersationem remeauerint.

I give the readings of Maassen's MSS. in a table:

MSS.	Cent.	C.Arelat. 524		C.Aurelian. 538			ibid. 549
		2	3	4	5	6	7
C	6-7th						-sione
K	7th	-satione	-sio	-tione	-sationem	-sationis	-sione
R	8-9th	-satione	-sio	-sationem	-sationem	-sationis	-satione
H	8th	-satione	-sio	-sione	-sionem	-sionis	-satione
A	9th	-satione	-sio	-sione	-sionem	-sionis	-satione
B	10-11th			-sione	-sionem	-sionis	-satione
L	7-8th	-satione	-sio	-sione	-sionem	-sionis	-sione
P	9th	-sione	-sio	-sione	-sione	-sionis	
T	8-9th	-sione	-sio	-satione	-sationem	-sionis	-sione
I	9th	-sione	-sio	-sationem	-sationem	-sionis	-sione
N	9th	-sionem	-sio	-sione	-sionem	-sionis	-sione
S	9th	-sione	-sio				

Maassen's text is usually that of the oldest MS., with all its bad spellings. I have corrected these, for K is very wild.

1. In no. 3 all have *conuersio*, which is probably right on account of the correct cretici, *praem͞ssă cōnuersĭo*, for the canons have metrical endings.

2. But the same *praemissa conu.* appears also in 2, 4 and 7, and the readings are doubtful.

3. The best MS. of the fourth family, R, has *conuersatio* in all the remaining cases. The sub-family, HA with B, agrees in two places, but not in the council of 538. But precisely in these places R is supported by K or by K T I. Thus we trust the fourth family's spelling, since it is again supported by K and L in no. 2. Only in no. 7 does this family stand alone.

It seems clear, therefore, that H A B have a later reading in the council of 538, and that *conuersatio* is the right reading in all places, except no. 3.

The same result is reached by noticing that the MSS. which never have *conuersatio* are P, N, S, all of the ninth century. The evidence suggests that in the eighth century it was a habit to correct *conuersatio* into *conuersio*. We saw that later MSS. had substituted *conuersio* in St. Gregory once or twice. We shall see the same in the Rule of St. Benedict.

More than half a century after St. Gregory's death, St. Aldhelm still uses *conuersatio* as the natural word for monasticism. But I do not see (from Ehwald's Index in M.G.) that he uses it ' absolutely '. He has *monastica conuersatio* thrice, *casta c.* thrice, *sancta c.* 4 times, *pudica. rigida, practica,* and so forth ; and he uses *conuersari* in the monastic sense, e.g., ' sub regimine *coenobii conuersantium.* I have not found the absolute use in the middle of the seventh century ; and though my researches have not been thorough, I venture to infer that it was no longer so common, and I regard it as a sixth century usage in the main.

Turning back to contemporaries of St. Benedict, I find some examples in the life of St. Fulgentius (by Ferrandus of Carthage, as it seems), both of *conuersari* and of *conuersatio :*

Vita Fulg. c. 3. (7), et sub ipsa professione laica, iam monachus CONUERSABATUR.

c. 8 (5), ambo (monks) moribus similes, ambo meliores proposito, CONUERSATIONE aequales, unus scientia superior (' equal in their monastic observance ', not ' with the same length of monastic life ').

Prol. 2. ne obliuione longa CONUERSATIONIS eius bona nescirentur (the excellence of his ascetic life).

c. 14 (29), plurimosque ad *conuersionem* piis monitis inuitando, monachorum numerum multiplicat, et magnae CONUERSATIONIS (so MS., but edd. have ' congregationis ') efficitur. (Here the distinction between *conuersio*, the entrance, and *conuersatio*, the continued life, is evident).[1]

Cassiodorus, five or ten years younger than St. Benedict, has *conuersatio* in the monastic sense:

Inst. diu. litt. 29: 'Secundus illis [rusticis] ordo CONUERSA-TIONIS purissimus imponatur', (see above, p. 159).

Hist. trip. I. 11: 'qui[1] CONUERSATIONE *monachica* illo tempore fruebantur . . . Haec ergo philosophia (monachism) [2]*conuersatione* miranda . . . docet . . . Animae uero puritate et bonorum actum [3]*conuersatione*, . . . [4]*conuersatione* solitaria . . . huius uitae [5]*conuersatio*. Alii dicunt huic causam fuisse [6]*conuersationi* persecutiones, quae religionis causa per tempora prouenerunt . . . hanc [in] [7]*conuersationem* usque perduxit Antonius, maximus monachorum.' This is all from Sozomen I 12-3, whose Greek has [1]τήν μοναστικὴν πολιτείαν, ([2] not in the Greek) [3]πολιτείᾳ πράξεων ἀγαθῶν, [4]μεμονωμένους, [5]ταυτμν τοῦ βίου τὴν διαγωγήν, [6]ταύτῃ (τῇ φιλοσοφίᾳ), (om in) cap. 13, τοῦ βίου τὴν διαγωγὴν. We see how Cassiodorus regards *conuersatio* as the regular word for 'monastic life', whatever the Greek.

VIII, 1, *tit.* 'De CONUERSATIONE, miraculis et responsionibus uel scriptis diuersorum monachorum, necnon et episcoporum.

ib. propter abstinentiam, *conuersationem* (βίου) mores atque miracula. *ib.*, fin: *conuersationem* (βίου).

VIII, 1. 'usque ad senium optime conuersatus' (πολιτευ--σάμενον, Soz. VI 29), etc. etc.

In Ps. 33, v. 6, P.L. 70, col. III (235): 'Quod accidere solet iustis, quando *in sancta conuersatione* animas reddunt.

In Ps. 36, v. 38, col. 126-7 (269): qui transierit ad Deum *sanctissima conuersatione.*

---

[1] *Conuersio* for 'entrance' is frequent:

3. (8), (*conuersio sui cordis*),

Prol. 3, salutiferis eius monitis ad suscipiendam professionem monachorum *conuersus.*

3. (7), inter ipsa conuersionis initia (yet it is possible that better MSS. might give us conuersationis!)

5. (12), ex toto corde *conuersum.*

19. (39), si quos autem nouos monachos uel in isto uel in illo monasterio Christus acquireret, tempus inter se *conuersionis* ordinemque seruarent.

In another contemporary Abbot, Eugippius,[1] there is only

Vita S. Severini, 4: daturus nihilominus formam, sollicitius admonebat beatorum patrum uestigiis inhaerere, quibus sanctae CONUERSATIONIS adquireretur instructio.

Cp. *Paschasius, Ep. ad Eugippium*, 3 'facilius uirtutes magistrorum a discipulis exponuntur, quae suggeruntur crebrius CONUERSATIONE docentium.

I think in both places the 'monastic' use was in the mind of the writers, 'ascetic life'.

Enough has now been given of sixth century evidence. It is time to turn to St. Benedict himself.

1. *Prologus*: Processu uero CONUERSATIONIS et fidei, dilatato corde, inenarrabili dilectionis dulcedine curritur uia mandatorum Dei. '*In the progress of monastic observance and of faith*'.

2. c. 1 non CONUERSATIONIS feruore nouitio. 'Not in the first fervour of religious life '.

3. *ibid*. De quorum omnium horum miserrima CONUERSATIONE melius est silere quam loqui. 'Of whose religious observance, the most pitiable among those here mentioned, it is better to be silent than to speak '.

4. c. 21 fratres boni testimonii et sanctae CONUERSATIONIS, 'brethren of good report and holy observance '.

5. c. 22. lectisternia pro modo CONUERSATIONIS . . . accipiant, 'let them be given bedding suited to their monastic state '.

6. c. 58 *init*. Nouiter ueniens quis ad CONUERSATIONEM, non ei facilis tribuatur ingressus, 'one who comes for the first time to religious life '.

7. *ibid*. promittat de stabilitate sua et CONUERSATIONEM MORUM SUORUM.

8. c. 63. ordines suos . . . ita conseruent, ut CONUERSATIONIS tempus et uitae meritum discernit, 'according as they

[1] A somewhat older Abbot than St. Benedict, Dionysius Exiguus, has *sancta conuersatio* (of Pope Gelasius, in letter to Julianus presb., in Thiel, *Epp. Rom. Pontt.* p. 286), and in translations, *recta conu., angelica conuersatio. Sancta conuersatione* in Pelagius I. to Bp. of Arles, P.L. 69, 405. The expression is frequent enough in most writers.

are distinguished by length of religious profession and merit of life, and '.

9. c. 73, ut . . . uel honestatem morum aut initium CONUERSATIONIS nos demonstremus habere, ' in order that we may prove that we possess both morality of conduct and also a beginning of religious observance '.

10. ibid. ceterum ad perfectionem CONUERSATIONIS qui festinat, sunt doctrinae SS. Patrum, ' however for one who is hastening on to the perfection of religious observance there are the teachings of the holy Fathers.

c. 2, non conuertenti ex seruitio praeponatur ingenuus, ' the free-born is not to be given higher rank than one who becomes a monk from a servile condition.

c. 63. reliqui omnes ut conuertuntur ita sint, ' as for the rest, let them remain in the rank of their date of entrance.[1]

There seems to be no doubt that St. Benedict wrote *conuersatio* in every one of these places. He does not happen to use the verb *conuersari*, nor the substantive *conuersio ;* but he has the verb of the latter, *conuerti*, of which he uses the present participle in an intransitive sense, as in Ps. 84 v. 6, where the reading ' Deus tu conuertens uiuificabis nos ' is an ancient variant for *conuersus*, which is still followed in the Missale Romanum.

There seems also to be no doubt that the sense of *conuersatio* is usually ' monastic observance ' (as in St. Gregory) of necessity, and in all cases it is more probably to be rendered thus : in fact it would everywhere be awkward to translate it merely as ' behaviour ' neither good nor bad. Even in Nos. 3 and 4, where there is an epithet, the sense implies

[1] I give the MS. variants from Dom Butler's notes, *Reg. Monast.* 2d ed., 1927, ' Lectiones selectae '. No. 2, conuersationis A B C T K O V S, conuersionis X *recentes edd.* No. 6, ad conuersationem A K X O V *al*, ad conuersionem B T S. No. 7, conuersatione A B X O V S, conuersione T K *Paul, Hild, Smaragd.* No. 8, conuersationis A B T K O *al* Hild, conuersionis V S *recc. Paul.* A is St. Gall 914, which represents the autograph. D is the 7th cent. Bodleian codex, the leader of the opposition. For the other MSS. see Butler. Of course I should regularly follow A against the rest, (with Traube, Plenkers, Morin, etc., against Abbot Butler's theories).

'monastic' behaviour; and in No. 10, the sense is fixed by No. 9.

The former conclusion must therefore be repeated here: *conuerti* and *conuersio* are of the entrance to religion; *conuersari* and *conuersatio* are of the practice of religious life.

The meaning of CONVERSATIO MORUM is therefore plain enough.

But it is difficult to translate, because we have no single word for this peculiar sense of *conuersatio* either in Latin or in modern languages.   There is no substantive from *monachicus* or *monasticus*; and *conuersatio* was used precisely for the want of some barbarism like *monachicitas* or *monasticitas*! In Greek ἄσκησις is near enough. But in Latin, *exercitatio* did not take on this specialized meaning, —just because *conuersatio* did.

Let us boldly say in English

' MONASTICITY OF BEHAVIOUR '

or ' OF CONDUCT ', though ' behaviour ' and ' conduct' are both slightly more external than *mores*.

For we cannot use a double word with a genitive, or a word with two genitives, as for example,

> Religious-behaviour of morals
> Monastic-behaviour of morals
> Strictness-of-life of behaviour.

The only way is to paraphrase the genitive by ' as to ' or ' in ',

> Religious observance as to conduct,
> Monastic conduct as to my behaviour,
> Monastic observance in my conduct

Consequently a literal translation is quite impossible; and the only exact rendering must be a solecism, as I have said ; ' MONASTICITY of conduct, of life, of behaviour '. The best paraphrase will be simply ' *let him promise to live as a monk should live* '.

There is nothing astonishing in the fact that *conuersatio* in the sixth century acquired a technical sense besides its usual sense. The phenomenon is common enough ; yet it may be well to give examples.

' Virtue ' is far more common (in Latin, Italian, French, English) in its restricted sense of a *good* habit, than in its original meaning of strength, power.

' Religion ' is still far commonest (in the same languages) in its general sense. But ' religion ', ' religious ' have a restricted sense which is easily understood when we say ' he entered religion ', ' religious life '.

' Order ' is common in its general and original sense. But ' holy Orders ' and ' Religious order ' give narrower senses, which are easily understood without the epithet, if we say ' he is taking orders ', or ' what order will he join? ' Here is an exact parallel to *sancta conuersatio* or *monachica conuersatio* with the epithet dropped, as we have found it in St. Gregory.

Again, ' good cheap ' became so common, and ' dear cheap ' so unusual, that ' cheap ' alone, without epithet, survived, and the original senses of ' market ' or ' bargains ' are now obsolete. But in the case of ' bargain ' the general sense remains, and we still say, ' a good bargain ' or ' a bad bargain '; yet ' a bargain ', ' a bargain sale ' have the restricted sense of ' good for the purchaser ', less good (except indirectly) for the seller. This is again exactly parallel to the use of *couversatio* without adjective.

The verb *conuersari* only takes on this limited meaning when the sense of the sentence demands it : it seems not to have become a cant phrase like the noun *conuersatio*.

As for *conuerti* and *conuersio*, their general sense of ' turn-ing towards ' had long since been used in particular of change of religion ; the use for the change from secular to monastic life was simple and obvious, like the modern use by certain sects in England and America of ' con-version ' for a particular form of religious emotion.[1]

If we turn to the *Thesaurus Linguae Latinae*, vol. 4 (1906–9), we find two verbs rightly distinguished :

1. *conuersare*, a frequentative of *conuerto*, used once by Cicero, and by five later writers, so it is rare enough ; and 2. *conuersari*, the very common compound from *uersari ;* so that the two words, identical in form, have been derived from *uertere* by different lines of descent.

Correspondingly the *Thesaurus* distinguishes two sub-stantives of identical form : CONUERSATIO (1) from *con-uersare*, and CONUERSATIO (2) from *conuersari*.

For *conuersatio* (1) the quotations are few : Ps. Aur. Vict. ; Caelius Aurelius *twice ;* Hilary and Tertullian once ; the Vulgate of Ecclesiasticus twice. These last are important, as we have the Greek, in 18²⁴ ἀποστροφή, and in 18²¹ ἐπιστροφή. The *Acta Petri* 26 are quoted for *in conuersatione peccatorum suorum*, whatever that may mean ; and *Passio Petri* 14 has the remarkable *conuersione uidelicet et conuersatione atque cum fide paenitentia hominis*. Out of all these passages, the two from Ecclus., and the two from Caelius (rolling the eyes and turning over in bed) are certain, and suffice to prove the existence of the word. But the *Thesaurus* adds three quotations from ' *Conc. Aurel* a. 524 ' (a misprint for *Conc. Arelat.* in the case of the first two of them) which we have already seen to mean

---

[1] For this ' conversion ', the expression ' he has got religion ' may be employed, so that ' religion ' becomes a cant name for the result of this experience. William James in his amusing book on Religious Experience seems conversely to identify ' religion ' in its abstract sense with these experi-ences, just as if one should think there is no order except holy Order, or no virtue but moral virtue.

'monastic life'; and the last sentence is also clearly wrong: 'Huc pertinet GLOSS. IV, 325, 4, "conuersatio, continentia".' On the contrary, this belongs to *conuersatio* (2).

In fact the evidence given so far leaves no doubt as to the origin of the monastic use of *conuersatio* as a cant word for 'monasticity'. It is simply *conuersatio* (2) for *monastica conuersatio*, like 'cheap' for 'good cheap', 'orders' for 'holy orders'. It had nothing originally to do with 'conversion'.

But it is probable that this cant use did not begin to be common before the sixth century, and did not last long into the seventh. In the eighth and ninth centuries it was obsolete, and wherever an adjective or the form of the sentence did not explain it, the scribe was inclined to turn it into *conuersio*. This corruption in MSS. began soon after St. Gregory the Great, as we saw in the codices of Gallican councils, of St. Benedict, of St. Gregory, etc. In the Carolingian age the cant use had disappeared.

This result seems clear and inevitable. It is quite inconsistent with the suggestions made within the last thirty years, that is, since Dr. Traube in 1898 pointed out the true text of the Holy Rule. Abbot Butler wrote recently, 1927 (*Reg. Mon.* 2d ed. p. 151): 'Scriptores Benedictini recentes uerterunt *conuersatio morum suorum* : "conduct of life according to the Rule"; "Leben und Klösterliche Zucht"; "Lebenswandel in seinen Sitten", "sa manière de vivre".' These are certainly not correct glosses, even if they are (of course) not far from the road.[1]

---

[1] The most elaborate discussion of *conuersatio morum* is by Dom Matthäus Rothenhäusler; it takes 63 pages. (*Zur Aufnahmeordnung der Regula S. Benedicti*, in *Beiträge zur Geschichte des alten Mönchtums*, Heft III, 1; Münster in Westfalen, 1912, pp. 20-82). The moral teaching of St. Benedict is first examined; then follows an interesting account of *abrenuntio prima* and *secunda* in Cassian, his use of *conuersatio*, and especially of *conuersatio actualis*. As St. Benedict used Cassian so freely in the Rule, the essay which comes next, on

If we turn back to Cassian, a good hundred years before St. Benedict (the *Institutes* are of 417-8), we find *conuersatio* a common word, both in its ordinary sense, and (especially) of monastic observance. Yet I cannot find a single instance where it can be said for certain that it means absolutely ' monasticity '; for the turn of the sentence or the epithet gives the shade of meaning. I give some chosen instances, which are sufficient to show that the word is very nearly a technical term, especially nᵒ 7 :

1. *Instit.* II 5, ut etiam his qui erant religionis expertes stupori esset tam ardua *conuersationis* eorum professio.
2. VI 7, angelis imitatione *conuersationis* aequantur.
3. X 7, diuersorum *conuersationes* explorantes (examining the religious observances of others).
4. XII 33, quanto longius a meritis eorum et *conuersatione* distamus (their observance).

    A passage which paraphrases St. Paul (2 Thess. 3⁹) is noticeable:
5. X 10, saltim *conuersationis* exempla sub oculorum fide uobis tradita memoria retineretis . . . et *conuersationis* formam meo labore praeberem.
6. X 18, graue nobis suae *conuersationis* reliquit exemplum.

In these words we recognise that *conuersatio* more easily means good conduct than worldly conduct.

---

moral perfection and contemplation in Cassian, is valuable. The conclusion is reached that *conuersatio morum* in St. Benedict is the equivalent of *abrenuntiatio* in Cassian, and that *conuersatio* merely means *conuersio*. *Conuersio morum* is an expression found in St. Ambrose (on Ps. 118, 59; P.L. 15, 1306), —so Dom Rothenhäusler points out. Cassian uses the verb *abrenuntiari, abrenuntiatio;* for which St. Benedict (he says) uses *conuerti* and *conuersatio.* Dom Rothenhäusler argues from the moral teaching of Cassian to the moral teaching of St. Benedict, in order to define accurately what *conuersio morum* must mean. But though the monastic virtues are (of course) taught in much the same way by both, it does not follow that *abrenuntiatio* corresponds to *conuersatio :* in fact it certainly does not; nor is *conuersatio* the substantive corresponding to *conuerti*, but to *conuersari.* It is a pity so painstaking and learned an investigation should not have led to the right result, because it argued from Cassian to St. Benedict a hundred years later, instead of starting with St. Benedict's own times. In England two hundred years ago ' conversation ' meant ' behaviour '; now it means ' talk '.

Other passages are echoed by St. Benedict, and he took them, presumably, in the technical sense of ' observance ' or ' monasticity ' :

7. *Inst.* IV 39, Per hunc [timorem] et initium CONUERSA-
TIONIS (so S¹ H L T , but conuersationis G S² *v*) et uitiorum purgatio et uirtutum custodia his qui inbuuntur ad uiam perfectionis adquiritur. So *S. Reg.* 73, ' uel honestatem morum aut initium CONUERSATIONIS ', so Petschenig is wrong in reading *conuersionis* with G. as St. Benedict testifies for the sixth century; for the rest of this very chapter is used by St. Benedict to make up most of his twelve steps of humility.

8. *Inst.* XII 30, quod est deterius, etiam perfectionem sibi ex hoc ipso miserabili statu et CONUERSATIONE promittit.
Cp. *S. Reg.* c.i, ' omnium horum miserrima *conuersatione* ', of *gyrouagi*, who resemble the monks of whom Cassian is speaking,—who want to become hermits, or to found a new monastery where they can be superiors.

9. *Coll.* III 15, initium CONUERSATIONIS *et fidei.* So
S. Reg. prol. processu uero *conuersationis et fidei*. But Cassian is using St. Jerome, *Reg. Pachomii*, 190, or half recollecting it: ' fratres probatae *conuersationis et fidei* '. The same words are quoted by the *Reg. Orient.* (Vigilius) c. 21: ' probatae fratres *conuersationis ac fidei* '.

Let us look at St. Jerome:

Reg. S. Pach., praef. (ad fin.), et de fontibus potius quam de riuulis bibant, quos *sanctae conuersationis* studia delectant.
Praecepta et leges S. Pach. 188, quando praepositi domorum fratres de *conuersatione sanctae uitae* docebunt, absque grauissima necessitate nullus aberit.
Vita S. Hilarionis, 14. " Ille fundator et eruditor huius *conuersationis* et studii in hac prouincia fuit.
ibid. 24, in tantum enim a Domino fuerat eleuatus gloriam, ut beatus Antonius, audiens *conuersationem* eius, scriberet ei.
ibid. 1, mihi tanti uiri *conuersatio* uitaque dicenda est.

Sulpitius Severus has ' in monasterii *conuersatione* ' (*Dial.* I. 15, 3). The word is evidently already on the way to the cant meaning.[1]

St. Paulinus of Nola (died 431) has some approximations :

Ep. 5, 13: ' conspectu et uicinia *aemulae conuersationis.* '

10, 3: ' per *conuersationem piam* '.

11, 6: ' ut uno tenore propositi et tempore CONUERSA-TIONIS nostrae apparuit '. (*conuersationis.* O; *conuersionis* F L M P V[2].

Paulinus to Aug. (Aug. Ep. 94. 2, ed. Goldbacher): ' ut de CONUERSATIONIS gloria (of religious life) ad gloriam resurrectionis communem cum matre (Melania) requiem coronamque capturus '.

With the genitive the word is common, e.g.

Victor Vitensis, (died 491) *Hist.* II 6: ' Eugenius coepit per *conuersationem operum bonorum* uenerabilis et reuerendus fieri '.

Faustus Reiensis, *Sermo* 29, p. 338: ' conuersatio uitae bonae '.

Cassiodorus, *Hist. trip.* I, 11; ' bonorum actum *conuersatione* ' (of monks).

The Regula Orientalis (Vigilius diaconus, died 430)[3] has :

[1] In St. Augustine's letters (ed. Goldbacher) I find (of course) *bona conuersatio* (69, 1; 140, 83; 149, 17) and *mala conu.* (65, 1 and 2), and also *sancta conuersatio* (48, 4), *laudabilis conu.* (140, 33); but note also 126, 8: ' propter infirmos, quibus nos praebere ad exemplum bonorum operum *qualicumque conuersatione* conamur ', where a good sense is implied.

[2] Hartel notes, p. XIV: ' Codicis O igitur summam esse sinceritatem atque auctoritatem, qui longe plurimis locis scripturam ueram uel quae a uera proxime abest, offert '. Yet unfortunately he has here written *conuersionis*.

[3] A great monk and bishop, St. Hilary of Arles (bishop 429-49) in the panegyric of St. Honoratus his former abbot, the founder of Lerins:

I. 3: ' sapientis conuersatio in conuersationis fine laudatur '.

1, 8: ' sed illico (in meditatione) in flammam conuersionis nutrita huiusmodi scintilla prorupit '.

ibid : ' condemnari itaque se senectus patris, aetatis illius *conuersatione* (*al.* conuersione) credebat '.

2. 9: ' exemplo ipsius ad conuersionem uocatus '.

2. 9: ' priuatus . . . tunc in *conuersatione* eorum episcopus gerebatur '.

2. 12: ' sanctum Caprasium, *angelica* adhuc in insulis *conuersatione* degentem '.

4. 18: ' Fortissimos quosque et recenti CONUERSATIONE praeualidos in ieiuniis uigiliisque, impar uiribus, pari lege comitatus est '.

c. 1: disciplina iuniorum . . . quae abbatis CONUERSA-
TIONE stabilita firma sit.

c. 2: diligentiam circa omnia quae ad quotidianam custodiam et *conuersationem* monasterii pertinet adhibendam.

c. 17: nec ignoret (praepositus) *conuersationem* suorum, nec
ad eorum scientiam caecus existat.

In the Latin translation of Palladius we find 'hanc
exercuit *conuersationem*' (μέθοδον, II. 7), and 'granderr
uitae *conuersationem* (πολιτείαν, I. 6).

The 'passion of seven monks' (C.S.E.L. VII) c. 12:
'Nemo me separat a sancto patre meo Liberato abbate
et a fratribus meis, qui me in monasterio nutrierunt.
Cum ipsis sum in timore Dei CONUERSATUS, cum ipsis
desidero passionem suscipere'.[1]

These examples from the scanty monastic writings of
the fifth century establish, it seems, that *conuersatio* was
regularly used of monastic life as early as St. Jerome and
Cassian; but it needed an epithet or the form of the sentence
to particularise its meaning. The sparse instances from
Paulinus and Vigilius diaconus are, however, clearer, and
the few later quotations lead us up gradually to the
developed use in the Holy Rule. *I think we may gather
that the 'absolute' use of ' conuersatio' for 'monasticity' had
long been current in the spoken language when St. Benedict wrote,
about 526. But the literary usage had lagged behind, preserving a
greater precision by the addition of suitable adjectives.*

In the seventh century, except in the learned Aldhelm,
the cant employment of *conuersatio* was on the wane, and
in the Carolingian revival it disappeared; so that scribes
habitually altered the word into *conuersio*. Thus the
familiar *conuersio morum* came at an early date into Benedictine tradition.

---

[1] Ennodius has *conuersatio* 52 times, and with the epithet *sancta*, etc.; but
apparently never of religious life in the technical sense.

INDEX

A

Abbot, election of, Justinian's laws compared with H. Rule, 59–63; blessing by Bp., 10, 60n.

Adresponsum, 73n.; see Responsum

Adscripticii, 152n., 154; equivalent , under Justinian to serui, 155

Aldhelm, St., *conuersatio*, 220, 231

Ambrose, St., uses *conuersio morum*, 228n.

Amelli, Abbot, on Cassiodorus's references to the H. Rule, 93–4, 95n.

Apollinarius Sidonius, on dignity of patricius, 186; his nurse's daughter marries son of the nurse of Pudens, 157n.

Aptonius, lately dead in 593, 139; age of his son, 139–40

Augustine, St., son of a decurio, 176; much used by St. Benedict, 33; on slaves, freedmen and rustics becoming monks, 184n.; use of conuersatio, 230n.

B

Baluze, 150n.

Bamberg MS. of Cassiodorus, 159n.

Basil, St., Rule of, 24, 35

Batiffol, 98n.

Bäumer, 98, 103n.

Bede, St., the only monk wellknown as an author or a saint, 172

Bethmann, 134

Benedict I, Pope, 151

Benedict, St., of Nursia (see also Rule H.), first mentioned by St. Gregory, 1; his fame due to reputation for miracles, 9–11, 13, 189; inventor of Compline, 98; of the eighth canonical hour, 98; completed the form of the Little Hours, 103n.; introduced Hymns as a regular part of Office, 103n.; common date

for his death founded on forgeries, 125; saw visions of St. Germanus in 541, 126; received Totila in 542–3, 127; visited by St. Sabinus in 546, 127–8; friendship with St. Constantius of Aquinum, 129; date of his death, 145; a suggested chronology, 146; never mentions rustics, 169–70; of good family, 184–5; wrote H. Rule at suggestion of Dionysius Exiguus by order of Pope St. Hormisdas, 203–4

Benedict, St., of Aniane, his Codex and Concordia compared with H. Rule, 32–3

Benedictio (relic), 142; (present), 197

Bernard, St., 10; his miracles, 12

Bishop, Edmund, 149n.; his views incorporated in Bäumer's Hist. of the Breviary, 98, 103n.

Blessing of an Abbot by the Bishop *inter missarum solemnia*, 10, 60n.

Butler, Abbot Cuthbert, 48n., 71n.; on ' This present rule ' (S. Reg. 64), 22n.; on the reading aloud of the Rule (S. Reg. 66), 24n.; on the instruments of Good Works, 34n.; on St. Benedict's sources, 33–4, 196

C

Caesarius, St., bp. of Arles, miracles recorded by eye-witnesses, 12; Caesarius and the H. Rule, 75–87; his Rules quote H. Rule, 75; date of his Rule *ad uirgines*, 76–81; signatures to it, 77–8; signatures to Bull of Hormisdas, 78; date of Rule *ad monachos*, 81–2, forbids Abbess to have attendant slave, 167; orders strict enclosure for nuns, 171

Casale, casarii, 152n., 154n., 160

Cassian, not the chief monastic authority of Cassiodorus, 88, 94–5;

DATE DUE